Before They Were the Black Sheep

UNIVERSITY PRESS OF FLORIDA

Florida A&M University, Tallahassee
Florida Atlantic University, Boca Raton
Florida Gulf Coast University, Ft. Myers
Florida International University, Miami
Florida State University, Tallahassee
New College of Florida, Sarasota
University of Central Florida, Orlando
University of Florida, Gainesville
University of North Florida, Jacksonville
University of South Florida, Tampa
University of West Florida, Pensacola

BEFORE THEY WERE

University Press of Florida

Gainesville | Tallahassee | Tampa | Boca Raton

Pensacola | Orlando | Miami | Jacksonville | Ft. Myers | Sarasota

THE BLACK SHEEP

**Marine Fighting Squadron
VMF-214 and the Battle
for the Solomon Islands**

Carl O. Dunbar, edited by Peter M. Dunbar

15 14 13 12 11 6 5 4 3 2 1

Library of Congress Cataloging-in-Publication Data
Dunbar, Carl O. (Carl Owen), 1891-1979.
Before they were the black sheep : Marine Fighting Squadron VMF-214
and the battle for the Solomon Islands / Carl O. Dunbar, edited by
Peter M. Dunbar.
p. cm.
Includes bibliographical references and index.
ISBN 978-0-8130-3725-7 (alk. paper)
1. Dunbar, Carl O. (Carl Owen), 1891-1979—Correspondence. 2. United
States. Marine Fighter Squadron, 214th 3. World War, 1939-1945—
Campaigns—Solomon Islands. 4. World War, 1939-1945—Aerial
operations, American. 5. World War, 1939-1945—Regimental histories—
United States. 6. World War, 1939-1945—Personal narratives, American.
I. Dunbar, Peter M. II. Title.
D790.473214th D86 2011
940.54'26593—dc22   2011011183

The University Press of Florida is the scholarly publishing agency for the
State University System of Florida, comprising Florida A&M University,
Florida Atlantic University, Florida Gulf Coast University, Florida Interna-
tional University, Florida State University, New College of Florida, Univer-
sity of Central Florida, University of Florida, University of North Florida,
University of South Florida, and University of West Florida.

University Press of Florida
15 Northwest 15th Street
Gainesville, FL 32611-2079
http://www.upf.com

Contents

Prologue

Following the bombing of Pearl Harbor on December 7, 1941, an entire generation of young Americans mobilized in response to the call of their country "to carry the heaviest burden, to fight in enemy territory and to keep the home-front secure and productive."[1] In all, more than 16 million men and women would serve in uniform during World War II, and "they came from everywhere and each had a story to tell."[2]

Like so many of the individuals who mobilized for their country and began the arduous journey to war, Carl Owen Dunbar Jr. stepped anonymously from his private life into the uniform of the U.S. Marine Corps and finally into the fight with the enemy far from his New England home. Like others in this new generation of citizen warriors, he began unversed in modern military strategies, tactics, and weaponry. As he tasked himself with the responsibility to master them before stepping into his role in the nation's global conflict, he described these experiences in letters home to his family. When his training was complete, his descriptive narrative continued from duty stations in the Pacific theater—many of the places isolated and remote with names that were virtually unknown and mostly irrelevant before the war began.

Carl Dunbar's journey began in New Haven, Connecticut, on the December 17, 1941. Dunbar chronicled his journey in the words of the letters that he wrote home to his family—letters read and then saved for more than half a century with other documents that reflect upon the events encountered during the course of his travels. Against the backdrop of the vivid and well-chronicled events of war, Carl's letters tell of his personal progression from home to a twenty-one-year-old aviation cadet, to a twenty-two-year-old carrier-qualified fighter pilot, and then on to his service in one the most elite and recognizable U.S. Marine Corps fighter squadrons in the Pacific theater during World War II.[3] When it began, the final destination of his odyssey was unknown, and as he traveled, the events of the time and the decisions of others determined the journey's end.

Names like the Coral Sea, Midway, Guadalcanal, New Georgia, Vella Lavella, Bougainville, Peleliu, Iwo Jima, and Okinawa marked the progress in the Pacific theater, and each in turn became commonplace and recognizable throughout America. The world press and the front pages of the newspapers recounted the battles being fought on the far side of the globe and the progress of the war being fought there. These accounts described the achievements and advances of military units and naval task forces as they engaged the enemy in places far away from the hometowns of the nation's young warriors. Some of these battles in the remote reaches of the Pacific helped to dictate the path of Carl Dunbar's odyssey, and others he witnessed firsthand during his three tours of combat duty there.

There are seventy-nine letters and postcards in all, written over a period of slightly less than two years. Stored with the letters was the flight logbook that accompanied Carl for much of the same period. The logbook entries describe each aircraft he piloted and the purposes for the flight time. The initial entries describe the training and his introduction to flight skills, combat strategies, tactics, and the weaponry of modern warfare. Later the logbook entries identify the remote locations in the Solomon Islands where he and his squadron engaged in sorties and combat missions against the enemy.

The accounts Carl Dunbar shared in his letters home were unique to him, yet the journey was not unlike those made by each of the individuals who found their way to the front lines in the global theaters of the war. When this war began, there was no hint of where the training and preparations would lead these young men, no knowledge of where they would be asked to meet the enemy, and no awareness of those they would be asked to fight beside. The words of Carl's letters gave his perspective to each of these experiences along the path of his journey.

The letters have not been edited in any way, and whatever information they contain has been included here unchanged in content, text, and punctuation. Carl's mother, Lora Dunbar, logged each letter by entering the date she received it in parenthesis below the date notation provided by Carl. If the stationery had a letterhead, an inside address, or a postscript, that information appears as well.

There are many names of friends, college classmates, fellow servicemen, and family members that appear incomplete in the letters because these individuals were readily known to the corresponding parties. "Mom and Dad" refer to Professor Carl Dunbar Sr. and his wife, Lora Dunbar, and "Sis" refers to Carl's sister, Lora Louise Dunbar (Johnson). References to "Tom" are found frequently in the early correspondence, and these references are to Carl's college roommate at Yale, Tom Schuller. Beyond that, the complete identity of many of the others has been lost to time. Carl's nickname, "Stuff," was unique to his immediate family; to my knowledge, it did not follow him into his life after the war and was left behind with the letters he wrote.

The original letters from my father to his family, his flight logbook, and the other documents from his military service have been donated to the Institute on World War II and the Human Experience at the Department of History at Florida State University. The records are part of the large collection of similar World War II materials maintained by the institute. They are available to researchers and others who are interested in the personal histories from the generation that was called upon to carry the nation's heaviest burden during World War II.

Squantum Naval Air Station and the
U.S. Naval Reserve Aviation Base in Atlanta,
December 17, 1941–March 9, 1942

I am the only Dodo left in the class.
Carl O. Dunbar Jr., January 6, 1942

Carl Dunbar began flying lessons as a novice civilian pilot while completing his undergraduate classes at Yale University. His degree was awarded in the spring of 1941, and two months later, on the first of July, he registered for the draft. According to a passage from the letter written on the second anniversary of his enlistment, Carl entered the United States Naval Reserves as an aviation cadet in September of 1941.

Within days of his commitment to the Naval Reserves, a world away in Tokyo, the Japanese Imperial Command had secretly given its approval to a plan prepared by Admiral Isoroku Yamamoto for a preemptive attack against the U.S. Pacific Fleet at Pearl Harbor in Hawaii.[1] When negotiations between Japan and the United States failed to resolve the growing hostilities between the two nations, Yamamoto's plan was carried out with shocking precision on December 7, 1941. Immediately, America was at war.

On December 17, 1941, ten days after the massive aerial assault on Oahu by the Japanese carrier fleet, Carl, then twenty-one years old, reported to New York City to begin the journey that is described in his letters, traveling first by boat and then by train, to his first duty station at the Squantum Naval Air Station in Quincy, Massachusetts. With this initial step, his odyssey to the war in the Pacific had begun, and the narrative of his experiences began two days later with a handwritten letter home to his mother.

As the training started for the young men at Squantum and for other young men at other training bases around the country, there was no meaningful correlation between their preparations and the planning by military commanders at the War Department in Washington or at the Japanese Imperial High Command in Tokyo. The decisions made by military leaders in both locales, however, became major factors in bringing together the author of these letters and two dozen other young pilots in the South Pacific to fight where time and circumstances dictated—each as a member of Marine Fighting Squadron VMF-214.

In Tokyo as the new year of 1942 began, Japanese military leaders looked to the Philippines and then on to other strategic locations for expansion of their empire. Admiral Yamamoto urged that the Imperial High Command consider the island of Midway north of the equator as an important objective in the Pacific, while other Japanese military planners pressed the advantages of securing strategic positions in the South Pacific. A move to the south, they reasoned, deprived Allied forces of key positions for a counterattack, intensified pressure on Australia, and hindered the use of Australia by the Allies as a staging area in the Pacific theater.[2]

A world away in Washington as the New Year began, America's leaders faced the daunting task of recovering from the surprise attack at Pearl Harbor and then countering the Japanese aggression in the Pacific. For President Roosevelt and his military advisors, two threshold questions loomed large in their discussions: (1) how would the nation prepare its defenses in the Pacific out of range of the Japanese offensive; and (2) where would the country begin its preparations for a counteroffensive against the Japanese aggression?[3]

At the head of the War Department, General George C. Marshall assigned the task of preparing the initial report on possible responses to the Japanese aggression to Dwight Eisenhower on his first day as a member of Marshall's staff.[4] When he had completed the assignment, Eisenhower acknowledged with the submission of his report that it was impossible to reinforce the Philippines in time to save the islands from the Japanese. Strategically, his recommendation urged the advantages of Australia as a base of operations. It was English speaking and a strong ally, it had modern port facilities, and it was beyond the current range of the aggressors. He urged Marshall to begin a program of expanding there and securing the supply lines from the West Coast of the United States to Hawaii and then from Hawaii to Australia.[5]

These strategic plans, and the events that surrounded the decisions made in Washington and Japan, later manifested themselves in a series of engagements between the warring powers in the Pacific theater, culminating in a confrontation in a group of sparsely populated tropical islands south of the equator. In this remote reach of the South Pacific Ocean, the Allied Forces began their first offensive against the Japanese in what history would come to know as the Battle of the Solomon Islands.[6] The correspondence and narrative that follow here chronicle the path of Carl Dunbar on his way to these islands, and it does so against the backdrop of the events that brought him to his final destination and into the history that was made there.

The letter written on December 19, 1941, from the Naval Air Station in Squantum, Massachusetts, describes the beginning of his journey.

Mailed December 19, 1941

U.S. Naval Air Station
Squantum, Mass
Wednesday
Dear Mom,

We are officially members of the U.S.N.R.—in dress and outlook. Arrived here at the base this morning about 11:40. Train from Providence to Boston. The boat from New York City was uneventful but most interesting. Didn't leave the pier until 6:30 and of course, the city was brilliant with lights. We traveled around the tip of Manhattan, up the East River through the Narrows and out Long Island Sound. We turned in shortly after 9:00. I woke up at 6:30 this morning, dressed, and went on deck, leaving the stateroom by the window so as not to wake Bill. Before sun-up, we were escorted through the channel entrance at Providence by a special pilot. The channel has been thickly mined.

Yesterday afternoon was eventful enough as a starter. Doc and Bill and I came into the City about noon. Doc left to visit and we agreed to meet at 1:00. Bill and I waited until 2:30. We were supposed to return to F.B. by 3:00. So we called to explain. They advised us to meet the group at Pier 11 by 5:00. We left word for Doc and went to a show. At 4:00, still no Doc. We subwayed to Pier 11, East River, only to find North River was our proper destination. A flying taxi-ride got us there in time, an hour before 6:00 sailing time. There was Doc waiting. Somehow we had missed connections. All three of us had been at the rendezvous, but in some way had not seen one another.

That was a flying start to what has been a marvelous two days. I know that the training is going to be a marvelous experience. Bill and Doc have turned out to be even finer gents than I had judged them. We have stuck together like fly-paper and will continue so, I know. Our uniforms were issued this afternoon—comfortable and well-fitted. The food is good and generously proportioned. One of the most pleasant surprises of the entire trip came this evening when someone mentioned singing. It turned out that Doc sang 1st base, Bill 2nd, while I carried the tenor. We spent an hour and a half after dinner singing—and believe me, it's the best singing of which I've been a part, I was going to say in a long time, but I should say ever. It won't be long before we'll be turning out some respectable harmony. What an amazing and pleasant surprise to find two really good voices, after two summers of monotones (except Marty).

Apparently, we will commence flying right away—probably Monday. One group left to make room for us, and another is to leave soon. Therefore, the base is not overcrowded. There should be enough planes for us. The base is brand new—two of the barracks are not yet finished. It is situated on a narrow peninsula-point with considerable surrounding water—just the right sort of place for Navy flying. There is some talk of weekends and Christmas leaves. On the other hand, schedules have been put on a seven-day week—so, as yet, I have no definite idea. We have not been officially welcomed or informed and there is a great deal about the place which is Greek to me.

You need only envy me for the present. We are in good hands and the treatment we receive is excellent. I am looking forward to the flying—it will be great to get in the air again.

My best wishes to you all, good health, and good fortune. I'll be glad to hear from you when you've time to write briefly. For now, goodnight.

Love,

COD, Jr.

Student C. O. D. Jr.

Naval Air Station

Squantum,

Mass.

In a passage from this initial letter Carl shares his enjoyment with the harmony and song experienced in the leisure hours of the second evening away from home. It is a casual, early observation of something with which he was familiar and that tied him to his days in college. An accomplished tenor, Carl sang as part of a quartet called the "White Washers" during his years at Yale, and this gift for music accompanied him throughout his training and into the Pacific theater.[7] Later in his journey, the evenings of song relieved the tedium from parts of his travels, and more than a year after he penned this first letter, the vocal harmonies of the "squadron quartet" were providing a regular diversion from the rigors of combat. For the squadron of pilots that journeyed together into the South Pacific, the quartet became the focal point for their camaraderie.[8]

Carl's first letter hints at some apprehension for not fully understanding what to expect in the new military surroundings, but it also reveals his eagerness to begin to fly. In the next three letters, the eagerness turns briefly to frustration when the opportunity does not materialize as quickly as he had initially expected.

Before Carl's next letter home, Eisenhower's assessment of the Philippines was becoming a reality. On December 23, General Douglas

MacArthur ordered the U.S. forces under his command on the island of Luzon to withdraw to the Bataan Peninsula as the Japanese advanced on Manila, and by December 27, Manila had fallen to the enemy invaders.[9]

Rec'd Jan. 2, 1942

Thursday
Dear Mom,

It was very disappointing not to have leave yesterday and last night to come home. Though I felt quite certain that any leave was out of the question, I didn't give up hope until the word had been definitely posted yesterday afternoon. I am thankful for the Christmas leave and that opportunity to be at home with all of you.

The visit with Dad Tuesday evening was a pleasant surprise. I shouldn't have imposed on his company, but he was good enough to invite me to the banquet, and I enjoyed very much accepting his invitation. Although the hours of securing here at the Base made it necessary to leave before the evening had hardly begun. As it was, I just did get back, with about five minutes to spare.

Flying at this place is a myth as far as I'm concerned. I am the last man now, and still haven't flown. Don't think that I'm not disgusted with this place, for I am. Never have wasted so much time in all my life as the two and one-half weeks up here. To absolutely no avail. Perhaps I'm due for a change. My name appears on the flight list for 8:10 tomorrow A.M., but the instructor has been ill for two days. I count on nothing. The weather is due for a bad turn.

Would you send me the suitcase key—in my right coat pocket— so that I can unlock the grip and send my dirty clothes to the laundry. Thank you.

I hope you are all in good health, and will keep it. My best wishes to you, with my goodnight.
Love,
Stuff

The U.S. Naval Air Station at Squantum began operations in 1923, and among its functions, the station served as a facility for initial ground school and preliminary flight training for new Naval Reserve aviation cadets. The training at Squantum lasted only two months before the cadets acquired the requisite experience and were reassigned to their next stage of preparation.

The base also served as a facility for seaplane flight training and as an airbase for coastal antisubmarine patrols in the North Atlantic. But in 1942, neither the facilities at Squantum nor at any other U.S. installation were able to provide a meaningful deterrent or response to the German U-boat threat that was about to materialize in the coastal waters of the Atlantic.[10]

Following the bombing of Pearl Harbor, Adolf Hitler lifted all restrictions on American shipping.[11] Soon after the training at the Naval Air Station got under way, German submarines were actively deployed off the Atlantic coast of the United States in search of vessels plying the waters of the Eastern Seaboard. By the middle of January, the U-boat threat became a reality and brought the war within sight of the nation's beaches.[12]

For the next six months, the toll on coastal shipping along the Atlantic seaboard was the worst of the war, and the results of the new German submarine campaign had a devastating impact.[13] The bright lights from the coastal communities, like those of New York City described in Carl's first letter, contributed significantly to the enemy U-boat successes.

As the student cadets moved among their first three duty stations—Squantum, Atlanta, and Jacksonville—the consequences of the German submarine activity became the first tangible evidence of war. Carl and his fellow cadets encountered the evidence firsthand during their training, but it came later in Jacksonville and not during their time at Squantum.

Mailed Jan 6, 1942

Monday
Dear Mom,
    Your package arrived last Friday. I have been wearing the contents, which couldn't be more satisfactory. Thank you for everything. I am still looking for the pipe.

It continues to be rather discouraging here with no flying. I believe that the last letter I wrote you, my name was on flight schedule for next morning. Just as surely the weather was bad and all flying was secured. Since then, my instructor has been on sick list. He is expected not to fly again tomorrow. I am the only Dodo left in the class. Most of the rest have at least three hours. Several have soloed. I have asked the Skipper for a change of instructor. But he advises me to sit tight. So I shall.

Tim sent me an enlarged framed picture of us this summer at the Trail. It seems mighty good to rehearse those scenes again. The picture doesn't leave the entire burden to memory. Also he wrote of a plan for he and Ruth and Jeanne to meet me the weekend of the 17th. I wish that my weekends could be longer to make the plan more practical. But I have written him of the circumstances and suggested that we wait until departure for Atlanta, when we will probably get two or three days off. I can spend one day at home and a day or two with Jeanne. It would be fun to drive up and spend a winter day and a log fire at Concord with Tim and Ruth.

I regret that there were no steel edges included in the ski outfit. I don't understand why the change, but that can wait until I am home. Did Sis get a ski-suit or did she decide to wait or to get something else? She wrote that she had been pretty busy during vacation. Sounds fine. I wrote her Sunday and sent the letter to Vassar. I don't have a doubt that the second half year will be more satisfactory for her. Seems to me she is getting into the swing of things.

What news of the trip to the West Coast and of Ray Jr.?

I'll close wishing you the very best of health. Also that by next letter I can report you no longer have a Dodo at Squantum. Keep smiling!

Love,

Stuff

During the cold days of early January as the rudimentary flight training for the cadets moved into its third week, the War Department in Washington began to secretly consider the possibility and viability of a plan urged by President Franklin Roosevelt to launch an air attack directly against Tokyo.[14] While never intended as a substitute for the primary strategies being developed by his senior military advisors, Roosevelt's objective was to strike back quickly in retaliation for Pearl Harbor. He envisioned the response to be one that would lift the spirits and morale of a nation still shaken by the surprise attack against the military installations on Oahu and strengthen the resolve of its citizens for what lay ahead in the Pacific theater.[15]

In the week following Carl's letter on January 9, the rough plans for the air attack suggested by the president germinated in the War Department. The concept for the raid was one to be carried out by Army bombers launched from the flight deck of a Navy carrier, combining the resources of both military branches in a single operation. After a week of secret, high-level analysis, the idea was believed to be feasible, and military commanders ordered a more detailed evaluation of the plan.[16]

In the warm tropical weather of the western Pacific on the day of Carl's next letter, Japanese forces on Luzon began their main assault into the Bataan Peninsula. By the end of January the invading army had broken through the initial line of the Allied defenses.[17]

Postcard

Postmarked January 9, 1942
North Quincy, Mass.
Thursday
Dear Mom,

Lot's of cold and wind here. Under 20 degrees all day and under 15 degrees most of it. Even the instructors shrink at the temperature. No flying for me yet, but with a change of instructor assigned to me, chances look good for tomorrow.

In case we have leave for a day next week, and one has been rumored, I shall take train to New Haven or plane to Hartford. I shall wire Jeanne, if she can meet me in New Haven.

Meantime would you hunt my Civil Aviation Authority instruction books on Navigation and Aerodynamics preferably the instructor's manual, if there is one? And if it isn't too expensive, send them along?

I hope you and Dad are keeping that good health!

Love to you both,

Stuff

The flight training for cadet pilots at Squantum was performed in Stearman N2S biplanes. The Stearman was an open-cockpit biplane nicknamed the "Yellow Peril," but despite its moniker, it was a sturdy and safe aircraft. The biplane had duplicate controls for the student pilot and the instructor. During initial training flights, the student cadet placed his hand on the stick and his feet on the pedals, and in this fashion, he could feel what the instructor was doing with the duplicate controls as the plane took off and landed. When it was the student's turn, he simply copied the techniques of the instructor.[18] When Carl's post card was mailed on January 9, he was still waiting for his first opportunity to mimic the flight techniques of his new instructor.

A biplane like the Stearman was a relatively easy aircraft to handle, but as a pilot moved from preliminary to primary flight training, he encountered a variety of aircraft that were increasingly more powerful and more complex.[19] Those who ultimately qualified to fly fighters piloted the most powerful and complex high-performance aircraft that the country had available to send into combat. None of these high-performance aircraft were biplanes, and none were flown from an open cockpit.

Before his letter on January 12, Carl finally made his first flight as a naval cadet in the Stearman biplane. With an interest in the friends at home and an eye to the financial obligations left behind, including the bill at David Dean Smith's music shop for phonograph records, the eagerness about the tasks that lay ahead returned to the words of his letters.[20]

Mailed Jan 12, 1942

Sunday

Dear Mom and Dad,

Finally the ugly duckling has commenced to sprout its pin feathers—perhaps its color will commence to change shortly—at least the color of the taste within its mouth.

I feel much encouraged after the second hour this morning. Although the instructor filled my ears with much reviling during the flight, he waxed complimentary about improvement after landing. Everything seemed woefully strange on Saturday, but today I began to get the feel of flying and this ship. The landings should be a cinch from now on. And the air-work will be a matter of practice.   Flying an open ship is far more interesting and satisfying than closed-cabin flying. Visibility is much increased. You feel much more aware of the reality of flying. Altogether, it is quite thrilling. I hope to solo in a day or two, but that may be too ambitious to fit my instructor's judgment.

I enjoyed both of your grand letters last week. However, they are no substitute for a visit at home. I look forward to a day and night of liberty so that I can join you. We had the day free yesterday, but Skipper refused to let me go farther than Metropolitan Boston. Had we been paid, I should have come anyway. Actually, I spent the afternoon in Concord with Tom. We had a grand visit. I managed an hour of hockey with the Middlesex team.

Fortunately, we are to be paid this Thursday. It has been a matter of borrowing and spending lightly the past couple of weeks. The welfare office took care of my food so that was no worry. We weren't paid because we hadn't been here the full two weeks on last payday—one day short. I plan to send B & K $20 on payday and the balance next month. My bill at D. D. Smith was paid. I have written them, hoping to clear the matter up. When all bills are paid here and there, I should still have some surplus, as salary, less flight-pay which we collect when we leave, comes to over $70.

Tim was coming to Boston this a.m. to consult the Navy Department about a commission in the Personnel Depart. I think he may

accept a commission if one is offered. Meantime, I am quite surprised to hear about Mickey. To my knowledge he had no intimation
that events would come to pass, as they have, so quickly. Happy
anyhow that he has been able to know the happiness of a happy
marriage this long!

Bill inquires about the camera. It has been sent from Hartford.

I have plenty of clothing—so don't worry about sending any-
more. The extra shirt and handkerchiefs were just enough.

Time to leave and study briefly for an aerodynamics test tomorrow. Forgive me if this letter is too sketchy. I'll write again soon. But
until I can get home, which will be soon, I hope, best wishes to you
both. Keep the health!

Love,

Stuff

In Washington, two days before Carl's next letter home to New Haven,
U.S. Army Lieutenant Colonel Jimmy Doolittle was secretly selected by
the War Department to undertake the detailed planning for the possible air assault on the Japanese homeland.[21] Doolittle's initial task
was to select a bomber that could take off from a narrow area, not over
seventy-five feet wide, become airborne in five hundred feet with a two-
thousand-pound bomb load, and fly two thousand miles to deliver its
payload. Doolittle determined that only one plane met the necessary
criteria, and as the training at Squantum continued, he selected the
Mitchell B-25 bomber as the aircraft around which the final planning
for his secret mission would proceed in earnest.[22]

With prior civilian flight experience, Carl progressed quickly, completing his solo check within a week of the first flight with his instructor.
On the day he soloed, he was intrigued by the speed and performance
of the Army's frontline P-40 Tomahawk mono-wing fighter that he encountered during his second solo flight of the day. His fascination with
the speed and performance of the aircraft remained with him as his
training continued.

For many young men called to the war, there were young women who had
been left behind at home. Some couples became engaged and married

during the difficult years of the war, but for others, their relationship would dissipate and fade over the time and separations brought on by the global conflict. Jeanne is introduced in these early letters, and Carl speaks of her periodically as he writes home, but in time, their relationship will wane and come to an end as Carl's journey to war continues.

Sunday

Dear Mom and Dad,

Last week seemed to be pretty full of everything but sleep. That's the cause of the silence at this end. We returned from liberty on Wednesday night only to be routed out in the slush and raw cold by an air-raid alarm. We wheeled out the planes and staked them down, finally returning to the barracks by midnight. They rolled us out at four to start the planes and prepare for emergency take-offs. Some of the fellows had to patrol watches all night. A rather trying night and following day.

It's no surprise to tell you that Jeanne drove up with Mr. Schuller. We had a grand time yesterday evening in Concord. Ruthie was with us for dinner and to spend the evening. I couldn't get overnight liberty but was allowed to return at two this morning. The evening flew by too terribly fast.

I felt ill this morning, combination of no sleep and an upset intestinal tract. But it didn't affect the flying. Passed the solo check this morning and soloed. On top of that I managed two hours of solo time, making a total of 2:15 solo, plus the 30-minute check and 30-minute warm-up dual. My instructor informed me that the check pilot had given me a good mark, which was very encouraging. Actually, I was pretty lucky on a couple of the maneuvers—hit'em for the first time on the check flight. The solo flying is wonderful. I sure enjoy every minute of it. I expected to be blasted out of the sky this afternoon by a couple of P-40's. They whizzed around and over me near the field in a most alarming fashion. Control tower gave me the red-light, which means stay away. So I opened the throttle and climbed, but aside those Army ships, I was moving backwards many times as fast as our ships go forward. They finally left without putting in here. But they made quite an impression.

Doc and Bill and I discovered a way to alleviate the tiring hours of a lazy afternoon. Last Friday, we eased our way into the hangar and into one of the service ships, which accommodated us handily. We just curled up and slept away the afternoon in peace and security.

With a fair break in the weather, I should finish preliminary flight training within two weeks. It's very possible I'll get two or three days leave the third weekend. It's too early yet to plan, but I shall hound the Flight Sergeant for all the extra flying time I can get, and then hope that the C.O. will get chicken-hearted.

I'm interested and glad to hear that Dad is taking air-raid warden instruction. I am impressed after last Wednesday with the need for preparedness for any eventuality. Somebody—the more the better—needs to know what to do when the emergency arises. This is another time when the cogs on the wheel are just as important as the machine.

My eyes are crying "quits" so I shall close and hop into bed. I'll be seeing you one of these days in the near future.

Keep smiling and stay healthy.

Love,

Stuff

P.S. We've moved to Quonset Point-Barracks 4.

As cadets adapted to the changes of military life and as their fourth week of instructions began, the onset of the war was also bringing changes to the routines of daily life at home. Reference to some of these changes appear sporadically in Carl's correspondence, and one of the first references is to preparations for a potential enemy attack on New Haven and his father's new role as an air-raid warden in the family's neighborhood. In hindsight, New Haven never experienced a bombing raid or other hostilities, but in the month following the bombing of Pearl Harbor, the city prepared for the possibility nonetheless. As the months of 1942 progressed, Dr. Dunbar took his responsibilities seriously, and on nights

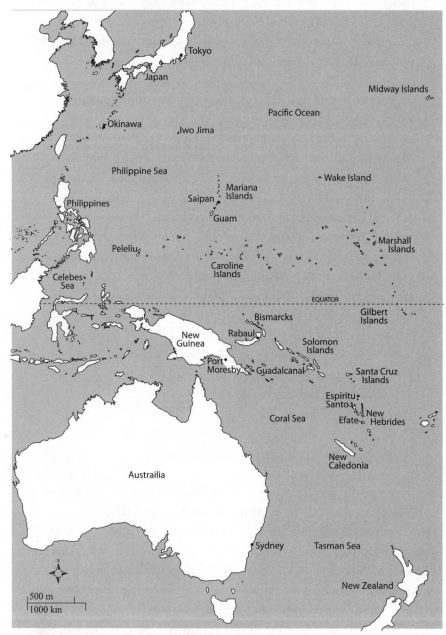

Map 1. Pacific theater of operations, 1941–1945.

when practice air raid warnings were sounded, he patrolled the neighborhood on foot to make sure residents had turned off their lights or pulled down dark shades to help ensure a blackout of the city.[23]

On January 23 the first in a series of events occurred in the South Pacific that contributed to the strategic importance of the island archipelagos found in the region. A small Japanese expeditionary force seized the northeastern tip on the island of New Britain in the Bismarck Archipelago that bordered the Solomon Islands to the north, securing the natural deep-water harbor at Rabaul.[24] It was a location able to sustain a major airfield complex supporting ground installations as well as a naval base, but the expedition was considered only a minor military operation by the Japanese at the time.[25] The Imperial High Command in Tokyo remained uncommitted to its next major offensive against United States forces in the Pacific.[26] The command continued to weigh the option of proceeding against Midway versus an expanded effort against Allied installations in New Guinea and the other island archipelagos south of the equator.[27]

As the Japanese were establishing their presence at Rabaul and continuing to plan, the blueprints to modify Doolittle's B-25 bombers for their special mission were being prepared in Washington, D.C., the armament for the aircraft was being readied, and the industrial targets in the Japanese home islands were being selected.[28]

At NAS Squantum, cadet flight training was progressing routinely, and the acclimation of the cadets to life in the military continued. Snow and wintery conditions detracted from the cadets' flight time, and the weather was in sharp contrast to the conditions in the South Pacific where the Japanese were securing a foothold on New Britain.

Jan 28, 1942

Wednesday

Dear Mom,

No news was good news, as you suspected. I had been relieved of my Sunday watch and so didn't need to be here even at 4:45. Fact is, I could have come in at any hour before sun-up Monday; no one would have known nor cared.

We have been hoping until today that we'd get back to Squantum before the weekend. The snow will undoubtedly upset flying considerably. Just how long no one knows. It will probably be two weeks hence—the third weekend—before and if we get a few days leave. It's possible that one of the Flight will be driving to Vassar the day we get off, in which case I'll join him and drop in for a short visit with Sis. It may not be practical, so better not mention word of it to her.

They had me literally "up in the air" yesterday afternoon. An air-raid alarm was sounded while I was out flying solo. Planes were dispersed about the field and key stations were manned. I returned to the field considerably perplexed by the state of affairs. I climbed to 1,000 feet and circled the field to watch and think, wiggling the wings in search of some signal, but none was forthcoming. After several circles, I decided to come down, having decided that there must be an air-raid alarm and feeling more of a menace in the air than on the runway. Moreover, I couldn't just wait for the gasoline to run out. Guess the other fellows had quite a laugh over my predicament, but it all ended harmlessly and without comment from superiors. I landed and taxied to the side of the runway and sat until word came to start the motor and taxi back to the hangar.

I stopped at this point last night to go to the movies. It's 7:00 A.M.—my turn at the watch until 9:00. We had a few tense moments last night after the show. One of the fellows, who stayed at Ship's Service for the evening to have a few short ones, asked us to pick him up before we returned to Barracks. I went after him, but 'twas almost ten o'clock and the hall was supposed to be locked. Bill was the last one in the room; he apparently had been writing letters and was accumulating odds and ends, taking his time about it. Meantime a lieutenant-commander was standing in his office doorway, outside the entrance to Ship's Service ordering an enlisted man to lock the doors. While I stood hollering at Bill to come, another chap, who had been drinking considerably, slipped in by me to pick up his box of writing paper he had left. The officer repeated his command to the gob, who hesitated somewhat to give the fellows a chance to get out. I asked the striper whether I could go in after them. He ignored me and repeated the order, adding that they could spend the night thinking it over. With that, the door was locked. I was very worried about the consequences of two of our unit being locked up in Ship's Service overnight and immediately started trying to reason with the officer. I managed to get out something about lack of knowledge of the regulations and inexperience when he drew himself up and blasted me, "Are you talking back to an officer?!" I retired at that instant meekly. Somehow, the two pals got out, but the drinking one tarried to stick up for the enlisted man who let them out. I fear that he will hear more of the incident, and it will be surprising if the whole unit doesn't reap some reprimand as a result. It was too bad that the show wasn't over a few minutes earlier, for I could have herded them both out and avoided any complications. We are hardly in a position to warrant any untoward attention.

Jeannie wrote that she very much appreciated your calls Saturday afternoon, when it caused you so much trouble to locate her. She was disappointed not to be able to come, but someone from out of town was coming and she didn't feel right about calling off the previous plans at the eleventh hour, nor would I have had her change them. She spoke of the few days leave I have been hoping for, and expressed the hope that we might spend them at home instead of traveling to Concord as we had tentatively planned for one day or two. She didn't know whether she would be welcome, when my time is so short but I have reassured her.

Tim was unable to pass the Navy physical, even for a desk job. So the commission seems to have slipped from his grasp, when it seemed so certain. He has not yet given up hope and may perhaps yet be able to get by. He mentioned another angle of attack, though said nothing of what it was.

I guess Sis will have plenty of skiing for awhile, and you two plenty of snow-shoeing and shoveling. Breathe deeply and get lots of sleep and fresh air while it's still free. See you soon.
Love,
Stuff

As early February approached, the evaluation of the flight skills of the Navy cadets at Squantum was concluding, and Carl began to anticipate his next duty station and the next step in his training. Pilots moving on to Atlanta had demonstrated basic skills in the Stearman, but of the many aircraft options that awaited Navy pilots after completing their training—torpedo planes, seaplanes, dive-bombers and fighters—there was still no hint as to which of these aircraft the cadet pilots leaving Squantum might be assigned.

Two days following Carl's next letter, two Army B-25 bombers were loaded aboard the newly commissioned USS *Hornet* in Norfolk, Virginia. Shortly after the aircraft were secured to her flight deck, the *Hornet* left its moorings, and later on the same day in the open Atlantic Ocean, the bombers raced down the gently sloping deck of the carrier and lifted easily into the air with space to spare. The concept that the modified medium-range Army bombers could take off in the short length of a carrier flight deck had been verified, and Lieutenant Colonel Doolittle's preparations for the mission against the enemy homeland continued to its next phase.[29]

Mailed Feb 2, 1942

Sunday

Dear Mom and Dad,

This is a bright evening for aviation cadets of Flight #72. Several of us have only an hour or two to go before finishing our flight program of this stage. If weather permits, we shall finish tomorrow and return to Squantum for final flight check and check-out in ground school. After that we are eligible for a long-awaited leave. The thought is very exciting! It's still a little difficult to plan, for there are too many provisions and unaccountables. Yet, the possibility of the coming weekend is quite conceivable. Conservatively speaking, weekend-after-next would be the time, but, as I say, they may push us through by next Thursday.

We were transferred to general mess today and no longer have to pay for meals. What a glorious surprise! Absolutely the best meals I've had since leaving home. To be sure, it is Sunday, but a week would not be too long to wait for such frugal repasts. Cereal, flap-jacks with molasses, fruit, hash, and coffee for breakfast; creamed chicken (real home-cooking), broccoli, sweet potatoes, hearts of lettuce, soup, apple pie á la mode, and coffee for lunch; oyster stew (like yours, with innumerable oysters), spaghetti and meatballs, fresh cabbage with dressing, bread and butter, fruit and coffee for dinner. The fruit is absolutely the best, California seedless oranges, fancy apples, and bananas. And you can have all the food you can eat. It's enough to hearten the most downcast soul, which has prac-tically been me.

Flying was secured yesterday afternoon and today since before ten o'clock. We've played a lot of volleyball both days. Six of us have been playing as a unit and we haven't been defeated. Fact is, no one has even come close. It seems like shadows of "Summer Island Nights." I guess volleyball is little enough start on the pro-gram which Mr. Secretary Knox outlined for publication today. I don't know how much of that training we'll get down South, but we could sure stand some. Doc and Bill and I spotted our forearms black and blue pummeling each other around last week one after-noon, so I guess there's plenty of spirit waiting to be released on someone.

My advanced check pilot caught me having quite a chuckle the other day when he unexpectedly peered into the mirror over the front cockpit. I had engineered a pretty satisfactory first landing on the check and came around to try a second. Well, I got the tail down all right, well down. (They insist on tail-first landings.) But my front wheels were still about six feet in the air. I want to tell you they really came down hard, hard enough to give him a good jolt, sitting right over the wheels. It tickled me anyway, but when he hollered through the gosport that I'd let her down pretty hard, I just natu-rally burst out laughing and opened my mouth in a broad grin. I don't know whether he heard me or felt some unaccustomed move-ment on the take-off, but first thing I knew was he was looking up at me with a curious expression. Guess he didn't mind too much, though, 'cause he gave me quite an interesting ride afterward, when we finished with instruction.

I'll be popping in on you soon. Meantime, my very best wishes to you for continued good health. Keep smiling!

Love,

Stuff

Completion of preliminary flight training at Squantum was followed by a short period of leave for the cadets; a few days at home in New Haven for Carl; and travel time to the next duty station for more ground school and flight training. In an era when trains still had names, Carl made his first trip into the South, traveling aboard the "Southerner" to the naval air station in Atlanta, where his preparations for war continued and the cold weather of the northeast was left behind.

The military installation in Atlanta had served initially as an infantry training facility during World War I, but the base was transferred to the Navy as the hostilities of World War II approached. In March of 1941, the facility was reopened as NAS Atlanta to train aspiring pilots for the Navy and Marine Corps.[30] The training regime in Atlanta included advanced ground school for the cadets; the aircraft used for their flight training were the same N3N Stearman biplanes used at Squantum; and the indoctrination into military life continued for the cadets.

Carl's first letter from Atlanta details observations about the changing terrain and describes the natural surroundings that he encountered as he traveled. As his journey proceeded, the descriptions of the places he visited and the things he observed continued, and these narratives are found in many of the other letters home. Some of the observations reveal the visual accounts of the war while others simply describe the places that he saw along the way that were different from those with which he was familiar back home in New England.

Saturday

Dear Mom and Dad,

While there are a few spare minutes here and there, I shall jot down a few lines to let you know I am safely arrived here and well situated.

I want to thank you both for driving me to the City Wednesday afternoon. There certainly wasn't much room to spare. Bill did manage to get the 7:15 plane and so made the journey in plenty of time, but I felt much securer to be aboard the "Southerner." I managed to push through the entrance gate at Penn Station without showing a ticket, as you saw. I ducked into one of the coaches, stowed the steamer trunk, and then proceeded to emulate Napoleon retreating from Moscow as I was ousted from one seat after another. There was a good deal of confusion which shielded me, and I occupied myself filling the cigarette case. I can honestly say, however, that it wasn't until the train pulled out of the station that I breathed easily. Eventually, the conductor came through and turned a benevolent ear upon my predicament. Upon scrutiny of the records, he found that New Haven Station had called ahead and reserved a seat for me. That was all there was to it, except that I had to disentrain at Washington, D.C., to buy a through ticket. There was none of the unpleasantness which I expected.

There were a couple of Ensigns in the dining car who invited me to join them. After dinner, we persuaded the belle of the train, a Lieutenant's wife returning from New York City to home in Birmingham, to join us in the Club Car. We spent time there until well after 12:00, though drinking stopped much earlier, when we entered Maryland. We finished the evening with a bit of bridge. Posing as the grand protector, I occupied the seat alongside my bridge partner, a much envied seat, I might add secured at distinct displeasure and surprise on the part of my senior officer, for the rest of the night. Consequently, I didn't get much sleep, only a great deal of enjoyment from the trip.

It was quite a disappointment to step out into clear Atlanta air Thursday morning and find it colder than the weather I had left in Connecticut. I saw several cars steaming with frozen radiators. Yesterday, it warmed up somewhat, so that in the afternoon the sun felt like spring, but there is still a definite chill in the air. I can't help feeling that this is only a cold snap, however, for the grass in Atlanta about residential areas is as green as late spring–early summer at home. It is remarkable country, from what I can see here and noticed from the train windows. The red clay which erodes so badly, appears bleak and fruitless. It is a mystery to me how the abundant Georgia pines grow so prosperously in such a locality. The ruggedness of the terrain strikes me especially. The country is flat as a whole, but there are myriads of sharply defined low hills, as though the region were a recently elevated peneplane that is now being dissected and in the early stages of a new cycle. I should recall the actual condition from my Geology, but I can't seem to. It is so distinctive that I shall be able to spot a similar geologic phenomenon, I believe.

There are plenty of watches to be stood here. In fact, that seems to be the main responsibility. Classes occupy the major part of the day, whenever watches do not interfere. My watch today lasts from 0800 to 1600, as messenger in the Central Office. Night watches are shorter. Reveille is sounded at 6:30. We muster and take exercise before breakfast. There is a supervised athletic period from four to five in the afternoon. I'm so stiff today from yesterday's exercises that I have no yen for physical exertion. This base is leaning over backwards to see that we get the much-needed discipline which heretofore has been so conspicuously lacking. Consequently, there are rather severe consequences for minor infractions of the well-defined rules. I shall not henceforth be sleeping in "ducks." Fact is, the discipline is rather refreshing, largely I imagine due to its novelty. They have told us that we can speed our stay here by two weeks if we can be in the upper half of the class with our ground school grades. I shall be pointing for that, to the exclusion of all else, even if it means giving up weekend liberties.

Leaving in such a flurry, I neglected to send the G. S. manual back to Squantum. Wonder if you would send it back, same class as the manuals you sent to me. The proper address, though not essential, is Lt. Channel, N.A.S., Squantum. If my college notebook (blue, loose-leaf) happens to be around and in fairly good shape, I could use it here. That is if postage isn't more than a few cents. It's not vital. I could use my soft white shirt, without the button down collar, too.

I had better close here. There must be an interruption soon anyway. My stationery is over in Barracks, but my address is: Student COD Jr., Sea 2/C USNR, Room 102, Barracks 8, N.A.S., Atlanta, Ga. I'll send along cash to cover my $15 loan and the bill at B-K as soon as we are paid. Meantime, my best wishes and my gratitude to you for the grand interlude at home between Squantum and Atlanta. See you soon!

Love,

Stuff

On the second of March 1942, the day he posted his next letter, cadet Carl Dunbar turned twenty-two years old as his journey to war continued.

For the Allied Command in the Pacific during the early months of 1942, the route between Hawaii and Australia became a priority as Eisenhower had recommended, and maintaining it became a desperate improvisation designed to secure and defend the links between these two strategic points.[31] Any attempt to engage the Japanese war machine as it moved south of the equator needed these links to support the movement of Allied troops, equipment, and supplies to the forward staging areas in the South Pacific islands north of Australia. The new strategic importance of these islands lay entirely in their geographic relationship to other areas.[32] This island region, one of the most primitive on earth, held nothing of inherent importance to attack or defend, and the airfields and military bases built on the islands as months passed became the only strategic objectives of importance.[33]

The Japanese had already made a preliminary advance to Rabaul, and as February turned to March, the strategic moves of both the United States and Japan in the South Pacific continued. The movements in the Pacific received little notice by the general population in the United States, however, as the nation focused on the presence and threat of the German submarines stalking merchant vessels off the major coastal cities along the Atlantic seaboard.

In Atlanta, weekend leave for the cadets preceded the next letter home. Carl's accounts of the weekend revelry include reference to a "milk punch" concoction, and this recipe from his college days traveled with him and would appear in other accounts of his leisure hours.

Mailed March 2, 1942

U. S. Naval Reserve Aviation Base
Atlanta, Georgia
Monday
Dear Mom and Dad,

Word from the sunny Southland, deep in the throes of a real old New England snow-storm. All the past week we have impatiently awaited the long-promised warm weather, only to wake up this morning and find this!

We had a big weekend in Atlanta, from Saturday mid-afternoon until last night. All the cadet reserves had the weekend liberty and most of them spent it in Atlanta. I believe our entire section from Squantum, except one or two stayed at the same hotel. That didn't make the weekend any less noisy. Bill and Pete and I roomed together across the hall from Doc, Andy, and Ed Moxey. We didn't get to bed until about four Saturday night and so slept 'til most eleven Sunday, when three chaps from another floor dropped in to visit us. We got out of bed then and trundled across the hall into Doc's room, and jumped into the double beds which they had wired together to accommodate three of them. The cry was for a milk-punch party, à la true college weekend Sunday. So from then until after 2, we raced about the room like a bunch of ten-year olds, breaking one of the beds doing swan dives onto it. When we finally decided to dress and eat, Bill and Pete and Andy climbed into the bath tub. I don't think you'd ever want to see a funnier performance. There must have been more water on the floor than in the tub. All in all, we had a pretty fine time. It afforded us the much-needed relaxation from the routine here at the base.

Again today I have the Central Office Messenger Duty, for the third time. It's about the first good break I've had on out-of-the-hat assignments. If I remember correctly, my last letter was written here in this office. I probably told you then that this is a regular office job. We do filing, some typing, and messenger duty for the C.O. and the regular office. There isn't a great deal to be done and no pressure about doing it. Meantime, we are excused from the day's classes and exercises. We can arise leisurely, skip the 6:30 muster and exercises and eat an early, unhurried breakfast. What's probably most important, we get a good night's sleep, for we don't have to stand a 4–8 or a 12–4 watch outdoors. Poor old Bill has had two 12–4's already, and there's another scheduled for him tonight. It means he has to get up and dress at 11:30, then stand out in the night until 4:00. With lights out at 10:00 and reveille at 6:00, you can imagine just how much sleep he gets. And he, as anyone, is expected to exhibit just as much enthusiasm and stamina next day as the rest of us. It's tough, but plenty of men are doing it all the time. I guess we have no kick coming. But I'm hoping to escape the duty, nevertheless.

I called, or tried to get in touch with, Anne Wagar, Maralyn's friend in Atlanta. But she goes to the University of Georgia in Athens and so was not at home this weekend. I can't remember M's last name for the life of me, so perhaps it is well she wasn't at home.

We have pretty definite word that our destination will be Jacksonville. Almost certainly, the student C.O. reports, we will not go to Corpus Christi. Of course that makes us all very unhappy. (Just had to deliver a message to the Captain and, as I breezed back into the office, practically knocked the Senior Flight Instructor off his feet. We both came around a blind corner at the same time.) I wrote Roy last week that we would probably be at Jacksonville in two weeks and I hope that we'll be able to spend a weekend together shortly. I had a good letter from him the day we left Squantum, but I hadn't time to reply until last Friday.

We are to be paid on Thursday, I understand. My stipend should amount to $48 or better. I shall send it along as soon as we are paid. Would it be too much trouble for you to take $27.50 of it to B-K? There should be a bill, too, from D.D.S. for about $3.60. I ordered an album of Show Boat melodies which was to be released late in February. If there's enough to pay for it, I'd appreciate it if you'd have them mail it to Jeanne. You have her address.

When we get South, I am planning to have $50 a month sent home. Would you suggest the New Haven Savings bank? And can arrangements be made for you to withdraw money to pay my endowment insurance as it comes due?

Atlanta had a black-out last week that was declared 98% effective. It was quite impressive here.

I hope you are both well. Anyhow best of luck. I'll write soon.
Love,
Stuff

Six friends from in and around New Haven—Carl, Bill Stuhlman, Pete Prudden, Doc, Andy and Ed Moxey—are introduced in the initial letters; these cadets began their training together at Squantum. Their first names appear frequently in Carl's letters, but with the exception of Bill Stuhlman, Pete Prudden and Ed Moxey, the last names are never revealed to the reader. Before Carl reached his final destination, each of these friends qualified for assignments different from his, and none of them accompanied Carl into the islands of the South Pacific.

In early March in the archipelagos south of the equator, the focus of American military leaders was on the small jungle island of Efate in the southern New Hebrides island chain.[34] A three-hour flight northeast of Sydney, Australia, Efate was to be the first South Pacific island of strategic importance as the country prepared to respond to the southern expansion being directed by the Japanese Imperial Command. As training got under way for cadets at NAS Atlanta, a small U.S. Army detachment was deployed to the New Hebrides, literally sneaking in without the knowledge of the enemy, to occupy the little jungle island.[35]

A few weeks earlier and nearly one thousand miles northwest of Efate, a small expedition of Japanese army regulars landed on Bougainville at the northern end of the Solomon Islands chain. The purpose of the expeditionary force was to extend the influence of the military presence that had been established earlier on Rabaul during the third week of January.[36]

As the first week of March concluded, the cadets in Atlanta were beginning to look forward to their next duty stations, primary flight training, and more sophisticated airplanes. Carl speculated that his next assignment was likely to be the naval air station in Jacksonville, Florida, and before he wrote again, that destination was confirmed. The minor flu symptoms he describes in the letter posted on March 9 did not dampen his optimism about the change.

Mailed March 9, 1942

U.S. Naval Reserve Aviation Base
Atlanta, Georgia
Thursday
Dear Mom and Dad,

Letters from you both and the pictures of Jeanne made a very happy birthday here in Atlanta. The framed picture, which was a wonderful idea, arrived Tuesday, along with a letter from Roy and a card from Peter Bullis. The picture has been doubly satisfying in as much as I have been confined to the infirmary since Tuesday morning. A mild sore throat which I had been nursing for over a week finally caught up with me Monday night after the big weekend. I've been running a temperature between 99 and 101 degrees, but the Doc says it's nothing serious. I have a feeling that tomorrow will be a much better day and that the worst is behind me. Confinement isn't all sad news, however, for it means that I didn't have to stand a 12–4 watch last night.

Payday today didn't include travel disbursement. It may be another week or so until the order comes through. Meantime I'll send along the $27.00 which we did receive (apparently we still get flight pay) and hope that you can extend my personal loan until the rest comes through.

I have had no word from Jeanne, as you, too, write. I hope that she has not been ill, though I rather imagine that school-work which she missed plus some social obligations, have kept her too busy even to think of writing. Still, as I remember, Jeanne has been rather prompt about writing to you.

Roy writes that he has checked out as second pilot down at Banana River. He is now to be transferred to Norfolk for a period of squadron training and to check out as first pilot and instructor.

He logged over forty hours the week before he wrote, and that isn't marbles. He has bought a '41 Buick and reckons that he has considerable saving to do. Cocoa is about 136 miles from Jacksonville, he writes, and he plans to drive up for a weekend. I don't know whether it will be immediately, however, inasmuch as he is to be transferred about the middle of the month. And we may just cross paths.

Good news to hear that Sis enjoyed her weekend in New Haven and Wesleyan. I just wish that time hadn't been quite so limited and that I might have spent a bit more time with her. We had a great time gadding about together. If she doesn't decide not to go back, we'll have an opportunity yet.

Well, chow has just been brought in, so I'll close and dig into it. I probably won't get liberty this weekend because of my present sojourn. So perhaps, I can write again then.

My very best wishes to both of you for continued good health. And real thanks for sending along the pictures. Let me hear from you soon.

Love,

Stuff

When the cadet pilots departed Atlanta and settled into their new assignments in early March, Japanese forces in the Philippines continued to advance against the Allied defenses in the Bataan Peninsula. Admiral Yamamoto focused his planning on the U.S. installations at Midway in the central Pacific, and other Japanese leaders in the Imperial High Command continued to look to the South Pacific. Rabaul and Bougainville were already under their control, and the next objectives being considered included military installations at Port Moresby on New Guinea and the island of Tulagi in the southern Solomons.[37] Tulagi served as the traditional British administrative center for the Solomon Islands, and its location presented a strategic asset in the archipelago. From the harbor at Tulagi, its occupants would have the ability to launch long-range seaplanes to patrol across the entire southern region of the island group.[38]

Above: Carl Dunbar Jr. with mother, Lora, and father, Carl Sr., during undergraduate years at Yale. (Dunbar family collection.)

Right: Cadet Carl Dunbar in blue wool receiving ship jacket at home after basic flight training at NAS Squantum, February 1942. (Dunbar family collection.)

N2S-3'ₐ ON LINE (PRIMARY LANDPLANE SQUADRON)

"Yellow Peril" N2S-3 Stearman biplanes, used by cadets during primary flight training, on the flight line at NAS Jacksonville, 1942. (Courtesy of the State Archives of Florida.)

Unable to engage Japanese forces in serious battle during the early months of 1942, the new commander of the U.S. Pacific fleet, Admiral Chester Nimitz, chose to engage in harassing tactics against the enemy. From his headquarters at Pearl Harbor, Nimitz directed USS *Lexington*, USS *Enterprise*, and USS *Yorktown*—the three U.S. Fleet carriers in the South Pacific—to engage in hit-and-run attacks against the Japanese warships gathered near Rabaul. Admiral Nimitz hoped that these tactics would unsettle the Japanese and make their leaders cautious as they contemplated expansion to the south. During the weeks in late February and early March, the strategy proved successful, and the Japanese movement into the southern Pacific was slowed by the tactics of the carriers. The planned invasion of Port Moresby on New Guinea and further expansion in the region was postponed by the Japanese Imperial Command until later in the spring of 1942.[39]

2 ✈ ✈ ✈ ✈ ✈ ✈ ✈

U.S. Naval Air Station, Jacksonville, Florida, March 12, 1942–July 12, 1942

> *Yesterday started out clear and hot. By 10 o'clock, there were great white cumulus summer clouds over most of the sky, with a network of blue sky between. On my solo hop, I climbed up through the cracks, between and above the clouds. At 5,500 feet, I was over some and among others. I found the experience quite a thrill. Instead of little tufts of cotton fluff, as the clouds appear from the ground, I found great towering columns and veritable mountains of mist, two and three thousand feet high. I danced around and between them, having a great time. The clouds give one a feeling of great height when the ground appears between them far down.*
>
> Carl O. Dunbar Jr., May 7, 1942

Jacksonville Naval Air Station is located on the banks of the St. Johns River in northeast Florida, and it was Carl's next interim duty station. In addition to serving as a major primary flight-training center during the war years, NAS Jacksonville was also an operational base for PBY Catalina "flying boats" patrolling the southern Atlantic shipping lanes for enemy submarines.[1] At NAS Jacksonville, cadet pilots moved into the final phases of their preparation, and the letters from this station look forward to the completion of training and to a commission as an officer in either the United States Navy or the U.S. Marine Corps.

In addition to descriptions of the beaches, the ocean, and the tropical scenery found in the new Florida surroundings, there are also reminders of the war to be found in these letters. The oil tar on the white sand

A Cluster of Oranges, Florida

Postcard from Banana River NAS in Cocoa Beach. (Dunbar family collection.)

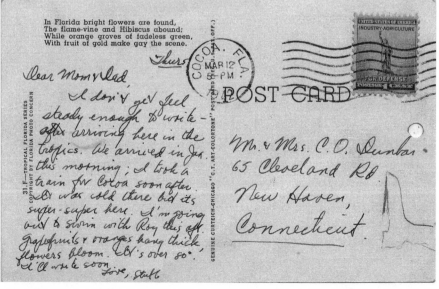

In Florida bright flowers are found,
The flame-vine and Hibiscus abound;
While orange groves of fadeless green,
With fruit of gold make gay the scene.

Thurs.

Dear Mom & Dad,

I don't yet feel steady enough to write — after arriving here in the tropics. We arrived in Jax this morning; I took a train for Cocoa soon after. It was cold there but it's super-super here. I'm going out to swim with Roy this aft. Grapefruits & oranges hang thick, flowers bloom. It's over 80°. I'll write soon.

Love, Stub

COCOA. FLA.
MAR 12
5 PM

POST CARD

Mr. & Mrs. C. O. Dunbar
65 Cleveland Rd.
New Haven,
Connecticut.

31. F—TROPICAL FLORIDA SERIES
COPYRIGHT BY FLORIDA PHOTO CONCERN

GENUINE CURTEICH-CHICAGO "C.T. ART-COLORTONE" POST CARD (REG. U.S. PAT. OFF.)

beaches and the flotsam and other remnants of sunken vessels washed ashore with the tide were vivid reminders of the conflict that awaited the pilots when their training was finished.

NAS Jacksonville was the longest training stop for the future pilots. It introduced them to the basic formations used by military squadrons, to the basic tactics of aerial combat, and to the instrument navigation techniques that aided on night missions and in bad weather conditions. The skills acquired and demonstrated during this phase of the training began the selection and separation process for the pilots. The scores and proficiencies achieved in Jacksonville became the criteria for the designation to the aircraft that each would fly when reporting for their combat assignments.

Postmarked March 12, 1942

> Cocoa, Florida
> Thursday
> Dear Mom and Dad,
> I don't yet feel steady enough to write after arriving here in the tropics. We arrived in Jacksonville this morning; I took a train for Cocoa soon after. It was cold there, but it's super-super here. I'm going out to swim with Roy this afternoon. Grapefruits and oranges hang thick, flowers bloom. It's over 80 degrees!
> I'll write soon.
> Love,
> Stuff

In the first letters from Florida, there are references and descriptions to the area around the naval facility at Banana River near Cocoa Beach. The Banana River facility opened in October of 1940, and it served as a subbase for the naval air station at Jacksonville. After the war the Navy transferred the Banana River facility to the United States Air Force, and it has subsequently become Patrick Air Force Base.

The facilities at Banana River were used as an operational base for Martin PBM seaplanes and Vought OS2U Kingfisher observation planes, and both were aircraft assigned to regular antisubmarine patrols along the southern Atlantic Coast.[2] Carl spent the final two days of his leave visiting at the Banana River Station before returning to Jacksonville for the next phase of his preparations, and he describes those days near Cocoa Beach in the letter written during his return train trip on March 16, 1942.

The letters that follow from Jacksonville describe the flight time in both of the observation aircraft based at Banana River as well as the flight time spent in the PBY Catalinas that were based at Jacksonville. Permanent assignment to these seaplanes was one of the options that awaited cadets after their training was complete, but Carl's encounter with the PBY Catalinas when he reached the Pacific theater was not as a pilot of the cumbersome flying boats.[3]

New York—Palm Beach—Miami

Pennsylvania Railroad
Richmond Fredericksburg & Potomac R.R.
Atlantic Coast Line Railroad
Florida East Coast Railway
Mailed March 16, 1942
Friday
Dear Mom and Dad

It has been a wonderful two day sojourn with Roy, and about as complete a change from what we have been doing as you can imagine. I have finally realized my fond ambition to go from winter into the middle of summer all in one quick jump. For it was just exactly midsummer Thursday in Cocoa as I disentrained. I rode out to the base, some 16 miles, with the mail truck. We stopped once while I scurried into an orange grove to pick an orange. It was a gorgeous day and the ride out was exciting to me. I just couldn't simmer down.

Roy and I spent the afternoon on the beach, played a little baseball and went for a grand swim. The water was about as warm as it ever gets at home and clear blue. Ted Cross, Elmo '40, was with us. Last night we started for a show, but instead stayed with one of Roy's buddies who had a date. We spent some time at her home—a

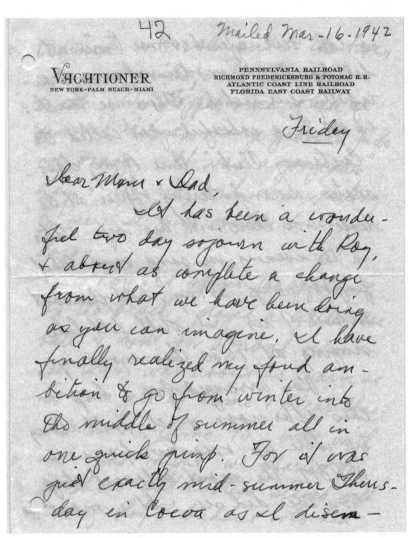

VACATIONER
NEW YORK~PALM BEACH~MIAMI

PENNSYLVANIA RAILROAD
RICHMOND FREDERICKSBURG & POTOMAC R.R.
ATLANTIC COAST LINE RAILROAD
FLORIDA EAST COAST RAILWAY

42 Mailed Mar-16-1942

Friday

Dear Mom & Dad,

It has been a wonderful two day sojourn with Roy, & about as complete a change from what we have been doing as you can imagine. I have finally realized my fond ambition & go from winter into the middle of summer all in one quick jump. For it was just exactly mid-summer Thursday in Cocoa as I discern —

Vacationer stationery letter. (Dunbar family collection.)

modern home beautifully furnished. Then we trucked off to a colorful spot called the "Castaway Club." One of my classmates, an engineering officer at the base, was there with his wife. Later in the evening, we sang some Whiffenpoof songs, "corny," but pleasant to both of us. I still felt like singing at 7:30 this morning.

Roy arranged for a "hop" this afternoon and I went along. We were up over two hours in a PBM, the most colossal ship you ever did see. It's most as big as the Clippers and looks even more grace-ful. Roy took off and landed the ship and flew a good part of the time. He was practicing under the hood while we were in the air. I profited by the experience for I sat right behind him, listened over an extra set of earphones, and followed the procedure. It was some thrill to have the privilege. I don't believe I can describe it except to say it was some experience!

Tonight, as I came to the station at Cocoa, the only person about was a man waiting on the platform with the mailbags. I went up to ask him about the train. I knew he was familiar when I was yet sev-eral steps away. So I greeted him with words to that effect. I asked him whether he'd ever been outside of Florida. He replied "yes, in Connecticut." Well, it was Pop Chrisman from Indian Neck. I bought a Ford battery from him. He's mail-clerking down here now. He's going to mail me Pondie's address in Miami, so I can write him about selling the sailboat.

I am going back to the base tonight. We are to report by 8:00 A.M. tomorrow. Bill Stuhlman and I are planning to room together, and I hope it works out that way.

My cash supply is low. I hope you can hold out until next payday. It grieves me to be such a poor debtor again, but this time I feel my money has not been frittered away, even though I have spent a goodly amount.

I'll write you my address at Jacksonville tomorrow. For now, my happy greetings and best wishes.
Love to both of you,
Stuff

As ground school got under way at NAS Jacksonville, training for the ca-dets intensified. The letters from Carl are sprinkled with descriptive ref-erences to the new Florida surroundings, the new aircraft being flown, and the scheduled tasks that awaited him as his training progressed.

In early March, west of Jacksonville at Eglin Army Air Force Base in the Florida panhandle, other pilots—these selected by Lieutenant Col-onel Doolittle—were also in training, simulating short-distance take-offs, practicing over-water navigation techniques, and learning cruise control for long-distant flights. While they prepared and honed these special skills, the pilots at the base at Eglin, like the cadets at Jacksonville, remained unaware of the roles for which they were preparing.

While the Army pilots trained at Elgin into the middle of the month, the USS *Hornet* passed through the Panama Canal and into the Pacific Ocean. The *Hornet*'s destination was the Alameda Naval Air Station near San Francisco, California, where she was to await the delivery of her special fleet of aircraft.[4]

Mailed March 18, 1942

Cadet Carl O. Dunbar, Jr.
Building 704, Room 244
U.S.N.A.B.
Jacksonville, Fla.
Sunday
Dear Mom and Dad,

Jacksonville is a tremendous place, but it is a grand place as well. We are all very favorably impressed and happy to be stationed here. Once again, we seem to be gentlemen. We were given liberty this weekend, but I remained aboard. I went swimming twice yesterday in one of the four pools and again this afternoon. The way my arms and back feel, I have had enough sunshine for the present.

Bill went to the infirmary yesterday with German measles. Two others of our section were confined yesterday also. There are a great many cases about, so I may well be coming down soon with measles. I am hoping to last out at least until Thursday when we are to be sworn in. For then I will receive cadet pay and have an opportunity to skip two weeks of waiting and start classes with the section ahead of us. There are at least five weeks of ground school before we start flying, which is a long prospect with so many planes flying overhead. It looks as though we would specialize earlier, skipping the usual procedure of training in all types of ships. Thus, we can spend proportionately more time in the type of flying we finally take up. We will have three months of intensive training after receiving our commissions here.

It's time to start thinking about chow, so I'll make this a short note. I talked with Bud Tator for awhile at the pool this afternoon. Met Carter Dye at Ship's Service yesterday. Coke Morton, an officer, walked by and I practically knocked the window out. I felt pretty foolish afterward.

I'll write soon and let you know how things are shaping up. How about that picture in the Register? I have one.

Best regards and good health.

Love,

Stuff

Carl did not come down with the German measles as he had supposed he would, and after his letter on March 18, he became one of fifty cadets to be accelerated in the training. In his next letter home, he begins his speculation about the aircraft options in his future. For Navy and Marine Corps pilots, these options included the seaplanes prevalent at Jacksonville, torpedo-bombers, dive-bombers, and carrier-based fighter planes. For most cadets, fighters were considered the elite assignment of the air fleet; to be considered for fighters, a pilot was required to master acrobatics, tactics, high-altitude flight, aerial gunnery, and proficiency in carrier landings and takeoffs.[5] Assignment to a fighter squadron came only after a pilot demonstrated competency in each of these essential skills.

The journey to war for the pilots was more than an arduous training regime and speculation about where their paths would lead. The young warriors were also learning to deal with uncertain futures and long absences from home. It brought about a reordering of personal priorities, and it was a time of changing personal relationships. For Carl, Jacksonville marked a time of change in his relationship with Jeanne and a time to reflect on the relationships of friends that had taken a different course.

On March 19 Carl was sworn into active duty as an Aviation Cadet in the United States Navy, and in his next letter home, he shares the news with the family along with some of the uncertainties that the future might hold as his odyssey continued.

Mailed March 21, 1942

U.S. Naval Air Station
Jacksonville, Florida
Friday

Dear Mom and Dad,

Your letters are certainly grand. I have just finished reading the word from home which arrived in this afternoon's mail. It's not hard to feel that I am sitting right at home listening instead of reading fifteen hundred miles away.

We were sworn in as Aviation Cadets Thursday afternoon. At the same time, fifty of us were advanced two weeks to take preliminary ground-school with the preceding class. Bill and Doc were among those advanced. It means that we will probably commence flying in the latter part of April, two or three weeks ahead of schedule. It will be nearer October than August when we are commissioned. This two weeks now will affect that date but little. The main result is that we will get started on the way sooner and cut out of two weeks marking time.

I went for an hour hop this morning in a PBY. It was very interesting, but I must admit that big-boat flying isn't very exciting. Right now, even if the choice were mine to make, I don't know whether it would be for fighters or for P-boats. Still minus the acrobatic training, I lean heavily toward the type of flying which fighter pilots do. On the other hand, I'd much prefer to be shore-based than carrier-based. And besides that, only a small percentage of those selected to go to Miami for further training make fighter pilots. The rest get torpedo and dive-bombing. I don't care much for either. Much will depend, of course, on the pressure-chamber test yet to come. Meantime, I shall try and make up my mind in case there is a chance of personal choice. That possibility is rather remote.

Fred Murphy, Yale '40, and I went to call on Ensign Cross, who is player-manager of the baseball team. He inquired about the positions we played and we replied. His next question was, "How many years of professional ball have you played?" It turned out that everyone on the team has played Class B professional ball or better.

Nevertheless, we are going to give them a sample of our offerings. We saw the team play the Atlanta Crackers this afternoon and they didn't look too impressive, at least not over awing. I may be forced to build up my past playing experience, but even so I probably won't get more than a glimpse of the team.

Glad to hear that you did the New York trip up round. This is a good time to indulge in a little relaxation to forget about the world for a few hours. Goodness knows the world is too much with us these days. I knew yesterday that you had called Jeanne for she wrote about it in her letter. I think it was very fine of you to call her. You would never be out of place calling Jeanne regardless of our relationship, for we shall always be the closest of friends, if no more. I can say that we are not enough more than that to consider marriage when I am commissioned, and, for that reason, it matters little whether we are more than close friends. The future is far too indefinite and the prospect of long absence too great to support any plans or hopes beyond that. At Squantum, I sensed the impossibility of making definite plans and the weekend before I left for Atlanta verified that premonition. It didn't make those happy days at home any less enjoyable and it has made me much happier since, for I have not been living in chimerical hope. The issue is definitely settled and it makes little difference to me what were the circumstances which decided the issue. I don't really know myself whether it was our mutual good judgment, or Jeanne's, or some external force as the ending of a summer aura or an interest in someone else. I have no reason to believe it is the latter. In any case, it has turned out for the best with nothing but happiness to remember and look forward to again this fall when I hope to be home for two weeks.

The letter from Boundbrook which you forwarded was an announcement of Wanda Anderson's marriage to Ensign Robert Owen, Yale '41. Murph and I both enjoyed the Alumni weeklies. Together with a visit with Scotty McLennan, they brought the class history pretty much up to date. He came up to the room Wednesday while I was away and left a message and his room number. We went to call on him that evening. There was some talk of cadet officer appointments. All cadet life is prescribed by cadet officers. But there has been nothing official. And I am quite certain that with this advance of two weeks, no appointments will concern me. (Scotty is a platoon sub-commander.) I read a good letter from Mrs. Murdoch with a good deal of campus news. Jake Dove is with Army Air in Washington (state), and Jack Schroder is at sea.

(Jeanne wrote that one of her good friends was on the tanker Bolivar which was torpedoed. He was one of the few survivors picked up by the Navy and taken to Guatemala. He returns again to the same duty.)

I must close here. I hope you will extend my best regards to everyone at home. I did write to the fellows in Department G at the factory, but as yet I've not fulfilled any other correspondence obligations. I envy you the spring cleaning outdoors, but most of all the next two months of spring.

You have all my best wishes for continued good health. Do let me hear from you soon.

Love,

Stuff

The passing reference to the torpedoing of the 15,000-ton tanker Bolivar in his letter of March 21 is the first of three descriptive accounts about the enemy submarine activity in the coastal proximity to NAS Jacksonville; activity that Jacksonville residents came to know firsthand during the spring and early summer of 1942.

The torpedo attack on the Esso Bolivar occurred on March 3 approximately thirty miles south of the naval base at Guantánamo Bay, Cuba. Despite the loss of the captain and seven crew members in the attack and "a gaping torpedo hole (that) had almost cut the ship in half," the badly damaged tanker was able to return to Guantánamo Bay (and not to Guatemala, as Carl had written).[6] The Bolivar was empty at the time the torpedo struck and on its way to take delivery of a full cargo of aviation fuel.

As the cadets progressed through their training at NAS Jacksonville, the Bolivar was one of many vessels lost in the U-boat carnage.[7] By March 4, German submarines had sunk or severely damaged sixty-five merchant ships in the coastal waters of the Atlantic and Caribbean, and many more were to follow.[8]

While training continued into the month of March against the backdrop of nearby U-boat activity, the Army pilots at Eglin completed their specialized training and prepared to move their B-25s to the naval air station at Alameda, California. When the bomber pilots left Florida, they were still unaware of the mission for which they had been chosen.[9]

Mailed March 31, 1942

Monday

Dear Mom and Dad,

Last week slipped by faster than I expected. With every day a full one now and two or three leisurely evenings last week when they were done, I just missed up on any writing. My letter tonight won't be long for I am very weary. I had an MOD watch Friday night for which I had to roll out at 5 A.M., and then we had a big weekend. So you see there is every reason for a weary head and tired body.

I said that our days are full. Since indoctrination began last Monday, we have a deadly routine. I think a straight away description will best illustrate it. Reveille, as before, 5:45. We muster outside in the dark. After cleaning and shaving and cleaning the room, we muster again at 6:25 for breakfast. At 7:25, we leave barracks to muster down the way for drill. Thence until 9:05, we march on the macadam mat with 12-pound rifles, ammunition belt and bayonets. Fifteen minutes from then until code and blinker class. Except for forty minutes out at lunchtime, classes continue without interruption until 4:00. Then we have another hour and a half of drill. Frankly, there's hardly time even to read mail until after evening chow. At the present rate, we are due to commence flying in three weeks. Already we have traded in our blue-wool receiving ship jackets for leather flying jackets.

Bill and Doc and I were measured for white uniforms this afternoon by the tailor who outfitted Roy. The government will issue us two sets of whites, but they will not be here for over a month yet, and whites become uniform-of-the-day week after next or sooner.

More to the point, however, is the need for more than just the government issue. Four is the minimum required of Ensigns when they receive commissions. This set will cost $17 complete, which can be paid on successive paydays by installment, if such is more convenient. I will need white shoes, and if I remember correctly, I have a pair there at home which are in good shape. Wonder if you could send them to me. Also I'd like the blue laundry bag. You asked about the records. Better wait until payday, sometime these next two weeks. I'll let you know definitely then. I am quite perturbed not to have reimbursed you sooner for the loan. Moving from Atlanta has upset the pay schedule considerably. I hope that you can forebear. As for the tobacco, it's well enough off with you, I believe. There really isn't much time to smoke. And soon it will be too hot to smoke anyway.

This last weekend was very windy and so somewhat chilly. Nevertheless, we spent most of Sunday on the beach or in trunks, at least. In the morning, we had to hide behind a bulkhead out of the wind to be warm enough lying on the sand. But in the afternoon, the sun took care of everything. The breakers and the long collar of sand were very enticing, but I couldn't work up enough enthusiasm to swim as we did the weekend before.

The Alumni Weekly came in this afternoon's mail. For the first time since leaving the hallowed halls, I felt a real longing to be back in school and a part of the campus again. Reading Liscum Borden's article on the campus activities and feeling the old undergraduate spirit certainly brought back many happy memories and tugged away at the old strings of longing.

I had a wonderful letter from Tim last week, about the longest and most sincere letter I've ever had. The greater part of it, he was writing about my present situation, not only mine but all of ours; it was his reply to some of my reactions which I had written and described to him. There were, however, a very unhappy few pages, too, that told of the end of Tim's and Ruthie's two years together. I never expected that anything would break them apart, and I don't believe that any external force could have. They decided that their aims in life were not as parallel as they had hoped and that in the long run, they could not make real happiness out of marriage and life together. So they concluded that friendship henceforth would be the basis of their relationship. I found it hard to comprehend what Tim's written words were saying; it left me feeling rather hollow when I had finished reading. But the bubble has bursted.

I haven't heard from Seaver, though I wrote him while we were at Atlanta. I looked into the decoding business as far as I could and sent along the dope to him. I have been hoping that he would let me know whether he made any inquiries and also whether Ruthie is back at home in Pennsylvania yet.

Taps has just been announced so I must close. I wish that I could send some of the sunshine and azaleas and tan along with my letter. There's more than any of us can use. I'll be writing again this week, but meantime take good care and let me know that all is well. For the present,
Love,
Stuff

As March turned to April in Jacksonville, Carl's focus away from the training regime was on the details for his new uniforms, memories of the campus back at Yale, and the end of the relationship between two of his friends. During this same period, at the War Department in Washington, military leaders who believed that the fastest way to defeat Japan was to attack directly across the Central Pacific were confronted with the official surrender of the remaining U.S. forces on the Bataan Peninsula in the Philippines,[10] a seriously depleted Pacific naval fleet, and no realistic opportunity to pursue a Central Pacific offensive strategy. By default, the only American offensive operation to be launched against the Japanese from north of the equator in 1942 fell to the pilots commanded by Lieutenant Colonel Doolittle.

In the South Pacific, the harassing tactics ordered by Admiral Nimitz and carried out by the three U.S. Fleet carriers—USS *Lexington*, *Enterprise*, and *Yorktown*—had slowed Japanese advances in the region, but by any comparison, the enemy still possessed overall superiority in the theater. With Australia and New Zealand serving as a foundation of Allied support, however, the opportunity to concentrate forces somewhere north of Australia in the South Pacific presented a realistic option to offer an armed response to the enemy before 1942 came to an end, and the Allied strategists focused their attention on this alterative.[11]

In Tokyo, two options for an expanded Pacific offensive remained under consideration—Yamamoto's plan to move against the Central Pacific island of Midway and the alternative strategy that called for increased presence in the South Pacific to sever the link between Australia and the United States. The Imperial High Command was aware of the increasing strength of the Allies in Australia. As U.S. men and supplies continued to flow into Australia in the spring of 1942, Japan countered with a slow and steady build up of their own in the islands north of the Coral Sea at Rabaul on New Britain and on Bougainville in the northern Solomon Islands.[12]

As April began and the opposing forces considered their options, primary ground school continued for the cadets at NAS Jacksonville, and their hours of leisure time were spent enjoying the Atlantic beaches and the waters of the St. Johns River in the warming spring weather.

On the second of April on the other side of the continent, the USS *Hornet* departed San Francisco to begin its voyage west into the Central Pacific. Tied to its flight deck were 16 newly arrived B-25 Mitchell bombers commanded by Lieutenant Colonel Doolittle.[13] The following day, Doolittle's Army Air Corps pilots who had trained at Eglin were told of their destination and the purpose of the mission.[14]

Mailed Apr 7, 1942

Naval Air Station
Jacksonville
Monday
Dear Mom and Dad,
    Bill and Doc and Andy—all four of us—skipped the first part of study hour a short while ago tonight to take a swim in the new pool just outside our back door. We were sticky and hot after two games of horseshoes and the swim was just what we needed. We're sitting around the table in shorts now, feeling very comfortable. I imagine

that fans will be in order tonight, unless the breeze swings around to our side of the building.

We finished ground school on Friday with no particular trouble and no studying except for an hour or so before the exams. And today we began ground school, engines, aerodynamics, aerology, radio voice procedure, and continued code and blinker. Only two weeks now until we commence flying. The way time has been speeding by, two weeks will be more like two days. We will all be happy to get in the air again, although it will mean the end of our weekends. Two days at the beach every week have spelled the time well-nigh perfectly. We recuperate just about in time to begin all over again. This week we're having a beach party with all the fixings.

Last Saturday afternoon, four of us went for a sail in one of the sloops which are available here at the base for cadets and officers. Because the basin is also used by PBY's and observation planes, sailboats are obliged to remain close to shore until they reach 2 or 3 miles upstream. We proceeded upstream and across to the other side of the river and the wind died completely. However, we were close to shore and Doc and Bill and Andy hopped ashore and up to a nearby store to buy some cold beer; the hot sun wasn't bad at all with a little refreshment. Well, about that time, we spied a little girl sunning herself on the end of a pier. We hauled down the sails and pulled out the paddles. It was a little tough, bucking the current, but we were soon within range of her charm. It was my duty as skipper to ask permission to call the base and explain our plight. She was very obliging. I needn't tell you that it was a real treat to walk into a well-furnished, clean house and chat for a few minutes with her family. The house was almost hidden behind a screen of Spanish moss–laden trees on the river bank and orange trees in the yard. Everyone came back down to the pier to wish us bon voyage; now I'm just waiting for a free Sunday afternoon to invite Nancy over here to the cadet club for one of the tea dances. You surely can't tell what will happen next down here.

I was very happy to receive the pictures of you and Sis. They greet me in the morning and bid me goodnight each day. I liked the one of you, Mom, which was in the folder; though I did change it from left to right. I don't want to always be asking for favors from home, but a box of your cookies certainly would hit the spot. Just sometime when you happen to be fussing around the kitchen.

I've had a little trouble with my right ear this past week, but it's practically well again. Apparently, some fine sand blew into it a week ago Sunday while we were seeking some sun on the beach. The ear began aching Monday night. I saw the Doc Tuesday a.m., but he could find no infection and suggested a foreign particle which had caused tension on the drum. I couldn't hear a thing all week until yesterday afternoon. I have been a little apprehensive, especially with the old right ear and it's a relief to be nearly recovered.

Taps is about to catch me so I'll close here. Hope all is well in the Elm City and that spring is already with you. Best of health.

Love,

Stuff

The basin of the St. Johns River adjacent to NAS Jacksonville provided safe harborage not only for the sailboats used by the cadets for recreation but also for the PBY Catalina flying boats and the OS2U Kingfisher seaplanes used to patrol the coastal waters in search of enemy submarines. In the merchant shipping lanes adjacent to the Atlantic beaches, however, there was no "safe harbor."

Between February 19 and May 14, sixteen merchant ships were sunk inside the Florida territorial waters alone, and four other vessels were heavily damaged in German submarine attacks.[15] Among the casualties was the SS *Gulfamerica*, a 8,801-ton oil tanker on her maiden voyage up the Atlantic seaboard fully loaded with ninety thousand barrels of fuel oil from Port Arthur, Texas.

The *Gulfamerica* was torpedoed and sunk directly off the Jacksonville beaches by the German submarine U-123 on the night of April 11, 1942.[16] In the daylight hours before the attack, the commander of *U-123* had conned his boat close to the Atlantic beaches where the cadets spent parts of their leisure time and that Carl describes in his letters. From the submarine's periscope, the captain was able to recognize cabanas, beach houses, a pier, a roller coaster, and other amusement rides. He concluded in his log that *U-123* had arrived as planned off Jacksonville

Beach south of the mouth of the St. Johns River, and he began the wait for darkness and the opportunity to unleash the U-boat's deadly armaments.[17]

Not more than five minutes after the submarine's torpedo struck the *Gulfamerica*, PBY flying boats from NAS Jacksonville were over the site dropping magnesium flares into the night sky in search of *U-123*.[18] The efforts were for naught, however, and the submarine slipped away in the darkness. *U-123* was able to continue its attacks on the shipping along the Florida coast until its cargo of torpedoes was exhausted, and its last torpedo was expended in a successful sinking off the coast of Cape Canaveral. Search planes were dispatched again following the attack off Cape Canaveral, this time from the naval air station at Banana River, but as it had after the sinking of the *Gulfamerica*, *U-123* escaped into the night and ultimately returned safely to Germany.[19]

Remnants from the sinking of the *Gulfamerica* by *U-123* and the effects of other U-boat attacks off the Atlantic coast on the beaches of Jacksonville are described in two of Carl's next letters. The first letter was penned three days after the sinking of the *Gulfamerica*, and the other was written on April 23, after the cadets had returned to flight training at NAS Jacksonville.

Mailed April 14, 1942

> Naval Air Station
> Jacksonville
> Monday
> Dear Mom and Dad,
>   There is a little time now before chow that I can begin this letter, and then I'll finish it after dinner.
>   Shoes and laundry bag and the caricatures arrived this afternoon. Just in good season, too, for we expect to be wearing whites this coming weekend, which is our last one for a month or two. I very much appreciate your sending them along. It will save me about ten dollars and as soon as the government whites are distributed, it will give me a change of white shoes so that I can keep one

pair cleaned. I understand that the soles are usually white rubber. I shall probably have the edges of these painted white.

At present I am nursing a beautiful shiner and a great puffed cheek, with a fairly good cut just below and inside my left eye. It was quite a weekend! I've never had so many people stare at me, nor have I replied with the same answer—"I bumped into a door"— to so many. As soon as we climbed out of bed Sunday morning, I bought a pair of dark glasses. But late in the day, those were discarded. Perhaps I was hypersensitive about my eye, but it seemed to me that everyone on and driving over the beach looked at me, some smiling, some disgusted, some just wondering. The fellows had a time here today ribbing me and making all sorts of stories out of my simple answer. Actually, it's considerably less swollen today, but the coloring has increased. Oh yes, I suppose you are wondering how it happened. You'd never guess. Two of us were riding on the front fenders of Paul's station wagon Saturday night on the way to a barbecue in Neptune Forest. The car was packed full of people and food, and the fenders were our only place to ride. It was fine until a little polecat appeared down the dirt road ahead of us. Paul immediately gave chase and we bore closer and closer upon the doggone thing. Finally, when we were less than ten feet from it, I piled off the fender. As the car went by, the side mirror clipped me solidly just under the eye. So you see. (Oh, we didn't get scented. The skunk jumped into the underbrush just after I, too, jumped.)

We didn't get to the beach Saturday until 10:00. To begin with, we didn't leave the base until late and then we ran into a total blackout. After four tankers had sunk just off the beach in 48 hours, the blackout measure was put into effect. Apparently the silhouettes of the ships from the shore lights had made them excellent targets. So heading toward the beach, when we finally managed to get by the barriers, parking lights were obligatory and finally no lights at all. The blackout itself was very successful. There were wardens with red and green flashlights at every corner and frequently in-between. Civilian and army units joined in close collaboration to see that no lights were showing. Some places were boarded up with tar-paper, and we didn't even know they were open. I rather imagine that the blackout will be a permanent thing here for the duration. It probably will not alleviate the crucial situation regarding our shipping, but at least it is an attempt. There seems to be no defense against the subs. I wish we could begin sending our oil via the inland route.

Mom, you asked about calling Jeanne. I thought I urged you to go ahead as you were planning, but perhaps I forgot it. I should still be spending every weekend I could in Montclair if I were still working in New Haven. I think you can appreciate that the war alone would put a pretty big question mark in any relationship—it makes any plans impossible. Furthermore, I suspect there is something else. But it doesn't make me unhappy. Whether or not Jeanne and I are as close as I had thought and hoped, we have far too much experience in common, filled with wonderful memories, to be any less cordial friends. So you go right ahead, if you really enjoy being with Jeanne, and I hope that you do. She likes you very much and I know that she would like to hear from you. I imagine that her time on Saturday will be limited, but don't let that stop you. I haven't been too good a correspondent myself up until a week ago, when the novelty of our rather high-speed life here began to wear off. You know how I feel about Jeanne, but I don't think you can make much of a message of that. I'm still waiting for Jeanne's picture, which, she wrote, was in the offing.

I thought of you, Dad, as we lived through two evenings of blackouts last weekend. And I don't mind saying that, as far as individual homes are concerned, you are miles ahead of Jacksonville in the way of blackouts and air raid protection. I didn't see New Haven blacked-out, but I imagine that, too, is immeasurably ahead.

Well, I did finish before chow. However it's time to run off now. So I will close with many thanks and much love to you both.
Sincerely,
Stuff

Carl's black eye, suffered courtesy of the station wagon's rearview mirror during an evening of revelry, was of his own doing. His firsthand account of the "black-out" on the same evening, however, was as a result of the action taken by Florida governor Spessard Holland following the

shore-based officer to have a car. I couldn't understand that at first, when Roy was considering buying a new car. I thought, in the event that I should be shore-based, for some few months, perhaps I could begin making payments to you on the Ford and use it as long as I stay in the States. Just consider this a feeler and no idea on which I am counting. I wanted to let you know that I was giving the matter some thought in case it might make some difference in your plans.

Word from Roy yesterday finds him in Key West for the rest of the month and then back to Cocoa. I don't know whether that's for publication, so keep it more or less at home. I gather from his letter that the Divinity School has made a coup, though the word causes no great unhappiness down here. The night I stayed with Roy, we started the evening at the home of a girl whose family spends a good part of the year at Cocoa and the rest in Illinois. Roy was invited to her home for dinner the next evening and apparently, all went very well. For he writes that she drove down to Key West with a married couple and himself and stayed there with his shipmate's wife for a week or so. How much happier, really, that he can live normally without pining away for something which didn't deserve the heartache!

George writes that you sent him pictures of me in uniform. He seemed to appreciate them very much; though I find them a bit too boy-scoutish for satisfaction. With our white cap-covers, the uniforms look 100% better. I lost my own cap weekend before last and since then have been wearing an extra one I borrowed. Five of us had our caps hanging up in a rendezvous at the beach. Sometime during the evening, mine walked out. I imagined that it would turn up the next day under soberer conditions, but it didn't; so I chalk it off. I shall either buy the one I have borrowed or buy a new officer's cap and wear the cadet insignia. Most of the class went three weeks ago to have pictures taken for the yearbook in white uniform. Some of them are very good. I was at the baseball diamond when they went. Bill missed, too, and we have been planning to go over since. If my eye permits (it is practically well), we may go for a sitting this Saturday. I hope the pictures will turn out well enough to send one along.

I should close here and spend an hour or so studying for the three exams tomorrow on our first two weeks of ground school—Engines, Theory of Flight, and Radio Code Procedure. Bill and Doc and Pete are holding a seminar down the hall; so I shall run and join them over a cookie box.

Many thanks for word and gift. I hope you are both in best health and living right in the midst of springtime. I'll be writing again soon.

Love,

Stuff

As the cadets progressed through the ground school curriculum described in the letter mailed on April 17, Carl's interests were of events at home—the sale of his small sailboat that had been used during family summers at the shore and the resignation of Dr. Albert E. Parr as the director of the Peabody Museum of Natural History at Yale.[25] Carl expresses his hope that the university will consider Professor Dunbar as the successor to Dr. Parr, and he asks his father about his interest in the vacant post.

When the evaluation of candidates for the directorship of the museum got under way at Yale, in the central Pacific far from New Haven, the mission urged by President Roosevelt was in its final stage of readiness aboard the USS *Hornet* as the carrier continued to steam east toward Japan. Doolittle's squadron of B-25 bombers was aligned on the carrier's flight deck and readied for the mission. Ammunition and bombs were loaded into the airframes, aircraft engines were given last-minute run-ups, and by sunset the loading and positioning of all of the planes had been completed.[26]

The day after Carl's letter and a day earlier than originally planned, the muscular, medium-range Mitchell B-25 bombers launched successfully from the flight deck of the USS *Hornet* in heavy seas and strong morning winds.[27] After lifting off from the deck of the *Hornet*, Doolittle and the other pilots flew east toward Japan intent on delivering their planned surprise attack. Fifteen of the sixteen B-25s were successful in reaching their objectives, and the crews began to open their bomb bay doors over the target cities of Tokyo, Yokohama, Kobe, Osaka, and Nagoya shortly after the noon hour on April 18.[28]

Three days after the Doolittle raid, on April 21, 1942, the cadets at NAS Jacksonville were given their permanent military flight logbooks, and after a training flight in an N2S-1 Stearman biplane, Carl made his first entry into the logbook that remained with him until the end of the war.[29] The logbook kept by each pilot chronicled his progression toward proficiency, his flight time, his extensive and specialized training, the type of aircraft he used, and, for Carl, his combat missions in the South Pacific. By the end of April, fifteen hours of flight time had been entered in Carl's new logbook, and approximately half of his hours were as a solo pilot.[30]

Mailed April 23, 1942

Wednesday

Dear Mom and Dad,

While I sit by the P.A. system, an hour-and-a-half watch here at Cecil Field, I'll write a few words to let you know that we have begun flying and that all is well.

Yesterday was my first flight and again today, we flew for 1.5 hours. This week our wing flies in the morning and goes to ground-school in the afternoon; next week the procedure will be reversed. I didn't get off to a very auspicious start yesterday, being 15 minutes late to begin with. The flight schedule was changed while I was attending code class, and consequently, I didn't get word of the change. Not only that, I had forgotten my helmet and goggles, and finally, after chasing up an outfit, I started out to the line without a chute. However, my instructor was very good about everything and warned me only not to be late again. He is a keen chap and can really fly the airplane. In fact, all the instructors seem to be outstanding. I believe that will be my second choice after fighter pilots. Flying didn't go badly at all. These Stearmans fly much the same as the E-base N3N's, only they are a little heavier, have more power, and you fly almost as much with the tab control as the stick. Being heavier, the planes land sooner after you pull the nose up, but that is better, for the plane doesn't float along waiting for a gust to blow one wing up or down. Mr. Wisner told me today that he could put me up for solo check tomorrow if I wanted to check; he continued that I was entitled to seven hours of dual instruction, and if I wanted some advance instruction in slips and small-field procedure and acrobatics, we'd go ahead and take some more dual time for that. I'm all for the instruction and so will continue with him. We did eight spins, two at a time right and left this morning, and then he did some acrobatic maneuvers which I couldn't follow. I asked him when we came in what they were, and he replied that he was trying something new, what he would do if someone were on his tail. He did a slow roll, then a snap-roll, ending in a steep bank, and several others. My stomach was a little woozy from the spins and I wondered how much it would stand. He said there was nothing unusual about that after such a long lay-off from flying and with so few hours in the air. I'll need a few more days for acclimation I guess.

The results of our first two weeks exams were posted yesterday. Everything went satisfactorily, except that Doc had some trouble with voice procedure and will have to take a re-exam. Mine averaged up to about 3.5. I'll be happy if the rest of the courses will measure up to that, but they will probably be tougher.

We spent our last weekend together at the beach. Our good friends had more than enough beds for all of us. We didn't hit the hay until after 5:00 Sunday morning. We spent most of Sunday afternoon in the surf and on the beach. The water was wonderful, but the beach itself was covered with little blotches of sticky tar-oil from the torpedoed tankers and freighters, a half-dozen of them within a hundred miles a week ago. It took kerosene to clean up our feet and hands, and even now, I have black oil between my toes. One of the little lunch counters where we find our main subsistence on weekends, had a display of grim reminders of the torpedoeings which had washed up in front on the beach. A life raft, the rudder from a whaleboat, a case of shelves, with one panel shattered by shrapnel, a tar-soaked broom and a bunch of bananas all black with tar. All the articles were covered with oil and partially burned. There was a loon dragging about the beach last weekend. It's feathers were covered with fuel oil and he could not fly. In the water, only his neck appeared. I don't believe it did get back out in the ocean again, for each time it tried, the surf pounded it back again unmercifully.

It's almost time for the bus to leave so I'll have to close here to get this addressed and mailed back at the base. I'll try and get time to write again this week. Meantime, my best wishes to you both. All good health and love,
Stuff

The letter of April 23 describes the introduction to basic acrobatics as the cadets returned to the cockpit after weeks of advanced ground school. Flight training for the pilots was now in a newer version of the Stearman biplane, and Carl continued to express his preference for permanent assignment to fighters in his correspondence.

Jim Spencer, who also flew in the South Pacific as an Army bomber pilot, described the characteristics of an emerging fighter pilot that he had witnessed during his own training.

Potential fighter pilots made themselves visible in primary flight training school by the maneuvers they were willing to try. The standard aerobatics menu of loops and rolls was too unexciting. They taught themselves upside-down spins, snap rolls beginning and ending upside down, inverted loops, vertical snap rolls with three or four rotations. A few of us believed we could actually fly backward for a few feet by cutting power and reversing the controls when we lost flying speed at the top of a vertical climb. We were fortunate to be flying Stearman biplanes, a plane so sturdy that it could hardly matter what we did with it or at what speed, it seemed impossible to tear the wings off.[31]

As Carl contemplated spins, snap-rolls, and other acrobatics at Jacksonville, the events culminating with the Doolittle raid over Japan had become the catalyst for changing strategies in the Pacific. Damage to the target cities by the incendiary bombs from the B-25s was limited, and the estimates were that only 302 casualties had been suffered and only about 90 buildings destroyed. But the impact of the raid on the

Japanese national morale was profound, and it permanently altered the mind-set of Japanese military commanders.[32]

Further opposition to Admiral Yamamoto's planned attack on the U.S. Pacific Fleet and installations at Midway quickly faded following the Doolittle raid.[33] Two weeks after Doolittle's planes disappeared over the horizon, the attack on Midway was approved by the Japanese Imperial General Staff and planning for the battle began. The intention of the Imperial Staff was to extend Japan's defensive frontier.[34] Historians now credit the impact of Doolittle's surprise attack with luring the Japanese into the decisive confrontation with the U.S. Fleet at Midway in the central Pacific.[35]

As the first days of June began to unfold, in addition to accelerating preparations for an advance against Midway, the Japanese Combined Command also dispatched two fleet carriers to join its other warships gathering in the Coral Sea south of the equator. The primary objective of these carriers was to accompany the troop convoy preparing to invade Port Moresby on the northern coast of New Guinea. As a secondary objective, the carriers were also to provide support for a smaller forward echelon of troops that intended to occupy the port of Tulagi in the southern Solomon Islands.[36]

Mailed April 28, 1942

Naval Air Station
Jacksonville
Monday
Dear Mom and Dad,

Solo check today after a big weekend was passable, but rather unsatisfactory. I don't mean that there was doubt about passing it, but my flying was miserable. There were a lot of thermals which boosted and dropped the plane a couple of hundred feet at a clip, and, on top of that, I just wasn't on the ball. Coming in after my final instruction hop just before checking, I let the ship get away from me taxiing down-wind. It spun completely around like a top, and there was nothing I could do but sit and hope the wing didn't scrape. It didn't. My first landing on the mat during check flight so scared the check-pilot that he didn't give me full control on the rest of the landings. I came in faster than I expected with one wing down, bounced on one wheel and careened off into the air again. It was most embarrassing for I haven't had any trouble all along; that was really my first bum landing.

We had a great time swimming in the surf Sunday afternoon. It was a hot day and the waves came rolling in about ten or twelve feet high. We plodded, ducked, and thrashed our way out through the breakers and then picked a big one to ride in. When you get a good start and pick the right wave, they carry you along for a hundred yards or more. I say carry; actually, they pick you up, and you plane with body out of water from the waist up. It feels like you were flying through the water. I've never experienced anything quite like it. Working out against the breakers is hard work, but lots of fun, too. It's easiest to dive through them. The water rushes by madly, sometimes somersaulting you, but usually you come through and up on the other side. Sometimes, we stayed on top. Then, the great wall of water breaks over you and practically knocks your head and shoulders off. You come sputtering to the surface with thick spume popping thick all around you, like a giant bath of ginger ale. We don't have to worry more than to keep track of each other, for the beach extends far out, and between waves, you can touch bottom with no trouble.

Whites were just made uniform-of-the-day today, and believe me, they really look snappy. All the boys who went ashore this evening were immaculately decked out in white; I think probably more went ashore than would have, just to show off their new uniforms. My government issue whites arrived today, and by Wednesday, the necessary alterations will be completed. I'll have to try them Wednesday evening.

I would write longer tonight, but taps will be sounded in about two minutes; that means lights out, and I want this to go in the morning mail. I'll need all the sleep I can get tonight for the three hour stretch of solo flying tomorrow. Flew in shirt sleeves today and it's wonderful, free and refreshing and healthy.

I'll plan to write Wednesday or Thursday. Meantime, every best wish to you both. Hope to hear from you soon.

Love,

Stuff

Beginning in May, the pilots in Carl's squadron were in the air almost every day, and on most days, they flew twice as they progressed through the assigned curriculum to be mastered. Flight time was a priority, and the need for time in the cockpit was explained by former Navy flying instructor Robert Berta in an interview with author James Bradley in 2003.

"After the pilot has soloed, experience is the best teacher," Berta told Bradley. "Experience makes the pilot. The best pilots had the most experience. We'd give them plenty of time in the air."[37]

While the training prepared Carl for destinations ahead, interest in the events at home remained a regular part of his correspondence. In New Haven, his father, a professor of paleontology and a member of the National Academy of Sciences, was selected by the university to replace Dr. Parr as the new director of the Peabody Museum, and the news was greeted as a "wonderful surprise" in Carl's next letter from Jacksonville.

Mailed May 4, 1942

Naval Air Station

Jacksonville

Sunday

Dear Mom and Dad,

What a wonderful surprise to receive word from Dad Saturday afternoon about the museum directorship! I have been waiting anxiously for further development after Dr. Parr's resignation; of course, hoping that the corporation would make the right choice. I can only extend my sincere congratulations; the news makes me very happy as it does proud. Sometimes the inner Yale sanctum is a pretty "cliquey" affair, you know. The increase in salary is impressive, but, to me, it is far less important than the recognition which the new position bestows.

All good news seems to come from home in the same week. Bill and I have mused over spring at home many times. I very much enjoyed the description of budding and already blooming spring in your letter, Mom. I can't quite picture as many tulips as you numbered, but I can see the cherry tree and all the spring flowers. I'm sure that I could never stand to live anywhere else but in New England. It didn't take many weeks away from home to convince me of that. Wish you could get some colored pictures of this springtime that I could see in the late summer when we get home.

The flying goes satisfactorily. I've been getting in three hours a day every day, which you can well believe is a good deal of flying. However, the time flies by (not to pun!) Each hop is ninety minutes long, two every afternoon or morning, with only a ten-minute rest between, time for refueling and to drink a coke. After every three solo hops, we have an instruction period. The first check, probably next Wednesday, consists of small-field procedure (a prescribed pattern around a small-field which will permit a satisfactory forced landing anywhere between 400 and 1,000 feet altitude.) For different altitudes, there are different procedures, which demand first, the proper pattern; second, knowledge of what procedure to follow; and finally, judgment in getting the plane in. Meantime, constant climbing and gliding speeds must be maintained. Also required are four out of six circle shots—a semi-circular approach from 800 feet into a circle 100 feet in diameter. Flipper turns are the other required item—steep, near-vertical banks at constant altitudes. I've been having some trouble with slips, which are required in small-field procedure. The Navy puts the ship into a steep slip right down to the ground. You raise the ship's nose as you approach the ground, and just before it stalls in, you kick the tail around so the plane is heading straight. I have been ballooning, because I straighten out too high and with too much speed, or else I slip right into the ground, which is not recommended. It is amazing how much at home I have become in the ship in such short time. Rubbing shoulders with ten or fifteen other planes around the same small field, landing three or four abreast, no longer bothers me, and I really feel that I could ride the ship into almost any tight squeak and get it out all right. My instruction hop today was fairly good, quite surprising inasmuch as we didn't get in until 5:00 A.M. this morning. I spent the solo 90 minutes doing nothing but slips, and they seem to be coming a little better. Had some more acrobatics Saturday, rather Friday, which went well. I tried a couple of snap-rolls by myself yesterday, but they weren't too sharp.

I'd be glad if you could find out the name of the little girl from Duke, come June. We really have some pretty fine facilities here at the base, as well as some nice parties on Sunday afternoons. I haven't had anyone here, mostly because there's no one here in Jacksonville I've met who warranted that much attention.

I'm going to knock off and go to bed now. It's almost eight-thirty. This probably hasn't been much of a letter, but at least you know everything is going along well. And I did want to send my congratulations along. The whites are very comfortable wearing and quite impressive. We aim to have some pictures taken in them soon.

Give my best regards to people at home. Let me hear from you soon. Meantime, all the best of health and good fortune to you both.

Love,

Stuff

On the day that Carl wrote home to describe his progress with small-field procedures and basic tactics, the U.S. and Japanese warships that had gathered in the Coral Sea began the first major engagement between the warring adversaries following the Doolittle raid on the Japanese homeland. Between the fourth and eighth of May, the task force of American warships led by the carriers *Lexington* and *Yorktown* engaged the Japanese fleet carriers *Shokaku* and *Zuikaku* and their supporting warships that had been deployed for the invasion of Port Moresby.[38] In a confusing battle of carrier-based aircraft in which naval gunfire was never exchanged between the enemy warships, neither side gained a decisive victory.[39]

For both sides, the losses in carrier strength during the Battle of the Coral Sea were significant. American carrier planes severely damaged the *Shokaku* and badly mangled the air group of the *Zuikaku*. In response, Japanese carrier planes succeeded in sinking the *Lexington* and damaging the *Yorktown* badly enough to force its return to Pearl Harbor for repairs. Lacking adequate aircraft after the battle to support the invasion of Port Moresby, however, the Japanese were forced to recall the invasion fleet after the five-day encounter, and the Imperial High Command delayed the assault on its next primary objective in the South Pacific until later in the summer.[40]

While the primary offensive against Port Moresby had been turned back as a consequence of the sea battle, the Japanese did succeed in capturing Tulagi. The new outpost was then promptly converted to a military facility, and the harbor at Tulagi became a new base for enemy seaplane operations in the southern Solomon Islands.[41] With major Japanese installations in the north on Bougainville and a new island facility in the south, the obscure Solomon Island archipelago began to emerge as a strategic part in the geography of the Pacific conflict.

Mailed May 7, 1942

Naval Air Station
Jacksonville
Wednesday
Dear Mom and Dad,

You may find this note scratchy and unintelligible at times, for I am writing from afternoon code-class where we take alternate code and blinker, the latter with shades pulled and lights out.

I flew some better this morning passing the twenty hour check than on the previous solo check. I could have flown better and I have flown worse. However, the first stage of the flying is passed, and tomorrow's instruction hop commences acrobatics. My check pilot was a wild man from way back. After I had finished shooting circles (he stays on the ground beside the circle), he climbed in and took over. He whipped down the sandy field about 30 m.p.h. spun around and tore off over three planes sitting near the circle. He banked sharply around the field after climbing a few hundred feet, and with full throttle, went into a shallow dive, zooming the circle and several other check pilots standing there. He forgot to neutralize the tab before take-off, so I did that. Also, he forgot to lock the tail wheel as he found out when he made his final landing on the mat (the tail of the plane about did a hula). On the way back to Cecil Field, he did an inverted spin, which is some maneuver. Whereas in most maneuvers, centrifugal force tends to hold you in the plane, in the inverted spin it tends to throw you out. You hang by the safety belt and try with all your might to keep your feet on the rudder bars and your hand on the stick. You don't practice inverted spins. They're just the result of a bad acrobatic maneuver and the pilot must know how to recover from one. If you can't get your feet on the controls, you need only unbuckle the safety belt and pull the rip-cord.

Yesterday started out clear and hot. By 10 o'clock, there were great white cumulus summer clouds over most of the sky, with a network of blue sky between. On my solo hop, I climbed up through the cracks, between and above the clouds. At 5,500 feet, I was over some and among others. I found the experience quite a thrill. Instead of little tufts of cotton fluff, as the clouds appear from the ground, I found great towering columns and veritable mountains of mist, two and three thousand feet high. I danced around and between them, having a great time. The clouds give one a feeling of great height, when the ground appears between them far down. They also give a relatively stationary medium by which one can judge just how fast he is going.

I have been admiring the hyacinths which are blooming profusely this past two weeks. They must be at their peak now. They grow wild here, as you probably know, in the greatest abundance. Everywhere along the river banks they are thick, and I noticed from the plane this morning that in one stretch of the river, for about a half mile above the dam, they completely cover the water. The field of pinkish-purple blossoms over a blanket of those shiny green leaves sitting on the blue water makes a very beautiful sight, one which would do a Kodachrome proud. There are some yellow flowers in the meadows, which very much resemble a daffodil in size and color, only they bend in bell-like fashion. I haven't yet seen one close, so cannot describe them accurately.

I believe that I haven't written to you before about the marvelous weather. Since we arrived, there has been only one day of rain, three hours one afternoon. There have been a couple of showers during the night.

All for now. I'll be writing again soon. Hope you will, too.

Love,

Stuff

On May 15 Carl's training squadron left their Stearman biplanes for Ryan NR-1 "Recruits."[42] The Ryans were mono-wing trainers with 160-horse power engines. They were used in the final stages of primary training, and in these planes the pilots began their orientation to the basic flight formations used by military aircraft. For ten days Carl accumulated hours and acclimated to the characteristics of the mono-wing airplane, and on May 26 he and the other qualifying cadets moved on to yet another new and more powerful training aircraft—the Texan SNJ.

One of the choices available to the Navy cadets when their training concluded was the option to be commissioned as an officer in the U.S. Marine Corps, and in the letters written as the summer of 1942 approached, Carl tells his family that he is considering the option of flying for the Marines. In later years in rare comments about his time during the war, he would say to me that only the most skilled of the pilots were selected to fly for the Marine Corps, and that it was something much sought after by many of the Naval cadets. Although not a part of the considerations expressed in his letters, before the end of the summer the U.S. Marines Corps—both the ground forces and the pilots—were to emerge as the spearhead of the new Allied offensive in the South Pacific.[43]

Mailed May 25, 1942

Sunday

Dear Mom and Dad,

For well over a week now, I have been hoping to find time to let you know that everything is well here in Jacksonville. I have felt very uneasy receiving your good letters without returning any of them. However, life has been so busy there just hasn't been time. I checked out of primary squadron Friday and into Squadron 12 yesterday. The thirty-three hour check and preliminary formation flying in low-winged Ryans is behind me. Tomorrow will probably be my first hop in the SNJ, which is a real airplane, 750 hp, an instrument panel to end all—radio, and refrigerator with bar attachment for guests. I got a real kick out of the formation flying last week. Much of the time we were flying 6–10 feet apart, which, believe me, is plenty close. You just never take your eye off the leader's plane; your left hand is constantly jockeying the throttle and your feet are moving ceaselessly on the rudder bars to maintain the distance by slipping in or out, closer or farther away. The basic formation is a "V"; the cross-over turns the "V" into an echelon, either right or left (see letter excerpt below).

In V-formation, the two rear planes are stepped up about six feet, and in echelon all three are stepped one over the other. To change from one to the other, the leader gives the signal, which is acknowledged by the wingman. At the signal of execution, the No. 2 or 3 man, whichever is to move, climbs slightly so as to leave ten to twenty feet between himself and the other wingman and kicks rudder, sliding across the formation and then settles down into his new position (see letter excerpt next page).

knowledged by the wingman. At the signal of execution, the No. 2 or 3 man, whichever is to move, climbs slightly so as to leave ten to twenty feet between himself & the other wingman & kicks

From a left echelon, the lead can be changed. No. 2 man takes over and No. 1 slides back and under to a wing position (see letter excerpt below).

& then settles down into his new position. From a left echelon the lead can be changed. No. 2 man takes over & No. 1 slides back & under to a wing position. There is

There is quite a satisfaction in successfully flying the formations, and you also get to know where your plane is and how to control it—you have to!

Night flying was equally interesting to me. Last Monday night, I flew dual from 9:45 'til 10:45. Half of the time we spent on touch-and-go landings and takeoffs; the rest circling at 2,000 feet while the other section practiced landings. I can't deny that it was exciting to take off into the night right toward the stars and sometimes the moon. I didn't use the instrument lights, as I preferred just the radium dials; that way my eyes grew and stayed accustomed to the dark. On the ground, there were two trucks with batteries of lights illuminating a strip of the mat. We landed between the trucks across the lighted strip. All around the circular mat, red lights were spaced to outline the landing area. The tower gave us signals before each landing. Circling to two thousand feet, after the signal to climb, a showering red flare from the ground, we followed one another about, watching the tiny dots of light moving ahead of and across from us. More or less in horseplay, my instructor joined close formation with one of the other planes in the circle. That was my first taste of formation, and at night, it was doubly impressive. Tuesday night, I flew solo through the same procedure, without the formation. The night air was smooth as glass and my landings were somewhat better than during the day, in spite of the fact that at night you must feel your way down as distance perception close to the ground is practically nil.

I had a little run-in with one of the civilian instructors in communications over a little matter of inattention. He went out of his way to be obnoxious and put me on report, and I did likewise to tell him what I thought of him. Originally, I was awarded 10 demerits and 5 hours of marching on the mat, but Cmdr. Hills tore up the charge after we had a little conference. Since then, however, I have tried to toe the mark a little better, for there is a general tendency to clamp down around here, and hours can only be marched off on Sundays and Wednesdays, our only liberty days.

We are about to join the Marines, that is Doc and Bill and myself. That seems to be the best outfit for advancement and for organization. We hate to give up our Navy uniforms, but that is really of little lasting importance. I applied for carrier duty with the hope of getting fighters. That, of course, will be strictly up to me, if I am selected for carrier training. Carrier pilots go to Miami for six weeks after finishing instrument flying here (five or six weeks hence for me). There they are divided up into groups of 12 during the six-week period. Of those 12, the top 5, based on flight marks and gunnery, are chosen as fighter pilots; the next five get dive-bombing; and the last two get torpedo-bombing. Doc and Bill both have asked for P-boats and hope to get land-based bombers. It will probably be a week or more before we know what branch we will get, and another week or two after that before we know about the Marines. Only a small part of each class is selected from volunteers.

V FORMATION OF NINE NR-1½
(RYAN TRAINERS IN PRIMARY SQUADRON)

NR-1 Ryans in basic military formation flight during training at NAS Jacksonville, 1942. NR-1s were the first mono-wing aircraft introduced to cadets as they progressed through primary flight training. (Courtesy of the State Archives of Florida.)

PBY PATROL PLANE APPROACHING BEACH

"Dumbo" PBY Catalina flying boat in the harbor at NAS Jacksonville, 1942. The PBY was used for antisubmarine patrols off the Atlanta coast. In the Pacific theater, the "flying boats" were the primary equipment used for search and recovery of downed Allied pilots in the waters surrounding the Solomon Islands. (Courtesy of the State Archives of Florida.)

I got a little whap on the head swimming last Sunday that required three stitches, but it is practically recovered now and I am no worse for the wear. It looks now like it would be late July or early August when we are commissioned. Don't you be working too hard! Hope to hear from you soon. Meantime, love and good health.
Stuff

The last week in May introduced the cadets to the controls of the Texan SNJ.[44] The Texan was the universal, all-purpose training aircraft for pilots in all branches of the service during World War II. It was the transitional airplane used in preparation for duty in frontline combat aircraft, and it was faster, heavier, and more powerful than any of the previous planes flown by the cadets.[45]

As the pilots began their flight time in the cockpit of the Texan, in the Pacific theater, the Japanese Imperial Command ordered Admiral Yamamoto to deploy his assembled armada of warships into the Central Pacific against the United States. On May 27, two days after Carl's squadron began to train in the Texans at NAS Jacksonville, the Japanese fleet carriers and accompanying ships began their move toward Midway.[46] The armada sailed with nearly two hundred ships. The fleet included carriers to launch aerial attacks and to defend against air raids on the fleet. The carriers were accompanied by other warships to bombard the U.S. military installations defending Midway, and bringing up the rear were transports packed with troops and supplies for the invasion of the island.[47]

Unknown to the Imperial Command, however, American military intelligence had broken the Japanese code used for military communiqués, first to learn of the assembling naval strike force, and then to determine that the intended target of the task force was Midway.[48] Forewarned of the attack, U.S. warships and carriers with their supporting aircraft were deployed to the Central Pacific to meet the Japanese armada. The aircraft carrier USS *Kitty Hawk* arrived at Midway on May 26. On May 28 the USS *Enterprise* and USS *Hornet* were dispatched from Pearl Harbor to join the *Kitty Hawk*. They were followed two days later by the USS *Yorktown*, which had been hastily repaired at Pearl Harbor following the Battle of the Coral Sea.[49]

Seven days passed before the opposing naval forces met in the Central Pacific. In Jacksonville, the cadets spent the week in the cockpit of the SNJ, making a routine progression to high altitude flight conditions.

Mailed May 29, 1942

Thursday

Dear Mom and Dad,

There is a bit more time these days here at Squadron 12. Until after solo in the SJN's anyhow, which should be Saturday for me. I still feel very uncertain about these heavy fast ships, not particularly in the air, for they fly easily and beautifully. But I don't feel that I have much control after landings, and a ground-loop here is worth 3 to 5 thousand dollars. Perhaps things will go better after I solo. My instructor makes me rather jumpy and rattles me somewhat for he is continually on my neck. He wants things done faster than I seem to think of them. And then I dope off occasionally, too.

We had the oxygen chamber test yesterday, went up to 16,000 feet for 20 minutes without oxygen and then on up to 26,000 for another 20 minutes with oxygen. They have been going up to 35,000 feet, but the doctor on duty this week gets the bends; so until better equipment arrives for him, the ceiling is 26,000. They say there is very little difference with oxygen anyhow. After sitting at 16,000 for 20 minutes, we were given a 12 wpm code-test and a navigation problem. Things are just a little fuzzy and you feel a little light-headed, though I encountered little trouble. The lights grow dimmer and your fingernails and tongue turn bluish. The oxygen mask sets all right immediately, and there is little sensation going higher up; except a gradual decrease of pressure on the ears and expansion of the gas on your stomach. The chap next to me had to have oxygen on the way up at 13,000; he would have passed out and nearly did anyway. He definitely won't get fighters. My ears gave me no trouble coming down or going up. We kept clearing them on the way down. One chap had trouble and it was necessary to level off and climb 1,000 feet several times.

There was a package this week—a carton of cigarettes—from the service club of Department G at the factory with a short note from Mr. Guinan, our timekeeper and the club secretary. It was good to receive greetings from the men; they asked for more word from here which I shall try to provide soon. We are just beginning work on gunnery—machine guns next week—so perhaps I can drop George a note soon and tell him what we are doing in gunnery. I believe we work only on .30-caliber guns, but there is a great similarity between them and the .50's.

Doc decided not to apply for the Marine Corps, so that leaves Bill and me holding the fort. We are neither one completely convinced that it is the only thing, though it still appears more attractive. I guess our minds won't be definitely made up until final applications are called for, sometime in the next two weeks.

All this work on planting sounds very ambitious. I am not surprised at the favorable comments, however, for I've yet to see anything but the best when you put your hand to landscaping or garden-planting, Mom. Someday I'd like to see you with a greenhouse there off the northwest corner of the house; it might be a bit of a chore at times, but there's something about flowers the year round, and all kinds of plants, tropical, etc., that appeals to me very much. Maybe you are glad enough for a rest by the time the gardening season is over.

I was just wondering, Dad, whether you had moved your office or whether the official seat had moved. I suppose for awhile there will be all sorts of details and problems which will plague you with their frequency and trifling nature. Perhaps that is to be expected in a day's work now.

Well, I'll paddle off for today wishing you all good health. Hope to hear from you soon.

Love,

Stuff

As May came to an end, 62.3 hours of accumulated flight time had been recorded in Carl's logbook—37.8 hours were in the Stearman N2S, 17.5

hours were in the Ryan NR-1, 7 hours were in the SNJ Texan, and of the total, 35.8 hours were solo.[50]

In June cadets moved to another new aircraft—the Vought OS2U-2 "Kingfisher" mid-wing monoplane.[51] The OS2U-2 was designed as a floatplane, and it saw combat action in all theaters of the war as a battleship-based plane used for air-sea rescue, antisubmarine patrol, and general utility. Modified versions of the Kingfisher, like those at the Jacksonville and Banana River Stations, were shore-based, and these aircraft were used primarily for antisubmarine patrols and could be mounted with two 350-pound, antisubmarine depth charges.

The modified land-based Kingfishers were also used for training at NAS Jacksonville, and as the summer approached, Carl and the other squadron pilots were assigned to the OS2U-2 as they continued to familiarize themselves with the basics of military flight formations. With the arrival of the first week in June, Carl entered his final month of training at Jacksonville.

Mailed June 3, 1942

Tuesday

Dear Mom and Dad,

Another graduation here for me since the last letter. I believe last week when I wrote, the SNJ was pretty much a muddle; it seemed like too much airplane to handle after only 6 hours of dual instruction. Well, the fourth period things all seemed to fall into line, and after the first few minutes of solo yesterday, I really began to feel at home in it. I spent most of the first hour and a half doing touch and go landings, first on an outlying grass field and then on the asphalt mat back here at the station. The second period, another chap and I went for a bit of an excursion some fifty or sixty miles down the coast. It seems incredible that Bob, just the previous hour, had flown over his hometown and over his house 110 miles south of here by car, about 80 by air. He made the round trip in an hour and a half. I can't quite conceive of dropping up for a quick visit from

New York City, but Bob did even better than that. Of course, it is illegal to fly more than about twenty miles from the base, especially along the coast which is a Civil Airway. But we were trusting and just hoped no one would see us or report us. On the way back home, we flew formation and buzzed back and forth at each other on our radios. The J's are beautiful ships in the air with their landing gear retracted. If you see a picture of them in flight, you can believe that it is not flattering. I pulled the sliding hood over my head, pushed off my goggles with blue sky above, clouds below, warm sun beating through the glass into the cockpit, with 750 hp throbbing in front of me as we cruised along beside each other at 160 mph. Need I tell you it was quite a thrill? If I get carrier duty, I will have 60 to 70 hours in the J. I look forward to them.

Well, after those two periods yesterday totaling three hours, I kissed the J's good-bye and today soloed an entirely different ship, the OS2U-2, an observation scout which is used on cruisers and battleships, as well as inshore patrol. We have an hour and a half of instruction, which is largely a solo flight with corrections; for the instructor is in the rear cockpit with practically no vision, only three instruments and a very abbreviated stick. And after that, we solo the ship for two periods. It is simple to fly, but it broadens your flying experience. Next on the schedule is a week of formation flying, 3 & 9 planes, in the OS's. After that, we have two and a half weeks of instrument flying and then off to Miami.

We have given up the idea of the Marines. So unless we are drafted, we shall stick to the Navy. I thought that you might be relieved, for it is true that the Marines get the hot end of the poker.

Jeanne asked me to send Dad her congratulations. I read this week's Yale Alumni Weekly with pleasure and pride, and I might add that the list of accomplishments and honors ascribed to the new director was very impressive. I had no idea that they were so extensive.

I must close now and get about my celestial navigation homework. Hello to Sis, who must be home with you now. Hope she'll have time to drop me a line soon. And I hope the finals turned out well.

For tonight, best of health and good fortune still.

All love,

Stuff

For four successive days after Carl's letter on June 3, the Battle of Midway raged between the American and Japanese fleets in what became one of the decisive naval engagements of the Pacific War.[52] On the first day of the engagement, Japanese carrier planes initially tangled with an attacking squadron of low-flying U.S. Navy torpedo bombers, and of the forty-one Navy planes that took off in this first wave against the Japanese invasion fleet, only four returned to their home carriers.[53] But unknown to the Japanese pilots fighting off the first wave of American planes at deck level, an additional squadron of high-flying TBD-1 Devastator torpedo bombers was following behind the first wave.[54]

Within a matter of hours on the first day of the battle, this second wave of torpedo bombers had mortally wounded three of the Japanese carriers, and on the following day, the American carrier-based planes sank a fourth Japanese flattop.[55] The American fleet lost the carrier *Yorktown* on the final day of the battle, but the destruction of the four Japanese carriers proved to be a decisive blow by the American fleet, and Admiral Yamamoto's armada was forced to withdraw to safety and abandon the planned invasion of Midway.

Before Carl penned his letter home on June 9, Yamamoto's gamble with Japan's Pacific fleet at Midway had ended in catastrophic failure.[56] By necessity, the Japanese focus in the Pacific theater turned from the Central Pacific to the islands south of the equator and northeast of the Coral Sea.

Mailed June 9, 1942

Saturday

Dear Mom and Dad,

This is one of those very rare occasions when we have a few free moments—a Saturday afternoon with no scheduled activities. So while I recline here in the sun, these few lines to you. After two cloudy days, the sun feels mighty fine.

Duties were announced yesterday at squadron. Doc and Bill got their P-boat duty, and I got my carriers. You can be sure that I'll do everything possible to get fighters once we get to Miami. I still have three and possibly four weeks here yet, however. The way things started this morning, it may be even longer. We were up for our first solo formation in the OS's. And it was a miserable flight for sure. My radio was not working properly and I was unable to hear the chase pilot. However, I didn't find out until we were in the air in formation, when he came alongside talking into his mike. I suspected that all was not well as I waited on the ground and had the mechanic go over the radio to check it. However, my suspicions were not strong enough. When I realized that I wasn't receiving the pilot's call, I began trying to adjust the frequency. It was a pretty tough assignment turning the dial at my right side with one hand and trying to keep my proper distance and position in the formation with the other hand, for one must constantly jockey with throttle and controls. I considered dropping out of the formation and there trying to find the right adjustment. Meantime, our chase pilot was screaming madly at us, and there I sat dumb as a dodo. Finally, I heard his call faintly. I picked up my mike, called him, and asked his frequency. No answer. Well, we finally got back. Besides the poor formation we flew, I learned from the chase pilot in no uncertain terms that my action in asking his frequency was a court martial offense. He didn't turn me in and I guess the station didn't hear me; so this time, I am lucky. However, it was a rather disheartening morning.

I called Antoinette Trout last night. Only talked with her a few moments; told her I'd like to come visit soon. A week from tomorrow was the earliest time we could both make it; so then it shall be. If there is time this weekend, possibly tomorrow, I hope to pay Mrs. Trout a visit and get to know her.

I'll send along the photograph which we had taken last Wednesday evening at the Hotel Roosevelt. We intended to have a group picture taken at the photographer's, but he was closed when we got in town. There are two faces in this picture which don't belong in the group, 3rd from left top, extreme right below; otherwise, it's a pretty typical group, except for Bill who seems intently fixed on something and far soberer than usual. Left to right seated, there's Tim Donovan, Andy, Doc, X, Gerry Connor (our flight at Squantum); top row; Bill, Paul, (Sam Kevan), and Pete. Poor Pete doesn't know what his parents will think when they see him in this shot. Actually, he never shows it when he's been drinking to any extent. The flowerpot in front of me is not a begonia, it's a mint julep.

Jeanne has a job in the city designing jewelry for a rather exclusive concern—the name has slipped my mind. She wrote that Bill has received his wings and will be stationed at Pensacola as an instructor. However, he won't get his leave until next October as he starts instructor's school immediately.

The sun is getting pretty warm and I think it's about time for another swim. So I'll close for today. Every good wish to all of you. Let me hear from you soon.

Love,

Stuff

P.S. Picture later—no envelopes available.

After more than six months together, the three cadets who began military service with an evening of song on their way from New Haven to Squantum prepared to part ways and travel different paths. Carl's letter described the transition—his assignment was to carrier training in Miami, and Doc and Bill Stuhlman would stay in Jacksonville and train in the Catalina PBY flying boats. The assignment to NAS Miami meant that Carl's aircraft options had been narrowed to torpedo bombers, dive bombers, or fighters.

While these routine decisions were being made in Jacksonville, the

Imperial Command in Japan was considering renewed efforts to secure Port Moresby and expand the Imperial presence in the Solomon Islands. Anticipating Japan's expansion, American commanders had been making preparations of their own. In mid-April, a team of U.S. Marines had been dispatched to the island of Efate in the New Hebrides approximately seven hundred miles south of Tulagi.[57] Their assignment was to construct a new airfield on the island. Designed to serve as a staging area for a planned Allied offensive into the Solomon Islands, the airfield on Efate was declared operational on April 13.

As flight training at Jacksonville continued into the early summer, so did the planning by Allied commanders for new facilities north of Efate and closer to the Solomon archipelago. In June, using the newly completed facilities on Efate, the Allies began construction of an advanced staging installation on Espiritu Santo.[58] The island of Espiritu Santo was two hundred miles closer to the Solomons and an easy one-way flight to the southern Solomon Islands for American fighter planes.[59]

Mailed June 13, 1942

Friday

Dear Mom and Dad,

I knew that there must be something out of the ordinary brewing at home with no word from you this week until today. It was good to hear today; however, no one knows better that myself how lack of time and interference from outside can put a stop to letter-writing. So, though I do like to hear from you both, it musn't cause you worry when there are busy days. You especially, Mom; sounds to me as if you needed a general slow-up. After all, this is no time for anyone to be in anything but tip-top shape; one cannot see what each of us may yet have to bear!

Flying slowed up this week with several days of non-flying, at least for formation hops, weather. (My, what a sentence!) In spite of all, I should check out of Squadron 12 tomorrow, or at least the first of next week. That means two weeks and a half of instrument flying—half of it in the Link trainer and half under the hood of a

"J." I look forward very much to getting back in the SNJ's again, with their greater speed and stability. They are a whole lot more airplane than the OS's. The 9-plane formations today were a great deal simpler than they sound. We had two hops. Only trouble was our section leader—and he was plenty; all over the sky, no precision or constancy about air speed or position. I was so mad that I'd have shot him down myself just to get him out of the way. Guess it got on my nerves a bit for I'm just recuperating from a good case of food poisoning which flattened me yesterday afternoon and a miserable night last night. I was grounded this morning, but got myself ungrounded this afternoon when our formation was scheduled for 2 hops. And I felt amazingly better anyway after getting my system well purged.

We had last Tuesday afternoon and evening off, due to rain. I called Antoinette and invited her to join us in town for dinner which she accepted. She is a grand girl, as you wrote, and we had a good evening together. Mrs. Trout invited me to bring all the chaps out Sunday afternoon to swim in the pool. And wouldn't you know, for the first time in well over a month, we have to fly this Sunday! All the gang was anxious to go, and perhaps we will draw a rain check on the invitation. If I am only to be here another three weeks, there's not much chance to enjoy the friendship. But perhaps the others, Doc, Bill, Pete, Paul, who have P-boat duty, and Tim, who is now AVS, will take advantage of it.

Roy was here for a few hours on Monday. I was sleeping down at Squadron when a messenger wakened me with the news that the S.D.O. (Squadron Duty Officer) wanted me. And there was Roy chatting with him! He had flown their C.O. up from Banana River and they couldn't stay long for their departure time was indefinite. I hoped they'd stay overnight, but I heard the ship go out as I returned home from evening chow. Roy is happy to be back at the home base again, in spite of long flying hours, and he was hoping for some cross-country ferry hops.

Chances are pretty good that I'll get 6 months or a year of instructor's duty after Miami and I might even be near home. However, it's nothing to count on, only a possibility.

Do your best to stay healthy. I'll be seeing you in another couple of months!

Love,

Stuff

Three nights after Carl's letter, the coastal community of Ponte Vedra, immediately south of Jacksonville Beach, became the site of an unusual submarine-related incursion. In the hours of darkness, a German U-boat disembarked four enemy operatives onto the beach at Ponte Vedra. The saboteurs were dressed as Americans, armed with explosives, and carried U.S. currency. Their intent was to slip into the country, blend into the populace and then target and destroy power plants, railroad systems, bridges, and other infrastructure. Three days earlier, four other German operatives had been put ashore on Long Island by another submarine for the same purposes.[60]

Both groups of enemy saboteurs were quickly captured by the FBI, and there was no opportunity for the agents to carry out their intended acts of sabotage. The enemy incursion south of Jacksonville Beach had no impact on the cadets at the Naval Air Station, and the incident became little more than an obscure and inconsequential footnote to the war and a part of the local lore among the residents in the area.[61]

Mailed June 18, 1942

U.S. Naval Air Station

Jacksonville

Wednesday

Dear Mom and Dad,

Two or three leisure hours beside the pool this morning are another pleasant reminder that my stay here at N.A.S. Jacksonville is almost over. Just another two weeks is all, or possibly three. Many times I have marched to or from classes envying the advanced students who found time to bask in the sun. And at last, I am on the opposite end of the envying.

My flying this week is on the ground—in the Link trainers. We fly two hours in the morning this week, and the rest of the time until classes at 2:30 is free. Until today, flying under the hood has consisted of familiarization with the instruments and their actual use in blind flying. Level flight, climbs, glides, turns, regular and timed turns to odd headings, spins and stalls with recovery. This morning, we commenced radio orientation. By use of the radio beam, you have to discover your position and then using a knee map, follow a definite procedure down one of the beams and over the cone of silence, which is located a given distance from the airport. All your movements in the trainer are recorded on a mimeographed map of the area. I'll send this morning's map copy along. There isn't anything too difficult about the instrument flying, and it's a lot of fun. I don't know how it will be flying real airplanes, but I'll let you know.

I had word from the fellow who lived next door before he left for Miami two weeks ago. He's very enthusiastic about the base and the flying. He writes that the cadets are treated as officers, that there are no stringent regulations, à la this kindergarten; after three hours of dual, two checks and one instruction, you're on your own to really learn flying inside out. That's going to be some sweet program, 60 or 70 hours of solo time in real fast ships, the latter part in fighters, I hope!

We've lost a good many Squantum cadets in the course of the training. Some of them are staying on and will be commissioned as AVS's, teaching ground school, etc. We lost about ¼ of our class at Squantum, and down here we've lost at least another ¼ and probably more. Most of the ones who dropped out here busted their 33-hour check, acrobatics and general control of the ship on small-field procedure, slips, pylons, etc. Fortunately, none of us had any trouble except Tim, who is now AVS.

I'm sending home a money order which was made out a couple of weeks ago. I had to wait to be sure I wouldn't need it. It will be a little something for when I get home. If you can use it now, do, and perhaps I can borrow some from you if I need it then. I don't know how much I'll be able to save towards leave, but I hope to have enough not to worry about it and to do some of the things which surely will pop into my head. Unfortunately, the weekends we've been having weren't at all conducive to economy.

Bill and Doc and I may possibly be commissioned about the same time. Just now, Bill and I are at the same stage, but his advanced training is about a week shorter than mine. Doc is over a week behind us. He can make that up, however. If we can't ride home together, perhaps at least we can be home at the same time.

Keep cool and healthy and happy, both of you.

Love,

Stuff

(Lake Butler Range Chart enclosed.)

As training at NAS Jacksonville neared its conclusion in June of 1942, more than half of the cadets who began at Squantum had washed out of the program and were assigned to other duties. Those that remained in the program turned their attention to instrument navigation and looked ahead to the next phase of training.

In the aftermath of the naval engagements in the Coral Sea and at Midway, June of 1942 found both Japanese and American carrier fleets in the Pacific theater significantly weakened. The Japanese Combined Fleet abandoned the planned invasion of Port Moresby, and the surviving carriers in the American fleet employed a strategy that avoided direct confrontation with the enemy.[62] Without effective carrier strength, island airfields in the South Pacific became the new strategic priority.

The Japanese High Command began to consolidate its positions at Rabaul in the Bismarck Archipelago and in the Solomon Islands. Already in control of Bougainville in the north, Japan expanded its presence to the island of New Georgia in the central Solomons and turned attention to a new airfield installation in the southern region of the archipelago. From the southern islands, Japan's land-based air assets would be able to extend their range to the shipping lanes farther south, threatening the link between the United States and Australia.[63] As July approached a small cadre of the Japanese Airfield Construction Unit began to burn kunai grass from the Lunga Plain in preparation for construction of a new airfield adjacent to the Japanese seaplane base at Tulagi on a sparsely populated jungle island known as Guadalcanal.[64]

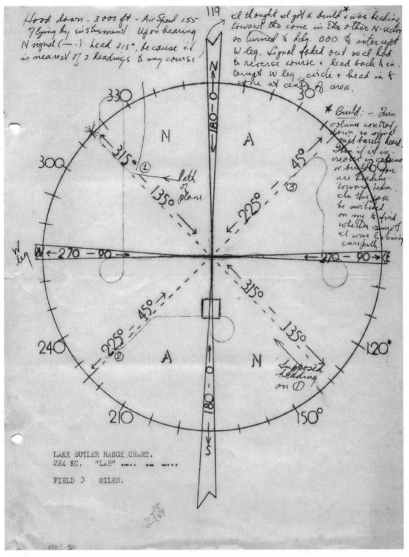

Lake Butler Range Chart prepared by Carl Dunbar during instrument navigation training at NAS Jacksonville, June 1942. (Dunbar family collection.)

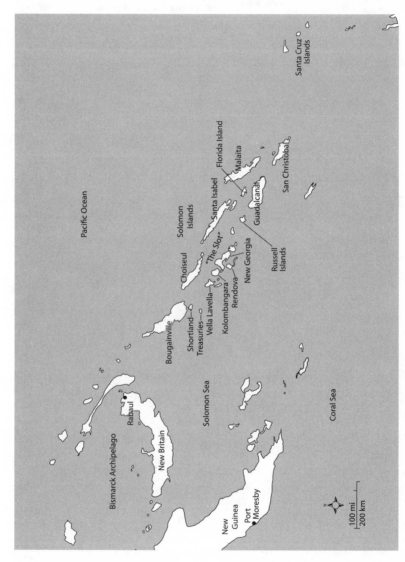

Map 2. South Pacific battle zone, 1942–1943.

A hundred miles long by 50 miles at the width, [Guadalcanal] was shrouded in a dense vegetation that thrived on the heavy rainfall from dense clouds trapped by a mountain backbone 8,000 feet high. Except where the lower slopes opened on meadows of razor-sharp Kunai grass, the tropical vegetation was so dense that little sunlight penetrated into the tangled undergrowth, where white cockatoos and mynah birds screeched through the green twilight. A rich variety of tropical insect life grew bloated on the rotting vegetation that sent a heavy stench of decay drifting out across the Indispensable Strait to Florida Island, where the tiny islet of Tulagi nestled in its bight.[65]

Mailed June 24, 1942

U.S. Naval Air Station
Jacksonville
Tuesday
Dear Mom,

Word of Tom's engagement in your last letter was no less of a surprise to me than it was to you. I knew that Tom and Ruth had reached a parting of the ways, a final parting, but I didn't realize that the trips to Wellesley since that break-up were to prove so fruitful. You must remember, however, that the engagement does not come from as short a courtship as you might at first think. Last summer was probably as excellent an opportunity as anyone ever had to get to know someone. Hira is a wonderful girl with a very serious-thinking head on her shoulders. There is no doubt in my mind that she and Tom are far more compatible in thought and per-sonality than Tom and Ruth ever could have been. Knowing Ruth as I do, I never could quite feel convinced that they would make a successful pair. Basically, they were too different. With Hira and Tom, it is quite different. There never was a more natural couple. For all the truth and feeling of your observation of Ruth's devotion to Tom, especially last spring, I think you, too, will be convinced that Hira is the girl for Tom, and that things really have turned out for the best. You will see it when you get to know Hira and can see Ruth a bit more in her natural element. We should be happy with Tom, for this marriage is bound to be successful; the match which we expected for a long time seemed hardly destined to prosper in the final analysis.

I'm surprised that Tom didn't stop on his way through. Or I was until I read about his engagement, which no doubt had him all agog. For he had written, just before school closed, that he was hoping to have a visit with you. He recalled with pleasure our parties and visits with you and Dad and spoke again with gratitude of your friendship and kindness to him. I've no doubt that you will be seeing him shortly.

Dad's mission to Tennessee was quite a mystery to me until your letter. However, I didn't much care inasmuch as I expected that he would come the rest of the way to pay me a visit after he had traveled that far. I still haven't heard from him, though the week is young yet. 'Course he may be planning to drop in unannounced. It would be just as much of a pleasant surprise, even though I am expecting and counting on a visit from him. Wish you could have come, too, though the base and airplanes would be much less interesting to you, I'm sure. Anyhow, it won't be long now until I'll be dropping in on you.

It's cheery news to hear that you're getting enough rest to be bouncing back. If you can just stay on the comeback trail and be the healthy person you always seem, it will make me and all of us very happy. You can afford to maintain a routine schedule and refuse to let anyone interrupt it. Might just as well be businesslike about it, 'cause it will make you happier in the long run.

Thanks for the news from home. It's amazing! Is anyone to be left single?

Best wishes to you and Sis, I'll be seeing you soon.

Love,

Stuff

As June came to a close, entries in the flight logbook recorded 30.5 hours of flight time for the month—21.5 hours in the OS2U-3 Kingfisher and

9 more hours in the more sophisticated SNJ-3 Texan that introduced the pilots to instrument flight and became the dominate aircraft for the balance of Carl's flight training.

The Texan was a two-seat, low-wing monoplane with a variable-pitch propeller, and it had a movable opaque hood that could be drawn inside the rear canopy.[66] When the opaque hood was drawn, the Texan's back-seat occupant was required to fly and navigate using the aircraft's navigation gauges. Once mastered by the pilot, the acquired skills became useful tools during night operations and in poor weather conditions. During these instrument-training flights under the hood, a safety pilot occupied the front seat of the Texan and kept a watchful eye outside while the back seat pilot flew blind relying on the gauges.[67]

Before completing instrument training at NAS Jacksonville on July 7, Carl accumulated twelve more hours in the SNJ and entered the flights into his logbook, much of the time recorded with the notation "under the hood."[68]

Mailed June 30, 1942

Naval Air Station
Jacksonville
Monday
Dear Mom and Dad,

Just about a week to go now; seven hops left in the SNJ under the hood is all. The instrument flying goes fairly well in actual practice. I had a two-hour hop this morning; glides, climbs, level flight, stalls with recovery, timed turns, etc. We sat down twice for about a half hour at two different fields, one about 50 miles from the base, the other about 70. My instructor promised to take me over to the Gulf of Mexico later in the week. All this demands a reorientation of my distance conception.

Bill and I are now candidates for Marine commissions. We were chosen for it last week. We didn't volunteer at the final call, only because we thought a little more time before active duty would be advisable. Well, we were selected anyhow—while many who had volunteered were turned down. Both of us are very happy at the news. Secretly, I guess, we both wished we had gone ahead and volunteered here. We never ceased to feel that it was the better organization with the higher morale. Now, if I can just make the grade and get fighters, perhaps you can be a little bit proud. I shall be very happy, you can be sure.

Jim Dern wrote last week that he has just been commissioned. He anticipated a transfer from his present job, but hadn't heard definitely yet. He was very surprised to read of Tom's engagement, still expecting, I guess, that it would one day be Ruthie and Tom. Another announcement which had rather startled him was that of Floyd to a Princeton senior. Apparently, Jim has been to New York City recently, though perhaps it was when he dropped by to see you. He said nothing of Lynn, except that he was with her.

I expected Dad to drop in one of these days this past week. Guess I counted on it too much from the beginning. Actually, there wouldn't have been so much to see except myriads of airplanes. I could have shown him the J which I'll be stunting and gunning at Miami for 40 or 50 hours. It's a mighty sweet ship!

We spent this afternoon on the gunnery range. Pistol shooting was satisfactory, but my trap-shooting wasn't worth a thing. I hit most of the dead ahead birds, but missed every one of the angle shots from right to left. It bodes ill for machine-gunning at the moving sleeve, but perhaps another day or two on the range will straighten me out.

I hope all of you are in the best of health. I know there must be lots of sunshine for you by now. Keep well and happy and let me hear from you. See you soon!

Love,

Stuff

During the infamous attack on Pearl Harbor, Japanese bombs and bullets also devastated three army airfields, two naval air bases, and the Marine Corps air station at Ewa that was located on the island of Oahu west of the anchorage at Pearl Harbor.[69] It took six long months before the base commander could begin the rebuilding process of the fighter squadrons at the base, but while Carl Dunbar was concluding his training in Jacksonville, the rebuilding of the Marine Corps squadrons at Ewa Air Station began.[70]

On the first day of July in 1942, two new fighter squadrons were commissioned at the station. The squadrons came into existence without fanfare, but one of them, Marine Fighting Squadron VMF-214, "would one day become the most famous squadron in Marine Corps history."[71] On the day of its commissioning at Ewa, however, the squadron consisted of only two officers, twenty enlisted men, and no aircraft.[72]

South of the equator in the days following the squadron's creation, American military reconnaissance discovered the work by the Japanese construction brigade on the new airstrip along the northeast coast on the large coastal plane of Guadalcanal. The discovery was greeted with alarm by Allied commanders, and it brought focus to the point where their forces needed to meet the enemy.[73] Two months after the discovery, a hastily assembled American amphibious assault force of U.S. Marines invaded Guadalcanal. Their mission was to seize the nearly completed airfield and blunt the Japanese expansion that threatened the Allied supply corridor into the South Pacific.[74] The August invasion of Guadalcanal would mark the emergence of the U.S. Marine Corps, which only two years earlier had numbered little more than twenty-five thousand men, into the forefront of the war in the Pacific theater.[75]

Mailed July 3, 1942

> Naval Air Station
> Jacksonville
> Thursday
> Dear Mom and Dad,
>   Yesterday was that trip to the Gulf. It was a grand vacation. The thirty minutes we spent there was like two weeks to me. I was under the hood most of the way over, so that when Mr. Dunn released it, the blue Gulf waters were already in sight. We flew over a strange

looking coastline for several miles—little islands and fingers sticking up out of the sea, which was everywhere extremely shallow; the land appeared to have been inundated by the sea with only the higher areas left between meandering streams rearing above the water. Shortly Cedar Key, our destination, appeared in sight. Four keys reaching well out into the Gulf. On one, a little fishing village was situated. The wharves and boats with rows of neat wooden cottages framed a very picturesque setting. On another key nearby was one long asphalt runway where we sat down. There were no houses, only a multitude of low trees. We climbed out of the ship and sat under the trees with a cooling salty breeze breathing over us. The air was warm, but not sticky and the sky was clear. There wasn't a sound, except for the occasional flopping of a fish somewhere in the blue water about us. The long-legged white herons poised motionless in the shallow water offshore were the very picture of all the unperturbed serenity. Need I say that it was hard to leave?

We didn't fly last Sunday. I called Mrs. Bull to invite she and Dr. Bull for cocktails at the Cadet Club. They had nowhere to leave the youngsters—mumps excluded the usual possibility—so they were unable to come. It appears now that there may be no other opportunity inasmuch as I shall be leaving early next week. With good weather, I could finish on Sunday, though that is probably too optimistic. I haven't heard from Roy this week to know whether he will be at Banana River. I have been hoping to spend overnight with him.

I must apologize for writing nothing of the box of cookies which were very delicious. I thought the package was from Sis, and I have been meaning to write her since the day they arrived. Let this be my belated thanks. I enjoyed the cookies ever so much. Next time, perhaps I can be sneaking one off the tray just after they come out of the oven.

Don't you have a trunk there at home which isn't being used? I shall have a great deal of clothing with all my uniforms and flight gear. Those fur-lined winter suits and boots take up a good deal of room. Let me know whether the trunk is still available and what you think of its capacity. Wouldn't it be just about the thing?

Lots of good wishes to all of you. I hope, Dad, you had some vacation and relaxation from your field-work. This will be a rather long scholastic year. Be seeing you!

Love,

Stuff

A total of 120.5 hours of flight time had accumulated in the logbook by the time Carl completed his training at NAS Jacksonville on July 7, 1942.[76] He and the other cadets who had successfully completed the training regime now looked forward to two weeks of leave and then to the new duty assignments for the final advance phase of their training.

Mailed July 10,1942

Naval Air Station
Jacksonville
Friday
Dear Mom and Dad,

Unbelievably, the good news has come to pass. I shall be leaving for New Haven this Sunday at midnight. Two enlisted men and myself are driving a Lt. Commander's car up. We don't plan to make any stops and so should not require more than 16 or 20 hours to make the trip to New York City. However, don't be alarmed if it takes longer, for we may encounter difficulty with gasoline for the car.

The ear is healing in good shape and needs only time to be good as new. I am told that beginning July 15, no more pilots will be sent to Miami for advanced training, but instead will remain here—this becoming an advance base (at Cecil Field). I had hoped for the change to Miami, but there is so little time left, it doesn't make much difference.

My best regards to you, and until early next week, I'll close here. No fanfare about my leave!

See you soon,

Love,

Stuff

During Carl's two-week leave, the Allied preparations in the South Pacific pressed forward. On July 12 the Marine 4th Defense Battalion, joined by the Navy Seabees and a detachment of Army engineers and soldiers, arrived on Espiritu Santo in the New Hebrides. The task assigned to the new arrivals was the construction of another new airfield amid the island's jungle and coconut trees.[77] With the construction of the new field, Espiritu Santo became the primary supply base in the New Hebrides, placing men and supplies for the Allied forces within easy range of Guadalcanal and the other islands in southern Solomons.[78]

On July 21 at Ewa Air Station in Hawaii, the temporary commanding officer of VMF-214 was reassigned, and Captain George Britt arrived to assume command of the new squadron. Captain Britt was twenty-eight years old with only two years of flying on his résumé, but he "exemplified the 'veterans' that commanded squadrons upon which Marine aviation was built early in World War II."[79] With the squadron's three initial pilots, Britt ordered the training to begin with dummy gunnery runs in aircraft borrowed from other units.[80] Over the next seven months, new pilots dribbled in as their stateside training concluded, and aircraft were alternatively assigned and taken away from the squadron as the pilots tried to create a level of combat readiness.[81]

Despite the speculation in his letter that the final phase of advanced training might be at Cecil Field near Jacksonville, Carl's hoped-for change to South Florida occurred. At the end of July with his basic and intermediate training complete, Carl's orders brought him to NAS Miami for the advanced syllabus expected of pilots qualifying for carrier duty.[82]

3 ✈ ✈ ✈ ✈ ✈ ✈ ✈

U.S. Naval Air Station, Miami, Florida, July 28, 1942–November 11, 1942

> *I can tell you that fighters were the biggest item to me in all this training program. I've been pointing for them since the beginning of C.A.A. training. So many others have gone ahead of me that there is nothing so momentous about getting fighters, except to myself. I've finally reached my goal and now I'm content to sit back and learn all they can teach me.*
>
> Carl O. Dunbar Jr., September 2, 1942

NAS Miami, or "Opa-Locka," as the naval air station was also known, housed the facilities and instructors for the final phase of training for carrier-bound Navy and Marine Corps pilots.[1] The training regime described in the letters from Miami includes gunnery runs, advanced acrobatics, aerial combat techniques, and practice for carrier takeoffs and landings, all designed to prepare the pilots for their roles in combat. Tom Blackburn, an initial member of the flight instruction cadre at NAS Miami, described the training regime at Opa-Locka in the biography of his war years published in 2006.

> As a finishing school for Navy and Marine pilots bound for operational Fleet combat units, [the] syllabus included ground school with the pilot's handbooks for both fighters and bombers, cockpit checkout, supervised touch-and-go landings at unpaved outlying fields, elementary formation work, and field carrier training-simulated carrier landings on a paved runway. Next all student pilots

learned air-to-air gunnery over the Everglades against towed target sleeves. If successful, they went on to dive-bombing, where it took three hits for five drops on a 50-foot circle to get an "up"—a passing grade. If the fighter student made it that far, he went on to dogfighting, which we called "grab-ass," and then on to aerobatics. The final leg was night-flying familiarization, mostly landings and takeoffs, rounded out with some extremely tame night formation flying.[2]

Time in the cockpit was a priority during the final phase of training, and Carl's logbook records a total of 152.1 hours of accrued flight time during his twelve-week stay at NAS Miami, most of the flight time spent in the Texan SNJ.

Mailed July 30, 1942

> U.S. Naval Air Station
> Miami, Florida
> Wednesday evening
> Dear Mom and Dad,
>   This briefly to let you know that I am safely arrived in Miami this afternoon. I stayed but two nights and one day in Jacksonville—checked out Monday and left Tuesday. Spent last night and this afternoon with Roy. We went out to dinner and the evening with a young married officer and his wife at their home. This morning, we went for a 2-½ hour hop in a PBM-1. I was to have flown it some, but the instruction hop was cancelled.
>   I am not yet straightened out here and so can tell you little about Miami. There are a good many of my friends here from Jacksonville and I've been visiting and learning things from them this evening.
>   Just know that all is well. I'll let you know more when I'm more settled.
>   It sure was grand to be home. I hated to leave. Keep all your health!
> Love,
> Stuff

The planes described in the next letter include the Stearman N3N and the Texan SNJ-both aircraft that the cadets had previously piloted at Squantum, Atlanta, and Jacksonville. The F2F, F3F, and F2A Buffalo, also mentioned in the letter, were new aircraft to the pilots, and all of them were operational in the fleet prior to the Japanese attack on Pearl Harbor. Each was more sophisticated than the training aircraft used by the cadets, but none of the planes could match the frontline enemy fighters being used in the Pacific battle zone.

The F2F and the F3F were biplane fighters used before the war, but neither type of aircraft saw action in the Pacific theater of combat. The mono-wing F2A Buffalo was the only fighter operational at NAS Miami that also saw limited use in the early months of the war in the Pacific, but the Buffalo proved to be utterly ineffective against the Japanese Zero.[3] It was quickly abandoned in favor of the Grumman F4F Wildcat, an aircraft the pilots were yet to experience during their stateside preparations.[4]

Later in their training, the F2A Buffalo became the first real fighter aircraft piloted by Carl and the other cadets, but as training got under way in early August, they found themselves back in the cockpit of the Texan SNJ.[5]

Mailed August 3, 1942

U.S. Naval Air Station

Miami, Florida

Sunday

Dear Mom and Dad,

Today finds us somewhat more settled. Our flight of twelve was completed yesterday (nothing transpires until the operating unit of 12 is complete. One waits for 12 cadets to arrive.) Today, we had lectures and tomorrow we are scheduled to begin flying. Our group consists of 8 chaps from Jacksonville and 4 from Pensacola, one of these a Lieutenant (U.S.N.) with three years of sea duty to his credit (he's a classmate of John Dunn) and another is a Marine Sergeant.

The attitude here is quite different than we have previously experienced. They treat us as officers and full-fledged fliers. The ability to fly is taken for granted; the emphasis is on tactics, aerial combat, gunnery, dive-bombing, strafing, and fleet formation flying, plus carrier landings. Everyone is crazy about the work. And, believe it or not, there are less accidents here than at any of the previous bases.

The base itself is smaller considerably than Jacksonville. It is older and hence more liveable. Grass and planting is under expert care. Furthermore, the barracks are further distant from the field and are consequently quieter. There are two fields on either side of a row of hangers, each with four different runways and including a grass landing area. One field is used for take-offs and the other for landings. This decreases congestion and taxiing, as we land toward the hangers and takeoff away from them. There are all kinds of ships here, F2F's and F3F's, F2A's, beside the J's and a few N3N's, which we have flown before. It isn't a very long time now until we shall be flying 1st line ships.

The training period here has been extended somewhat—from 8 to 12 weeks. As previously, we are to be commissioned after 8 weeks; the last four weeks are called pre-operational training advanced fleet-combat work and all to the good, as money in the bank. I wrote Smitty a note yesterday and will wait to hear from him. We get next Friday night and all day Saturday off, so I hope to see them.

I'd like copies of the pictures you took while I was home, Dad, whenever you have an opportunity to print some.

Hope you are both well. I'll send along some money as soon as I can get a money order.

Love to you,

Stuff

On August 7, 1942, three days before Carl's next letter, nineteen thousand U.S. Marines landed on Guadalcanal, marking the beginning of the first true Allied offensive of the Pacific theater.[6] The Marines met little initial resistance from Japanese troops who were unprepared to meet the invasion force and had withdrawn to the thick jungle of the inland portions of the island.[7] Only a brief and ineffective Japanese air raid against the troop transports and the escorting Navy warships in the harbor challenged the amphibious landing. Three days after the invasion, however, the land battle for Guadalcanal was joined in an initial firefight between the opposing troops, and it began a struggle for the previously unknown island that lasted more than six months before the victor was declared.[8] The focus of the war against Japan now turned to the South Pacific and the islands in the Solomon archipelago. The United States and Allied forces were intent on bringing in supplies, air support, and more troops to secure their toehold on Guadalcanal, and the Japanese Imperial Command, surprised by the initial invasion of the island, began efforts to repel the Marine invasion force. As Carl's training got under way at NAS Miami, the Battle of the Solomon Islands began in earnest, and Guadalcanal became the first objective in the archipelago.

The Solomon Islands are the third-largest archipelago in the South Pacific, and they are found northeast of Australia and east of New Guinea on the eastern reach of the Coral Sea. To the south of the Solomon group were the important Allied bases on the islands of the New Hebrides—Efate and Espiritu Santo—and to the north in the Bismarck Archipelago was the Japanese fortress of Rabaul on the island of New Britain.

Before World War II began, the Solomon Islands were nothing more than a remote and isolated part of the British Empire, a status they attained in the late nineteenth century.[9] When war came to the islands in 1942, lifestyles of the native Melanesian people had changed little over the centuries. The small population of European settlers that occupied portions of the island cultivated coconut plantations and engaged in other limited agricultural pursuits. To most of the world, the major islands in the Solomon archipelago with names like Guadalcanal, Tulagi, New Georgia, Kolombangara, Vella Lavella, and Bougainville held no meaning. But as the last months of 1942 became the early weeks of 1943, these islands, beginning with Guadalcanal, emerged from anonymity to appear regularly on the pages of the nation's daily newspapers.

Mailed August 10, 1942

U.S. Naval Air Station
Miami, Florida
Sunday
Dear Mom and Dad,

Don't be surprised if this letter lacks coherence. It won't be. For this is the day after our day off. One day and night in eight is ours to spend as we like. Friday night and Saturday, we spent at Miami Beach with not too much sleep and much exertion. None of us has felt particularly spry today, although we did have some snappy volleyball games late this afternoon after three hours of 9-plane, properly called "division" flying.

We have been getting about three hours a day since we began flying last Monday. And as you can judge, my ear has caused me no trouble. The weather has been grand for flying—most of our flying is done over the clouds between 5 and 6 thousand feet. The training is mighty interesting, too. They certainly baby us no longer. My first hop last week was divided between spin indoctrination in the SNJ-3, which we fly altogether now for awhile, and power and cut-gun landing procedure. Eighteen spins, plus flipper turn stalls with roll-outs, proved too much for me. The spin and stall characteristics of these J's, as with all low-winged monoplanes, are very violent. You can stall the plane at any speed if you pull back hard enough on the stick. On the level, they will snap-roll; if you are in a steep left turn, they cart-wheel with a vicious snap into a right flipper turn; and if you are in a steep right turn (or flipper turn), they snap over on their backs. To recover from spins, you kick full opposite rudder and slam the stick forward with both hands as sharply as you possibly can. This throws the tail out of the slip-stream; you are thrown hard against the safety belt and the plane is under control heading straight down. Well, after a half-hour of these, I managed just to get on the ground before my stomach revolted. Then we went ahead with landing procedure. Next day, on Tuesday, was my inverted spin hop in the N3N-3, primary bi-plane. We did inverted and normal spins for awhile and then commenced doing slow-rolls.

Again my stomach revolted, but I just kept on doing slow-rolls and looking over the side whenever the occasion demanded. It was quite a relief, believe me, to get by my dual acrobatics instruction Friday with no ill effects. The instruction consisted of slow-rolls, loops, immelmans, chandelles, more spins and stall procedure. We also did some snap-rolls and barrel-rolls. Probably tomorrow, I shall have my first acrobatics check. One must complete a regular procedure of stunts: viz.—two successive loops followed by two right slow rolls, then two left, followed by right and left chandelles, and then by right and left immelmans—all these must be completed within the area above the field and within a six minute time limit. It isn't particularly difficult, but you've got to know what you're doing.

Acrobatics, etc., haven't been the only flying by any means. After four hours of instruction and check on landing procedure, we took up three-plane, or section, formation flying and checked out on that. Now we are working on 9-plane division formation. It is fairly complicated, but I won't bother to explain it here.

I just did escape being put on the report sheet this afternoon with its consequent grounding and restriction. The charge was failing to take a "wave-off." There is a runway signal officer on the end of the runway (just as on carrier decks), whose job it is to direct planes down by semaphore or by his portable radio. He indicates whether you are fast or slow, high or low, or wing-heavy, etc., and pilots are obliged to answer his signals with appropriate controlling. If there is congestion on the runway, or a pilot's landing appears unsafe, or perhaps his wheels are still retracted, the signal officer gives the pilot a "wave-off" by swishing the flags vigorously over his head. The pilot then flies on around the landing circle. The wave-off I got this afternoon was below knee-level and I interpreted it as a signal to cut the engine and sit down. I was plenty indignant when they called the operations tower and put me on report. My statement on the report sheet must have reflected my feelings. The C.O. cleared me of the wave-off violation after talking with the runway officer and finding that his signal was incorrect. But he told me in a warning manner that my attitude in the statement I made was wrong. I was a student here and would be a junior on entering the fleet. I concurred.

One of the boys had to bail out Thursday. Two of them bumped wing and tail during formation work. The rudder and elevators jammed so that the plane turned in wide circles to the right and the elevators would not neutralize to permit level flight, but would fly the ship only up or down at fairly steep angles which would not permit landing. After almost an hour of deliberation while the planes circled over the airport while the pilot experimented and inspecting officers looked over the damaged controls from another plane, they decided for the pilot to jump. So from about 5,000 feet, we suddenly saw a black dot—the pilot chute—break out below the plane. And then the chute itself billowed out with the pilot swinging merrily down. Meantime, the plane nosed over and down, in response to the tab controls which the pilot had set before abandoning ship, and screamed its way down. The pilot landed safely, none the worse for his experience, only firmly convinced in the security of his parachute. It was reassuring to all of us.

Many thanks for the raincoat. I haven't needed it yet.

Don't mind if I have time only for a card later this week. It appears to be a pretty busy one. Best regards to you both.

Love,

Stuff

As flight tactics became more sophisticated and training flights longer at NAS Miami, the American Marines continued to solidify their position on Guadalcanal. On August 12, five days after the initial invasion, the Marines captured the seaplane facilities at Tulagi northeast of Guadalcanal.[10] Once the perimeter around the airfield on Guadalcanal itself was secure, the Marines began to lengthen the airfield runway to thirty-six hundred feet and ready it for Allied aircraft.[11]

On August 15 Navy transport destroyers delivered aviation fuel, bombs, ammunition, a cadre of aircraft mechanics, and an operations officer to manage the field on Guadalcanal and prepare for its anticipated aircraft.[12] By August 17 Marine General Alexander Vandegrift commanding the ground forces on Guadalcanal declared the field operational and christened the base "Henderson Field" in memory of Major Loften Henderson, who had lost his life leading a Marine torpedo-bomber squadron at Midway.[13]

Two days after Carl wrote home on August 18 describing the sites of Miami that he had seen from the air, the first American fighter planes and dive bombers were catapulted from the flight deck of the USS *Long Island* southeast of Guadalcanal to take up permanent station at Henderson Field.[14] The nineteen F4F Wildcat fighters and twelve Douglas SBD dive bombers from the *Long Island* became the nucleus of the "Cactus Air Force," the small group of American aircraft that were assigned to protect the U.S. Marines from air and sea attack as their efforts to secure the Allied foothold on Guadalcanal continued.[15]

Because both Japan and the United States were left with only skeleton carrier forces following the battles of the Coral Sea and Midway, the carriers had little direct impact on the air war in the South Pacific while the battle for Guadalcanal raged on into the fall of 1942.[16] Without the carrier platforms, the island airfields, like Henderson Field on Guadalcanal and Kahili on Bougainville, became the key installations for control of the air, and from the air, to provide protection for the land forces and naval vessels engaged in the battle for the islands in the Solomon archipelago.

The complex at Henderson Field became the focal point in the early struggle for both attackers and defenders, and it became emblematic of the months of conflict to follow.[17] Taking, holding, and defending the island airfield facilities became one of the important objectives in the sequential battles in the South Pacific, and Marine fighter and bomber pilots became the frontline warriors in the fight to control the air space over the islands.

Mailed August 18, 1942

> U.S. Naval Air Station
> Miami, Florida
> Tuesday
> Dear Mom and Dad,
>   Time seems to get away so swiftly! I haven't meant to be so long

writing. Even now this will probably be cut short by afternoon muster; but at least you will know that all is well.

Haven't been flying this week—we are standing by for gunnery. There aren't enough ships equipped and this results in more or less of a bottleneck. I checked out in acrobatics last Friday and flew a couple of hours of instrument flying Saturday. Flew over Hialeah Park, the Miami-Biltmore Hotel, Pan American's Clipper base, the Orange Bowl, or whatever it is, and really enjoyed the sightseeing. One of the boys tells me we are scheduled for night flying tonight. I hope that we are, for this sitting on the ground isn't very exciting.

The photographs arrived yesterday. I enjoyed seeing them. Wonder now if I am such a poor photographer that the pictures of you, Dad, didn't turn out. I was counting on them. The caricature in an earlier letter was very amusing and quite good, I thought. I liked the little write-up below.

Mom, you know that I'd be delighted to have you make a trip down here. I wanted both you and Dad to see the base at Jacksonville, and this is no less imposing. You wondered about my leave. Everyone is getting two to three weeks after they are commissioned, and I have every reason to believe that we will, too. So I should be home in late October or early November. However, if you want to make the trip, I'd be glad to have you stay here as long as you like. It is a long, wearisome journey, I must warn you, one that I wouldn't tackle by choice, but that's entirely up to you. Of course, there's always a chance that I might be based somewhere in the States for awhile without leave, and then a visit would really hit the spot. You plan as you like, and I'll let you know should any change in commissioning-leaves occur.

I fear time is a bit too short to tell you about the Officer's Club, which certainly bears description. So I'll leave that until next time. I haven't written Sis, so I hardly deserve word from her, but I do hope she's well and happy. For now, best wishes to you both, and
Love,
Stuff
P.S. If you can extend my credit, I'm in the midst of buying a trav-

eling bag and a cap. The former was a bargain which demanded immediate attention!

Air combat in the modern fighters of the day was still relatively new in 1942, and the use of aerial tactics was much more of an art than a science.[18] Carl's letters from Miami introduce the reader to flight tactics and aircraft maneuvers known to the pilots as snap rolls, flipper turns, stalls, Immelman maneuvers, chandelles, and inverted spins. Each put an aircraft through an aerial acrobatic move more extreme than routine flight intended, and the expectation was that each tactical maneuver would be mastered for use before a pilot headed into combat to encounter the enemy. Some of the maneuvers were considered relatively simple, like a loop-over or a barrel roll that were intended to provide an escape from a tailing enemy aircraft, but others were more complicated.[19] The Immelman maneuver, named for World War I ace Max Immelman, required a pilot to put his aircraft into a steep climb, change direction, and level out on a different course. The tactical flight path was essentially a half loop upward followed by a half roll. The Immelman was a challenging maneuver for any World War II fighter, and if it was not executed correctly, it could result in a stall.[20]

The chandelle was also a maneuver intended to provide a course change for the aircraft. It was a slow climbing turn leading to a 180-degree direction change while the plane gained altitude and lost speed, but like the Immelman, there were risks. If the chandelle was not executed properly by the pilot, the aerial tactic could result in a deadly spin and loss of the aircraft.[21] The flipper turns, stalls, snap rolls, and other tactical maneuvers had similar combat objectives—to change aerial attack angles or facilitate evasive maneuvers away from the gun sights of attacking enemy aircraft.

An inverted spin was executed when the aircraft was upside down, and this maneuver, too, was extremely difficult to recover from without a cool head and some altitude under the aircraft.[22] Carl was to discover the consequences of an inverted spin incorrectly performed later in his journey.[23]

Mailed August 21, 1942

U.S. Naval Air Station
Miami, Florida
CB-2 Rm 220
Thursday
Dear Mom and Dad,

We are still waiting on gunnery, 'though meantime, on Tuesday night, we commenced night flying—skipped last night, and we go again tonight for 3-plane or section work. There was nothing to the two hours of landing familiarization at night. The runway is lighted up brightly and the runway officer talks to you on the radio all the way. You just set your throttle to permit the plane to settle at a constant rate. When you are almost on the ground, you commence pulling back on the stick, raising the nose and pushing the tail down so it will hit first. Then, as soon as the ship touches the ground, you cut the throttle and there you are just as pretty as a ripe watermelon and just as pleased. I thought the day would come when we would feel just as much at home in the SNJ's as we did in the Stearmans. And the time has already come. I'd sooner fly the "J" than drive a car. I honestly feel safer. Of course, one mustn't go to sleep at the controls as I did last week on an instrument hop. I just plain forgot to put the wheels down before making a landing approach. Oh! I didn't land with wheels up—the plane won't let you! Not this one. But I did forget. So that when I hauled back on the throttle at 500 feet to lower my flaps, the warning horn blared away—and was my face red!

We had an oxygen familiarization hop yesterday. Three of us went up together solo to over 20,000 feet with regular oxygen equipment. We donned the masks at 12,000 feet going up and took them off at 14,000 feet coming down. We had to keep leaning the gas mixture out all the way up, and at 20,000 feet, the ship was rather sluggish. The manifold pressure gauge (a measure of power—actually recording in inches of Hg, the pressure of the vapor as it is impelled into the cylinder head by the supercharger) read only 17 inches, whereas at sea level, it reads 42 inches maximum. I could climb at only 200–250 feet per minute at that altitude, whereas at sea level, one can approach a rate-of-climb of 1,500 feet per minute. Nevertheless, we indulged in a bit of dogfighting and tail-chasing which was finally cut short when my motor began coughing and sputtering and I had to attend wholly to it. Then we commenced our descent.

It was beautifully clear up so high. Unlimited visibility really means something up there. I experienced no particular feeling of height—objects on the ground seemed about the same. I did notice a change in boats on the ocean. They were practically invisible, except for the long white tails which streamed out far behind them. They stood out like beacon lights. It was cold—about 10 degrees below zero, though under the closed canopy, it was very snug and comfortable. The oxygen equipment worked perfectly so that there was no physical discomfort. Frankly, I see little difference between operations at sea level and at altitudes, as long as oxygen is at hand. And I understand that for the Navy, 20,000 feet so far in this war has been the ceiling. We figured out today on the computer, that, because of decreased air density at high altitudes, our indicated airspeeds were far off. Instead of an indicated air speed of 140 miles per hour, we were cruising at a true air speed of 180 to 190 miles per hour; in our dives, which indicated 230 miles per hour or better, we were well over 300 miles per hour. I thought our relative positions changed rather rapidly!

Have to close rather abruptly for chow and night-flying. I hope this letter finds all well at home, even the weather.
Best wishes and love,
Stuff

On August 21, while the pilots at Miami trained in nighttime procedures and became familiar with high altitude flight, Japanese naval vessels landed Imperial Army reinforcements to mount a counterattack against the perimeter defenses surrounding Henderson Field.[24] The attack began two hours after midnight and continued through the hours of early morning darkness. With the arrival of daylight, enemy aircraft flying south from Bougainville appeared in the skies over Guadalcanal to join the battle and support the invasion force. But the incoming enemy aircraft were met by the newly arrived Wildcats of the Cactus Air Force, and before the noon hour, the defenders had succeeded in driving away the Japanese air support.[25]

The land battle on the island raged on through the day, but by the end of the afternoon, the Japanese attempt to break through American lines and seize the airfield had been turned back: 28 Marines died defending the field and 72 more were wounded in the fight. But the Japanese faired much worse, with a total of 871 soldiers killed during the day's action.[26]

In Hawaii at the Marine Corps air station at Ewa during the final week of August, the newly forming VMF-214 fighter squadron took delivery of its first eleven Grumman F4F Wildcat fighters. Shortly after the arrival of the new aircraft, two more Marine aviators joined the squadron, expanding the roster of pilots from three to five.[27]

Mailed August 26, 1942

U.S. Naval Air Station
Miami, Florida
Wednesday
Dear Mom and Dad,

I do hope that you got to New York City last Sunday to see the Dodgers take two from the Giants. Guess they'll need every point they can get the way things are going in St. Louis the past two nights.

We commenced gunnery last Thursday, since my last letter, I believe. We had one period of dual instruction, a demonstration of the various types of runs that can be made upon an enemy. The instructor blacked me out once and dimmed me out several times on pullouts. Since then, I have done a fairly good job myself on dim-outs. Following the instruction hop, we had two periods of dummy runs, which lack only the bullets. Then yesterday, we had our first of four live runs. It wasn't a very sparkling exhibition. We have 120 rounds to fire in 10 separate runs of 12 shots each. Well, because of lack of time through a poor join-up on the leader's part, plus a couple of bad runs on my part on which the chase pilot ordered me not to fire, I only fired 60 rounds. And out of that 60 rounds, I had only 5 hits. As it turned out, I was high man of the five of our flight firing yesterday, but even so, it is only average, and the first run is no indication of what the others can do. Aside from the total hits, which was disconcerting enough, the chase pilot just about completely unnerved me. He changed my run completely, ordered me out of my first two runs because he thought them unsatisfactory. It was tension aplenty firing the first day when the outcome of this gunnery means so much to me; having to learn the run all over again was almost the last straw. Well, there are three more hops; so it is yet only the beginning, and I think I can hit the sleeve. I just wish I was certain of it.

We finished up our night flying last week with a cross-country hop, a triangular 45-minute course. Three of us flew together throughout, and by the fifth night, we were flying a pretty good formation. When we were up alone, we did quite a bit of capering about. In all, we had two periods of landing practice, three periods of section formation, one of division, and one cross-country hop. Fortunately, we were flying with the first quarter and first half of the moon, which not only made the night-formation work easier, but provided quite a spectacle as well, flying over and around great puffs of cloud and over the ocean.

Perhaps I should have described briefly the procedure on the High Side Run, which we are making in these introductory gunnery runs. The tow-plane flies a straight course, trailing the sleeve some 900 feet behind. The sleeve is about fifteen feet long and approximately two feet in diameter—looks just like a wind sock at an airport, only without the taper. We, the attackers, fly just over a thousand feet above the tow-plane and a quarter to a half-mile ahead of it, one after another in column. The lead man charges his gun, flips the safety switch, rocks his wings and peels off, maintaining his altitude throughout the flipper turn. The attacker, after peeling off, reverses his original course, heading now toward the tow-plane, still 1,000 feet above it, but somewhat off to one side. As the distance between the attacker's plane and the target decreases, the pilot judges the proper timing and rolls over most on his back and dives down on the sleeve, picking it up in his sights as he dives. When you are about to hit the sleeve, you pull the trigger, and swish! You're by the sleeve and pulling out of your dive below the tow-plane, idling throttle and scouting out ahead to climb up into position for the next attack. Meantime, the next plane in line has peeled off for its attack. It's quite a pull when you pull out of the dive at 200 to 250 miles per hour. Usually, you don't see very much but a gray curtain for a second or two, though you remain in full possession of all other faculties. You probably don't have much idea of the run from this description—I can show you better with animation sometime.

Jim declares that he hasn't been north in over three months. If his job has been changed, he said nothing of it.

Well, it's another one of those chow-calls, so I'll have to close for the present. I hope Sis is home, well and happy. Give her my best and tell her I am really about to write.

Love to all of you,

Stuff

The gunnery training for would-be fighter pilots at Opa-Locka was "high-deflection-angle shooting," and the gunnery runs were made from the overhead, the high side, and the flat side. The gunnery techniques were designed to minimize the exposure of the attacking airplane to the flexible guns of enemy bombers, and they were extremely effective when mastered. Tom Blackburn described the techniques that were taught at NAS Miami in his biography.

> In the overhead run, one comes over the target on an opposite course and approximately 3,000 feet above it. At the right moment, the pilot goes into a half roll to an inverted position and pulls through a very steep dive. At the point of opening fire, approximately 500 feet from the target, the ideal is to be in a vertical dive perpendicular to the horizontal target. This requires maximum deflection—lead—because the relative motion of the target is greatest. As the dive progresses, the angle of the dive decreases and, thus, the amount of deflection needed also decreases.

If properly executed, a pass close aboard the target will find the attacker in about a 45-degree dive. With recovery beneath the target, the speed obtained in the dive is used to zoom back up to get ahead and in position for the next run.

The high-side run is somewhat similar to the overhead run, except that the dive starts about 1,000 feet to one side of the target. The attacker should be in a steep dive abeam of the target so that the shooting is done at a 45-degree deflection angle both in the vertical plane and at the four o'clock position or 8 o'clock position. (The target's nose is considered to be twelve o'clock.) The recovery is executed much as from an overhead run. In the flat-side run, the optimum position for opening fire is 90 degrees to the course of the target. This narrows to a maximum deflection of 45 degrees as the attacker passes astern of the target and recovers.[28]

Mailed September 2, 1942

U.S. Naval Air Station
Miami, Florida
Wednesday
Dear Mom and Dad,

This is what happens when you run out of stationery at the same time the end of the month rolls around and, to top it all, Ship's Service closes for inventory. I almost forgot, too, that yesterday was our day off.

I hadn't expected to know about our assignment to advanced training in time for this letter. But the selection was posted at afternoon muster. Four of us were given fighters, four scouts, and three torpedo-bombers. You wouldn't know the other three fighters; so I'll simply say that they were the one's we expected to be chosen, on the basis of gunnery scores and flying performance. None of the flight was particularly good on gunnery; I ended up with 58 hits in four runs; the rest went 42, 41, 21, 20 and lower.

Waiting for the final selection was not easy. After all the gunnery scores were in, I felt entitled to fighters, but according to scuttlebutt, the top gunners were getting torpedo-bombers. I can tell you that fighters were the biggest item to me in all this training program. I've been pointing for them since the beginning of C.A.A. training. So many others have gone ahead of me that there is nothing so momentous about getting fighters, except to myself. I've finally reached my goal and now I'm content to sit back and learn all they can teach me.

There have been some changes in the training program, so that it will probably be Christmas or after before we will be given leaves. It's tough on most of the fellows—and I am more and more thankful for those two weeks in July. As it has turned out, the flying time I missed then has made quite a difference already, but I can never complain. The boys I would have flown with, had I not ruptured an ear-drum will be finishing up and leaving this week. They trained under the old syllabus and so spent only about ⅓ as much time here as I shall spend.

Mom, if you are sure you want to brave the train ride down and back, I'd be very happy to see you the 19th, or whenever is best for you. My next day off is the 17th. I probably won't be able to get any time off during the days while you are here, but I can perhaps have 12 o'clock liberty in the evenings. Of course, I'll want you to see the base and the Officer's Club. I think the hotel where we've been spending our days off at Miami Beach would be comfortable and quiet for you. Again, I must warn you that the train ride is very dreary, especially if you have to make it alone. And, too, unless you spend a week or so down here, when time might drag a little on your hands. Florida is not very pretty this time of year and neither is the weather. Now, if you still think you want to make the trip, I shall say no more. At least you won't find it an anti-climax. I just wish I knew whether or not I would be stationed down here around Christmas time. For then, I would urge you very particularly to make it a two-week vacation and bring Dad and Sis along. That would be a real party, for I'd have my commission and only day-time obligations. However, I can't be certain of future plans.

We won't be flying likely for a couple of weeks. We must wait for the succeeding class to complete gunnery and be assigned, for two classes combine groups in advanced training. Flight 23 hasn't begun gunnery yet, so the prospect is for no immediate action. We may get an instrument hop meantime, and I plan to hop in the rear cockpit with a chase-pilot one of these days.

I didn't hear from Roy before the 26th, but I did have a long letter from Jim Murphy, my roommate at Jacksonville, who is undergoing transitional training at Banana River. In case you see Roy, if he's at home now, tell him that Jim is there. Maybe he'll have him for a check sometime and take it easy on him. Jim is a good flier anyhow and won't need a great deal of help.

I think it's time to run back down to squadron and see about a little skeet shooting. For a time, I guess they've made me flight-leader of the group, so I must seek to be on time.

My best wishes to all of you. Let's not be overdoing things! And for heaven's sake buy your tickets in advance next time!
Love,
Stuff

Live-fire gunnery was the final tactical skill to be mastered before pilots were chosen for fighters, and by the end of the first week of September, Carl had posted the highest gunnery scores in the training squadron. As he had speculated in his letter home, he became one of four pilots from the squadron to be selected for the coveted assignment. At NAS Miami, however, there were no first-line aircraft for the four newly qualified fighter pilots to fly, and the training and preparation to join the fleet continued in the Texan SNJ trainer.[29]

While the cadet fighter pilots acclimated to their new role in Miami, in the Solomon Islands the battle for Guadalcanal was entering its second month. The American pilots of the Cactus Air Force and their Grumman Wildcat fighters provided new defenses for the Allied troops on the ground, helping to fend off the daylight bombardment from Japanese warships and aerial bombing raids from the enemy planes based at Bougainville and Rabaul. With Henderson Field fully operational, Navy Seabees began work on a second adjacent airfield, dubbed Fighter One, to enhance the capabilities of the Cactus Air Force to control the airspace over the battle zone.[30]

In the northern Solomon group, the Japanese began a crash construction program of their own to speed the completion of an expanded airfield complex at Kahili airfield on the island of Bougainville. The complex at Kahili was intended to serve as a base for air support in counteroffensives against the American forces on Guadalcanal, and it was also intended as a staging area from which the Japanese could continue to expand their influence into the central islands of the Solomons.[31]

From Guadalcanal in the south to Bougainville in the north, the islands in the Solomon chain stretched in roughly parallel lines divided by the Pacific waters of New Georgia Sound—Florida Island, Santa Isabel, Choiseul, and Shortland Island bordered the sound to the north, and the Russell Islands, Kolombangara, Vella Lavella, Rendova, and New Georgia bordered it to the south. During the Battle of the Solomon Islands, the "no man's land" north and south through the waters of New Georgia Sound between these islands became known simply as "the Slot."[32]

From the staging areas on Bougainville and Rabaul, Japanese warships navigated south through the waters of the Slot on regular missions to shell the American Marines on Guadalcanal and to resupply and reinforce the ground troops attempting to retake the island. To Allied forces, the enemy ships making these regular excursions came to be known as the "Tokyo Express," and their missions were carried out during the hours of Pacific darkness when the planes from Henderson Field were unable to provide aerial defenses for the island.[33] When daylight approached, the Japanese warships were forced to retreat north before the planes of the Cactus Air Force were able to launch and seek out the enemy surface vessels.[34]

Mailed September 7, 1942

U.S. Naval Air Station
Miami, Florida
Sunday
Dear Mom and Dad,

Thanks to a Lt. Commander who lectured us for leaving the squadron without permission, we have begun our advanced training and are definitely on the final stretch drive toward those Navy wings. While the officer was reprimanding us, one of the flight spoke up and asked him if we were expected to flatten the cushions in the ready-room for three weeks, waiting for the flight ahead of us to finish gunnery so that the flight behind us, with whom we were scheduled to fly advanced training, could commence. "Hell no!" he snapped back. "You will have a flight tomorrow!" And so we did, joining with Flight #20, two ahead of us.

Yesterday and today, we have been making camera gunnery runs, learning new runs, beside the high side, which we used in tactical gunnery. Tomorrow or Tuesday, we will commence actual firing again. Henceforth, there might just as well be an enemy for a target—it's the real business!

I can't recall whether I wrote you about my second narrow escape from the "report" last week. Skip this if I did. This time the charge was dangerous flight conduct and taxiing too fast. It all came about when the target I was towing wouldn't release when I returned to the base after a firing run. It was my first tow; so when the sleeve didn't release first time, I thought my procedure hadn't been correct. (The nose of the ship is dipped rather sharply at the same time the release lever is pulled.) Well, I went around again, this time shaking the ship more severely and working the lever continually. Still the sleeve stayed with me. So the third time I really got violent. That's when the tower objected. They claimed I was gyrating violently enough that my ship was about to stall and that it mushed in to fifty feet. In the end, I had to land with the sleeve, which wasn't damaged. The tow-line had twisted around my tail-wheel. Fortunately, the chief flight instructor felt the charges weren't warranted, and I got off lightly with an admonition to caution.

Again it seemed like a small world day before yesterday when I was being examined by Brooks Knight's doctor. Everyone said the exam was to determine whether or not we were crazy. Actually, it is an experiment to determine whether or not a test can be devised to better allocate pilots in that branch of the service where they are best suited, and also to weed out the unfit. Dr. Draper spent some minutes explaining to me the theory of their exam. They seek to study all factors, physical, psychological, and emotional qualifications. The test was conducted at Norfolk—pilots were interviewed and studied; the board of doctors, none fliers, then rated them. And the results were compared with actual records. They were so close that the Navy is trying the thing out again here, this time using trainees as guinea pigs, and the predictions will be checked against actual records of our flying up to the time we are commissioned or through operational training.

Dr. Draper asked me where my home was—he's a Harvard grad from Massachusetts. When I mentioned about you, Dad, he immediately remarked that he had been talking with a very good friend of yours a few days before. Made a very interesting sidelight to the exam routine and also enabled me to find what it was all about.

We've decided, since we are to be here for awhile, to take advantage of the squash courts. Only we can't buy any racquets here in Miami—there aren't any. I wonder whether there's an old one there at home which you could send me. I'm not particular so long as the frame is whole, inasmuch as we haven't too long to play. Or if there's none at home, could you try the Sport Shop for something in the bargain line—that is if you can consider putting out the cash while I'm still owing you. I could pay up my debt now, but it would leave me about broke, and I will be drawing a real salary in another three weeks. If you do buy a racquet, I'll send you whatever it costs. But I'm hoping there will be a spare one around the house. We do definitely need three squash balls, however. We can't get them here.

The chief in charge of our machine guns, their operation and maintenance here at the base has been after me for more information about the .50-caliber, which George was telling me about when I was at home. I knew only that it fired much faster than the ones we now have, but could not explain why. It's not the sort of things to write letters about, but if you happen to pick up the principle involved, talking to George, and can carry it down here in your head, perhaps I can give him some dope that might prove valuable to him here or in the fleet.

It's hard for me to believe that the summer is almost over. In fact, football is covering the sports pages down here. I think of you and imagine you are sleeping under a blanket at night. What a welcome innovation that would be for me!

I'll be running off now—this time to bed. We had three hops this morning and there's prospect of the same tomorrow. It's grand, but wearing to keep moving that fast. I trust that you are all well and happy.

Love,

Stuff

When Carl's letter was written on September 7, the war in the Pacific was entering its ninth month. In the United States, the country's industrial complex was gearing up its massive war production effort, and American companies were developing innovations in equipment and weaponry. Among the thousands of innovations was the .50-caliber machine gun being developed at the Winchester Arms factory in New Haven where Carl had worked in Department G after graduation and before reporting to Squantum. The reference in his previous letter to George and the department is one of several made in his correspondence to the employees who remained behind to support the war effort in a different way.

On Guadalcanal, the jungle perimeter around the complex at Henderson Field created a virtually impenetrable barrier except for the established overland access trails that were well guarded by the American defenders.[35] But even with the secure perimeter, Marine general Vandegrift was concerned about the enemy build-up south of the Field, and on September 7, he ordered an intelligence gathering counteroffensive against outlying Japanese positions. Four days before Carl's next letter, the 1st Marine Raider Battalion, on Vandegrift's orders, boarded landing craft to begin the mission, and on the following day, the Raiders made a surprise amphibious landing against an enemy force south of Henderson Field estimated to be between one thousand and three thousand troops.[36]

With air support from the Cactus Air Force, the Raider Battalion's mission proved a successful incursion. The Marines killed thirty enemy soldiers and suffered only six casualties—two were killed and four wounded. Before withdrawing, the Raiders gathered valuable intelligence on the enemy build-up outside the Marine's defensive perimeter, disabled the radio equipment at the Japanese headquarters, and destroyed supplies of food and more than five hundred thousand rounds of enemy ammunition.[37]

At Ewa Air Station on Oahu, by the time the next letter was posted, VMF-214's new commander, George Britt, had been promoted to major, but the squadron's aircraft inventory still outnumbered the pilots available to fly them. As the days of September passed, Major Britt continued to wait for new pilots being trained back on the mainland to fill the vacant billets in his new squadron.[38]

Mailed September 11, 1942

U.S. Naval Air Station
Miami, Florida
Thursday
Dear Mom and Dad,

It's a bit late in the evening to begin writing, but, if this is a short letter, at least you'll understand. We've just returned from the daily evening show at the auditorium. This evening, beside the regular moving picture, the station's swing band entertained, with the help of some guest entertainers from Miami night clubs. It was very good.

Mom, I received your letter this afternoon with news of your arrival time. I spoke to the desk clerk at the Patrician yesterday about a room for you. In spite of the distance from here to the beach—it's about 18 miles and connections by bus are rather slow—I believe you'd be most comfortable at the beach. We'll not worry about getting hither and thither until you arrive. And you needn't worry about the room at the hotel. I'll take care of that. There are a couple of visits I want to make while you're here. Lt. Phillips, our flight leader from the Academy, has his mother here. She entertained all of us two weeks ago and I know she'd like to see you. Then Jim Flack and his wife are here—he's a Lieutenant in the physical training, a Yale Divinity School graduate, a teacher at Hopkins, and Smitty's and my boss at Goodwill Industries of Y.C.C. I was to have had dinner with them last Tuesday, but Jim had the O.D. duty and so we'll visit them together.

What did you think of the write-up of Peabody's "man of four professions"? I thought it very interesting and quite a tribute! I countenance no thought of worrying over the appearance of a hired press-agent. I think none is necessary, and no hired press agent could do as good a job.

The flying is progressing steadily. At the present rate, we shall be commissioned by the end of the month. Until today, I had been hitting the gunnery fairly well, 12 out of 43 one day, 19 for 120 tries on beam runs the next. That's about 19% hits, and the requirement is 5%. However, today I had no hits for 48 tries. I fear it was the result of yesterday's day-off. I couldn't fly worth a darn, and I knew it. In fact, I fired only 48 rounds because I knew the bullets weren't going in the sleeve. Still, they charged me with 120, claiming that if I were shooting an enemy, the rest of the bullets wouldn't do any good. I don't think much of that system of learning gunnery. It certainly doesn't do you much good to fire if you know you aren't on the target.

Very good news about Roy, I'd say. I've had the greatest respect for his ability. In fact, I've been shooting for his mark. And you can be sure I'm happy to see his merit recognized!

I'll plan to meet you at the train, Mom. For now, stay healthy, all of you! I'll be seeing you soon.

Love,

Stuff

The tribute referred to in Carl's previous letter about "Peabody's Man of Four Professions" was an article about his father, and it appeared in the *New Haven Register* on August 31, 1942.

As a scientist, he has been a world authority on historical geology; . . . as a teacher he has conducted Yale classes for 22 years; as a writer, he has published . . . a number of textbooks which are used yearly by thousands of students in this country and Britain; and as an executive he has . . . become the director of Yale University's Peabody Museum.

Over his desk are enlarged snapshots the director himself took of his son, a Yale graduate and now a flyer in the navy, and of his daughter, a sophomore at Vassar.[39] [Less than a month after the article appeared, the picture of Carl became outdated when he exchanged his Navy blue for the olive green of the U.S. Marine Corps.]

On the reverse side of the printed page of the *Register* was another feature article. This one describing Japan's invasion of the islands in the Pacific theater, and it recounted the "fanatical" courage demonstrated by Japanese pilots and soldiers during the battles being fought south of the equator.[40]

Late in September following the unsuccessful attempts to retake Guadalcanal earlier in the month, the Japanese Imperial Command prepared to intensify its efforts with more reinforcements. The Imperial Army 2nd Division was ordered to Rabaul on New Britain, and there the division was to prepare for an assault on Guadalcanal in an amphibious landing as early as it could be achieved. The Japanese objective remained unchanged—retake the island and the airfield from the occupying United States forces.[41]

On September 23, 1942, as the Japanese readied their forces on Rabaul for the new assault on Guadalcanal, in Miami, Cadet Carl Dunbar became Second Lieutenant Carl Dunbar and a new pilot in the U.S. Marine Corps. He was joined at the ceremonies by his mother, who had journeyed by train from New Haven to be present for his commissioning.

Mailed October 5, 1942

U.S. Naval Air Station
Miami, Florida
Sunday
Dear Mom and Dad,

It is just after 7:00 in the evening. The first night navigation hop will be going out shortly. I am scheduled for the second hop—going out at 9:25 and returning about 11:00. So for the first time since last Tuesday, I have two hours to write letters. Wednesday night we began night flying—two hours of landings with no lights, that is except boundary lights. It was amazing to find that landing in the dark is entirely possible, although I will admit that the first one found me quite apprehensive. I was glad to be on the ground at the end of the night's hop.

Thursday was the biggest flying day we've had, I guess. It was our initiation into first-line fighting ships. And it seemed scarcely credible that we successfully handled the F2-A's (Brewster Buffa-los) after training so long for just that climax. All Navy fighters are one-place ships; so consequently the first hop in the Brewster is also the solo hop. Well, believe me, it was a whole lot of airplane. I have no qualms whatever in admitting that I was just plain scared. 1,050 horsepower seems just like a flying engine and feels the same way. First hour, we did some touch and go landings at an outlying field, with radio and signal flag coaching from the ground. Muzz had a forced landing for his first attempt in the new ship, but handled it beautifully. He had come in for his approach, but apparently was a little high, so the flight-officer gave him a wave-off (go around again). Muzz poured on the coal, but got no response—his left gas tank had run dry because the mechanic here had failed to refuel the ship after the previous hop. Well, Muzz just nosed her over and brought her down through a fence, but with no personal damage and only a scratched wing where it hit one of the fence-posts. Next day, he had better luck.

By mistake, I got in an extra hour of Brewster landings. That was Friday. In the latter half of the period, I went up to 10,000 feet and made myself spin the ship right and left. Yesterday was a day-off, but today, we had another hour of air work familiarization. That's official language for "she's all yours, boys; go up and wring her out!" So we did. I slow-rolled, looped, immelmanned and chandelled until my stomach hollered quits. It's really an easier airplane to handle than the "J." Only things happen ever so much faster. I shall always have the greatest respect for these fighting ships, I hope!

You may wish for Florida sunshine, Mom, but you can be sure I envy you New England fall equally as much. We went to a football game here yesterday, but it certainly wasn't the football setting I know. You can have all the South, anytime you want it as far as I'm concerned.

My orders haven't arrived yet, but my commission came Wednesday. The orders are due sometime this next week. That's not too soon, for I can't see more than about two weeks of flying left here. Love to all,

Stuff

P.S. I hope Dad can throw off that throat pronto. I'm convinced that the whiskey cure is the only thing!

Miami was just a stopover in the pipeline between the primary flight schools and the combat assignments for new pilots. In the fall of 1942 NAS Miami had strictly limited facilities with which to train the ever-increasing number of cadets flowing out of the two Florida-based primary schools at Jacksonville and Pensacola, and the acute equipment shortages in the Fleet prevented the pilots from accruing any time in the cockpits of the aircraft they would fly in combat.[42] While almost all of the flight training was in SNJ Texans, there was one other option, and the pilots were able to log limited flight time in the cockpit of the aging F2A Brewster Buffalo after they had qualified for fighters. In total, the entries in Carl's logbook for time in the cockpit of a Buffalo totaled 20.8 hours before his preparations in Miami had concluded.[43]

At Ewa, the tedious rebuilding process for VMF-214 continued into the fall, and on October 8, nine new Marine Corps second lieutenants arrived from San Diego to take their places in the Squadron. Among the arriving aviators was Vince Carpenter, who later became one of the squadron's division commanders. The day after Carpenter and the others reported for duty at Ewa, two more pilots arrived, and the squadron strength increased to sixteen pilots.[44]

Mailed October 14, 1942

U.S. Naval Air Station
Miami, Florida

Tuesday

Dear Mom and Dad,

Today was my first flight since last Tuesday when I was grounded—for fatigue. Three nights of night flying and a heavy daily schedule prompted me to ask for an afternoon of rest. The doctor recommended two days. I took five! Six of us in the flight were grounded for the six days, and the authorities got a bit hot under the collar about it.

The time off wasn't exactly a rest cure, but it did take my mind off of flying. We "rendezvoused" in town every afternoon and celebrated long into the night. I felt ever so much more comfortable in the plane today, more alert, less jumpy and generally at ease. So my conscience is not stabbing me as hard as it was yesterday.

I neglected to write in the last letter that I bumped into Professor Hall here just after you left, Mom. It's Lt. Colonel Hall now. He's connected with foreign liaison. The first time I met him he was eating lunch with a pair of Ecuadorian ranking aviators. They spoke no English; so Professor Hall interpreted both ways, to and from me. I would like to have him out to the base, but I fear he is rather too busy.

We have a couple of weeks left of flying here and then a short time of actual carrier landings elsewhere. After that, I should get my 15-day leave before departing to take a crack at the Japs.

The apples (and McIntosh they were) certainly hit the spot! Made me very homesick as I bit into the first one and lay my head back on the pillow with closed eyelids and dreamed of Connecticut hills. Everyone enjoyed the rare treat of real apples. Muzz asked particularly this afternoon to have his appreciation included with mine. Guess we just don't see eye to eye on the place to live, Mom.

I'm going to close briefly tonight and turn in for a long sleep. This will let you know that all is well in Miami. Best wishes to you, and I'll be seeing you soon!

Love,

Stuff

The battle between the opposing ground forces on Guadalcanal dragged on into October, and a second new fighter strip was completed by the Navy Seabees adjacent to Henderson Field and Fighter One. While the American forces maintained the secure perimeter around the airfields on the northeast coast of the island, the Japanese remained in force in the jungles and mountain areas on other parts of the island. At night the Japanese warships of the Tokyo Express continued to shell American positions around Henderson Field and then retreated north out of range of the Allied aircraft during daylight.[45]

In addition to shelling from the enemy naval guns, Guadalcanal was also subjected to harassing enemy air raids by fighters and bombers based at the airfields on Bougainville and Rabaul. As the first weeks of October passed, the Marines defending the airfields remained under constant attack-bombing and strafing from the air, bombardment from the Tokyo Express, and artillery and sniper fire from the Japanese forces on the ground.[46]

The tentative progress by General Vandegrift's Marines and the inability to secure the island after more than two months of fighting became a source of growing concern among American military leaders, and it was finally decided that a change of leadership was necessary. On October 18, after days of deliberation, the commander of the Pacific theater, Admiral Nimitz, replaced the U.S. commander in the South Pacific with Admiral William Halsey in an effort to change the tide in the ongoing conflict.[47]

With the appointment of Admiral Halsey, a new attitude permeated the American forces in the South Pacific, and "defeatism and conservatism were replaced with a fighting spirit. From the time of Halsey's appointment onward, the course of the battle on Guadalcanal began to change."[48]

Mailed October 24, 1942

> U.S. Naval Air Station
> Miami, Florida
> Friday
> Dear Mom and Dad,

They've been trying to finish us up and send us elsewhere, but still I have four hops left. We are to fly all day tomorrow, and in that case, we shall probably finish. In any case, we haven't long to go here. I don't know what my orders will be after leaving here. Some of the Marines are going elsewhere, along with all the Naval pilots, for carrier training. That is not a long process, in the neighborhood of two weeks. On the other hand, if I don't go to the Wolverine my leave will commence immediately, and I shall be home sometime next week. I won't know until the last minute when my orders arrive, so I shall probably not have an opportunity to let you know I'm coming.

I am no longer a virgin pilot—just a bum and a hacker now. I ground-looped a Brewster this afternoon, and ground-looping is an offense for which I have no sympathy. It happened on take-off. I forgot to lock the tail wheel, and just as I was getting up good speed, it began to vibrate violently, spinning 'round and 'round like a top. I didn't know what was wrong. I only knew I didn't want to take it off the ground in that condition, so I chopped the throttle—and bingo! I was spinning around helplessly. Two and a half turns before the wing finally went down and smacked the runway. So that's why I am a bum. They assigned me a 1.0 in aptitude, that's equal to 25%, and I am to write this thesis on the "Importance of the Check-Off List."

Muzz and I were restricted for eight days for missing bunk check Monday night. His girl had a party for us at her home, and we just didn't get back. So daily, we trudge over to the Administration Building at 1900 and 2100 to muster. Last night, we had girls to dinner at the O-club, and so we drove up to muster at 2100 in Bunkie's convertible Packard. No dust on us! Then I drove ashore, and we played about so long that we missed the 2300 bunk-check. However, the OD was a good man and took care of us.

The girls caused us to eat 2 steak dinners apiece last night. They didn't arrive until 2045, one hour and a half late. The kitchen stops taking orders at 2000. So at 3 minutes to 8, I ordered four steaks. And when the girls didn't arrive, we started on their dinner, which we had very auspiciously safeguarded under napkins. I believe the guests around us were quite amused, for we made much ceremony of changing places to begin our second round and meantime carried on a swift pantomime with our absent guests.

Had a good letter from Bill Stuhlman this week. He is still doing pre-operational at Jacksonville. In two or three weeks, he will be home on leave; so there is a chance we may hit it together. The happiest word is that he, too, is reporting to San Diego (confidential) and so in all probability, we shall be together again.

Doc is in Atlanta at instrument instructors school. He brought "Grace" back with him from home and they are married now. Paul Cross has just finished instructors' school at Jacksonville and will go to an "E" base to instruct. Pete Prudden is still at Jacksonville in pre-operational training.

Well, I must close here and drop Tom a note. I have been trying to get a ferry hop to Pensacola, but without success.

Best of health to you both and to Grandmother Dunbar. I shall be seeing you all soon.

Love,
Stuff

On October 26, 1942, Second Lieutenant Carl Dunbar received his pilot instrument rating, concluding his time and training at NAS Miami.[49] On the day Carl received his instrument rating at Opa-Locka, Japanese and American naval forces in the South Pacific concluded a gigantic game of hide-and-seek in a naval engagement southeast of Guadalcanal, remembered today as the Battle of the Santa Cruz Islands.[50] The battle was a tactical defeat for the United States, but it also continued the attrition of the carrier-based aircraft on both sides.[51] The Japanese carrier *Zuiho* was severely damaged during the confrontation at the Santa Cruz Islands, and the Japanese suffered the loss of one hundred more carrier-based aircraft.[52]

The United States' losses included the USS *Hornet*, which had contributed significantly at the Battle of Midway and launched Doolittle's raiders against the Japanese homeland only six months earlier in the year.[53] The carrier was heavily damaged during the fight and finally sank before the battle ended. The loss of the *Hornet* left Admiral Halsey in the unenviable predicament of having only a single damaged aircraft carrier,

Flight line at NAS Miami, 1942. SNJ Texan trainers (used by Navy and Marine pilots for advance flight training, aerial gunnery, and carrier take-offs and landings) are shown in the foreground. Outdated F2A Brewster Buffaloes and F3F biplane fighters appear in the upper left. (Courtesy of the State Archives of Florida.)

the USS *Enterprise*, and one battleship to support a fleet of smaller war-ships fighting to keep open the sea supply lines to the besieged Marines on Guadalcanal.[54]

Fortunately for Halsey and the Allied forces, the Japanese carrier fleet was also badly battered, and once again the Imperial Command withdrew its warships to safety in the north to avoid the risks of an-other engagement.[55] As 1943 loomed on the horizon, the continuing attrition of the carrier assets on both sides following the Battle of the Santa Cruz Islands placed even more emphasis on the strategic impor-tance of the island airfields.[56]

From Miami, Carl moved on to the cold weather of Illinois, reporting on November 4 for duty aboard the USS *Wolverine* in Chicago Harbor on Lake Michigan.[57] The USS *Wolverine* had operated as a Great Lakes

Left: 11. Second Lieutenant Carl O. Dunbar Jr., USMC, following his commissioning at NAS Miami, 1942. (Dunbar family collection.)

Below: USS *Wolverine* based at Glenview, Illinois, on Lake Michigan and used for carrier qualification by Navy and Marine fighter pilots in 1942. Originally a Great Lakes steamer, the *Wolverine* was stripped and fitted with a carrier deck for pilots headed to Fleet duty. (National Archives.)

paddle-wheeled excursion ship before the war began, but after Pearl Harbor with all available carriers deployed to combat assignments, the *Wolverine* was reconfigured with a carrier flight deck. After its refitting, the *Wolverine* served as a primary platform for pilots headed to the fleet, allowing them to execute real takeoffs and landings from a sea-borne carrier deck.

On November 11, 1942, after five successful landings on the flight deck of the *Wolverine* in a Texan SNJ, Second Lieutenant Dunbar was certified as "carrier qualified" by the senior training officer.[58] With his logbook showing 280.9 hours of accumulated flight time, Carl Dunbar had completed his final phase of training and was available for assignment to an operational combat squadron.[59]

In the Pacific theater, admirals Halsey and Yamamoto continued efforts to build their manpower in the battle for the control of Guadalcanal. American ground forces had begun an offensive against the Japanese troops still occupying portions of the island on the second of November.[60] Each night, however, the cover of darkness permitted the Tokyo Express to land more troops to counter the advances by the U.S. Marines.[61]

On November 12, the day after Carl received his carrier certification, the American ground advance stalled in the face of a strong Japanese counterattack.[62] In the afternoon hours of the same day in the waters to the north of Guadalcanal, the warships from both navies prepared for another confrontation at sea.[63] This time, the battle would be fought without carrier support on either side.

Once it began, the Naval Battle of Guadalcanal continued through the long night of November 12. With the light of morning, "the waters off Guadalcanal were full of smoke and several burning vessels could be seen."[64] The Americans had taken a dreadful beating, losing six destroyers (either sunk or disabled) and four cruisers, two sunk and two more disabled. Despite the losses at sea, the U.S. forces had held their ground against the advances of the Japanese counteroffensive on the island. The Japanese warships had failed in their primary objective to smash Henderson Field with their naval guns, and the ground forces were unable to successfully challenge and overrun the perimeter of the Allied defenses that protected the airfield complex and its aircraft.[65]

Three days following the sea battle, on the morning of November 15, the Japanese tried yet again to land their full invasion force on Guadalcanal. Fighter aircraft from Kahili on Bougainville and a smaller airfield on the adjacent Shortland Island were dispatched to provide cover for the returning Japanese transports, but once again they were met and repelled by the defending Wildcats of the Cactus Air Force.[66]

When darkness fell on the evening of the fifteenth, Admiral Halsey could claim a clear-cut victory on Guadalcanal. The Japanese had set out to land ten thousand men on the island, supported by heavy equipment, big guns, and ammunition for an entire infantry division, but only two thousand men had actually made it to shore with limited supplies and equipment. In the three days between November 13 and 16, the Japanese lost at least thirty warships and transports and an estimated fifty combat airplanes.[67]

While the losses were heavy on both sides, the Americans succeeded in their efforts to land more reinforcements for the beleaguered Marines defending Guadalcanal, and Halsey's forces had turned back the attempt by the Japanese to do the same. "There was no doubt that the Americans had the best of it, and the outcome would vitally affect the struggle for Guadalcanal."[68]

4 ✈ ✈ ✈ ✈ ✈ ✈ ✈

San Diego to Espiritu Santo, New Hebrides, December 5, 1942–March 12, 1943

> *I had quite an unexpected experience week before last when my ship got into an inverted spin at low altitude and I had to hit the silk. I was so upset at losing the plane that the jump was very much of an anticlimax. Didn't even collect any bruises, largely, I guess because of the spot in which I landed—a shoulder-deep, muddy-water swamp. I straddled an old stump and started collecting my chute, but left that job to others who soon appeared on the scene. I doubt whether the weight of the world ever drooped heavier upon my shoulders than it did as I trudged back to the nearest telephone.*
>
> Carl O. Dunbar Jr., January 30, 1943

After spending two weeks of leave at home in New Haven, Carl left for the West Coast, traveling across the country by train to San Diego to await orders deploying him to his combat assignment. San Diego served as one of the major ports of embarkation to the Pacific theater, and it was the gathering place for thousands of young warriors—each one fresh from their training regimen, equipped with new skills, knowledgeable in sophisticated weaponry, and eager to use their new tactical proficiencies. Departing San Diego for their assignments, the soldiers, sailors, and pilots left for unknown destinations in the Pacific, places revealed to them only after their departure. Upon arrival, the destinations were places that they could not reveal in their letters home to family and friends.[1]

Carl arrived during the first week of December in 1942, almost one year to the day from the time he had departed New Haven for initial flight training at Squantum. Upon arriving, he reported to the naval air station where he was temporarily billeted with Air Regulatory Squadron Three to begin his wait for permanent assignment to an operational Marine Corps combat fighter squadron—one he expected within a matter of days.

On Oahu during the week of Carl's arrival in San Diego, Marine Fighting Squadron VMF-214 was approaching full operational strength, taking delivery of a few more new Grumman Wildcat fighters and awaiting the arrival of eight new pilots from the mainland, among them O. K. Williams.[2]

On Guadalcanal during the first weeks of December, Navy Seabees were completing the extension of the bomber strip at Henderson Field by laying Marston matting for a mile. The airfield at Fighter One and its companion fighter strip adjacent to Henderson Field were also being prepared with the steel matting so that the airfields could remain operational in the tropical climate that brought constant rain and muddy conditions to the surface of the runways.[3]

Two days after reporting at NAS San Diego, Carl posted his next letter home.

Mailed December 7, 1942

2nd Lt. Carl O. Dunbar, Jr.
Squadron ARS-3
Marine Aircraft Wing
NAS San Diego
Sunday
Dear Mom and Dad,

Arrived safely in San Diego Friday forenoon—the train was only ten hours late to L.A. However, I had miscalculated by one day and so was early instead of late reporting in. Except for the train ride, which is tedious for even the shortest distance, the trip was far more interesting than I had expected. Purely by chance, the company in Pullman 230 turned out to be congenial and full of fun. There were two Army captains, two lieutenants, four civilians, two lawyers and two mining engineers, one of whom has been practically all over the world; the rest of the complement included two young married ladies, each with a pair of grand youngsters. For more diversification, you'd have to delve into a magician's cauldron.

My baggage hasn't arrived yet, or hadn't yesterday afternoon. I am anxious about it, for unless it arrives in the next day or two, I am very apt to have to leave without it. I imagine the hold-up is due to the change of stations in Chicago. I took the N.Y.C. and sent baggage on the Penn. Baggage hadn't arrived when I got to Chicago. So I had to arrange to have the bags sent across to Dearborn Station and thence checked on to San Diego. It all depends, I guess, on how soon the baggage-transfer agent gets around to transferring my equipment.

San Diego is absolutely an impossible town. I thought I'd seen a lot of service men before, but that was all a myth. Perhaps it's because the town was small to begin with, but in any case one might just as well go to bed as bother going in town. I called Dodie Rollins first thing Friday evening to find that she was announcing an engagement next evening. I left the fellows and boarded a bus for La Jolla (about ten miles distant) where Dodie met me. It was only about a mile to their home, well up the mountainside overlooking the ocean. After a little chat with Mr. and Mrs. Rollins, we settled down to talk over Vassar-Yale days and the events which have transpired thus since they ended. I was terribly disappointed that Sem is not the lucky man. As we talked, the phonograph was softly playing Yale Glee Club records, and altogether, it was a painful as well as a glorious meeting. I noticed a big well of tears in Dodie's eyes as she told me of her trip east last summer and I looked away. She is a wonderful girl! Her fiancé is a lawyer, a Penn graduate, now a full Lieutenant with the Naval Air Operations Command. I guess they have known each other for many years.

Jim arrived same day as I did. The rest of the boys were already here. Very fortunately, they are all to fly together in a squadron of those ships Dad and I were looking at last week. Don't think I've not been wishing like the deuce that I could be with them.

I feel that I should write one or two other letters and so must close here. It was a wonderful visit at home. I am only sorry it went by so fast. Just have to wait for awhile until the next leave. Maybe by that time, we'll all be wearing "civies" again. Give my very best wishes to grandmother. Things happened so fast, I couldn't even say good-bye to her. Let me hear from you, especially that you're well and busy.

Love and best wishes,

Stuff

In an era before routine transcontinental commercial airline service, travel by rail was the norm for long distances, and trips across the country took days and not hours. Pullman car facilities provided sleeping and dining facilities for passengers on the train, and the opportunities for brief social interaction with other travelers like those described in Carl's letter were commonplace.

In San Diego, Carl's wait for a permanent assignment that was expected to be a few days became almost two weeks, and orders to a combat squadron remained an uncertainty when his next letter was written. Despite the uncertainty, the preparations of the gear and equipment that Carl intended to take with him into the Pacific continued, but the flight skills that were acquired and refined in months of training at Jacksonville and Miami got little use. Carl's only flight time during his first two weeks on the West Coast consisted of three flights. All of them took place on December 12, and all were in a SNJ-3 Texan.[4]

Mailed December 16, 1942

Tuesday

Dear Mom and Dad,

Surprise—to both of us! I'm still waiting. In fact there is even a chance that I'll get back to Florida again this week on a ferry-hop. I just missed going to Dallas yesterday. Don't know what kind of plane I may get to fly, though it will probably be a fighter.

I managed to get in four hours of flying Saturday, which will get me flight pay for December. I was piloting for free-gunnery training of rear-seat men. I got a big kick out of it, though I must admit the airplane and I seemed like perfect strangers at the outset. On the last two hops, it was my job to escort the tow-plane home, and I had a chance to do some gunnery runs myself. And I found that the lay-off has made me very rusty. They do all gunnery here out over the Pacific, which is very beautiful. The visibility is not too great, but the setting is picturesque, nonetheless. The very blue Pacific washes the well planned harbor, and the city of San Diego nestles comfortably between the sea and an imposing mountain range.

This California weather is not all it's cracked up to be. The days are warm enough, but the nights and mornings are uncomfortably cold and damp. I'm just about over the first cold I've had since Atlanta last March. I can't blame it all on the weather after the trip across the continent, but the weather had a lot to do with it.

Bill arrived last Monday, and of course we celebrated the re-union. Pete Prudden arrived yesterday, and we all got together last night. I haven't seen Jim yet this evening to talk with him about his first flight in the F4U. He had four hours in it today, time enough to make plenty of observations. He would have flown sooner, but he was grounded last week for doing a slow-roll 25 feet off the ground!

I received both your letters and was very glad for both of them. I would have written again sooner except that between celebrating and purchasing gear, I've had little time of my own. Fact is, I've been carrying the money-orders around with me nearly a week. My check was here in San Diego when I arrived, and so I've had plenty of money. But I've spent a good deal on such things as a sleeping bag, blankets, two pair of rugged marine boots, a sheath knife, raincoat, foot-locker (a small trunk), and any number of smaller items such as soap, toothpaste, etc.

Mom, if you will let me know how much I owe you for the wedding gift, I'll send along a money order next letter. And, too, I'll send some for a picture that Sis can pick out for her room while she's home. Wish you could persuade grandmother to stay for Christmas. If she'd stay and Larry and Imogene and Gevene could be with you, it would be a rather jolly time.

I'll try to keep you a bit better posted henceforth. My love to all of you at home. Lots of smiles!
Stuff

As the first anniversary of Pearl Harbor passed, Allied forces closed in on their initial objective at the southern end of the archipelago. The U.S. Marines began their final offensive push against the remaining Japanese military units on the northwest side of Guadalcanal, intent on driving them permanently from the island.[5] Farther up the Solomon chain, however, the formidable enemy installations on New Georgia and its adjacent central islands, and on Bougainville in the northern reach of the Solomons, were being refortified and expanded by the enemy.[6]

At NAS San Diego, the pilots temporarily assigned to Air Regulatory Squadron Three continued to wait for their permanent orders, their time spent watching the activity of others. Unlike Miami, however, the idol pilots were observing the performance of American's new line of combat fighters, including the F4U Corsairs, and not the outdated Brewster Buffaloes. The new Corsairs, like the new pilots, were also awaiting their initial deployment to combat in the Pacific.[7]

Among the thousands arriving to depart from San Diego in December of 1942 were Bill Stuhlman and Pete Prudden. They had begun their initial training at Squantum with Carl, but assignments to different types of aircraft had separated the friends in July after primary flight training in Jacksonville. San Diego provided a brief reunion opportunity for the young men from New England before they were separated again.

Mailed in San Diego, December 22, 1942

Monday

Dear Mom and Dad,

My emotions have just run the gauntlet this past half-hour. For about fifteen minutes, we were preparing to depart for Jacksonville on a ferry hop this afternoon. And then we learned to our great disappointment that we are not allowed to go farther than Dallas, because we are subject to immediate orders. It was a let-down, I can tell you, after two weeks of dropping into Operations each morning in the hope of getting a hop, to have one finally and have it taken away. Now we have settled back to the old grind of sitting and waiting and mustering three times a day. Sitting around getting stale and staler certainly is a discouraging build-up for what must be imminent action.

There is a bright spot on the horizon, however. I spoke briefly with Lt. Commander Clifton in mess-hall Saturday morning. He is Jim's skipper, organizer of the first Navy F4U squadron. I told him how anxious I was to fly the Corsair and how I had wanted to get in his squadron, although that was impossible for any Marine flyer. He asked my name, saying he had a former pupil who is organizing a Marine F4U outfit elsewhere and that he would get in touch with him and see what he could do for me.

I was speaking to him about a spectacular exhibition of dog-fighting the previous afternoon between a Corsair and an Army Mustang (P-51). I suspected that "Whispering Joe" was flying the F4U, but it turned out that he was in the P-51. The two planes were all over the sky, from 10,000 to 2,000 feet, chasing one and the other through screaming dives, all sorts of acrobatic maneuvers, tight lufbery circles. In tight turns and climbs, great trails of vapor streamed from both planes' wing-tips, leaving arcs hanging in the blue after the combatants had sped on across the sky.

The Zamsky proofs arrived this morning. I think they are far better than the photos by Tooley-Myron. You didn't mention which ones you liked, if any, however. Were I having the pictures made up, I should have them printed upon the woven paper. It is more expensive, but it has a distinction about it. That is only my preference, though, and the choice is naturally yours. As for the proofs, there doesn't seem to be a great deal of choice among the whites. Bill likes number 1. #4 in greens with the top-coat is easily the most real face. I like the other sitting pose (full-length) for reality, too, but it wouldn't make a good opposite for one of the whites, if that's what you had in mind. Number 8 or number 5 aren't too bad. I'll be interested to know what was your choice. I'll return the proofs, too, right away.

I would call on Christmas, but I know that the wires will be jammed with calls of fellows who haven't been home as recently as I have. So perhaps it is better that this be my Christmas greeting. I hope you will all make the best of the season. It is my first

Christmas away from home, at least from home or from the family, and I shall be thinking of you. Perhaps next year, it will be a different story and we will all be together. At any rate, it is a blessing still to be in the U.S.A. I feel for those who are less fortunate.

My deepest regards to you all and best wishes for a happy Christmas, lots of smiles and good health.

Love,

Stuff

While anxious to fly the new Corsair that he describes in his letter, Carl's opportunity to pilot the high-performance fighter did not come while he was at NAS San Diego. His logbook shows no time in the Corsair, and the "ferry hops" he had hoped for did not materialize. His time in the cockpit remained limited, and only two more flights were recorded during December. Both came on the day after Christmas, and both were in an SNJ-3.[8] With the purchases described in his next letter, the personal equipment for his journey into the Pacific had been assembled, but the uncertainty surrounding the date of departure remained when the letter was posted at the end of December. The paperwork and other details that preceded his deployment continued, and the weekends and evenings were spent in the nightspots of San Diego and Los Angeles. The wait, now almost a month, was not to be more months as Carl speculated in his next letter but was to end in three weeks when his orders to depart San Diego were issued.

Mailed December 30, 1942

Tuesday

Dear Mom and Dad,

Both your letters and the package arrived yesterday—a welcome Christmas greeting and gift each! I want to thank you for the wallet which seems almost too good to use, especially in the frontier regions; it is lovely indeed. I might add that I hope you were not expecting packages from here for Christmas. There is such a great deal of demand here, with so many service-men stationed nearby, and a limited supply, that I deemed it unwise to attempt to send anything.

I fear I shall have to admit my very bad memory on birthdays. Much as I am ashamed to say it, the 23rd and the 1st slipped up on me without my realizing what they signified. It would have been far better had I remembered in time, but as it is, you will both have to bear with me and attempt to forget that I am remembering a bit late. I want to do some more looking around before I pick out anything.

As for the wall decoration I promised Sis, I feel obliged to ask you to help me out. It will cramp me a little bit to send along the amount I had in mind until the 1st. I have a thirty dollar mess bill due now, and Bill and I figured up last night that I have spent over $105 on supplies, etc. necessary for embarking. If you can manage it without embarrassment and could finance the deal for me, I'll reimburse you come payday. I'd just as soon wait until then anyhow, except that Sis won't be able to pick out anything while she is home. Perhaps she could pick out something and wait until my payday to have it sent. I am planning on sending her $20.

The $105 which I mentioned is composed of relatively few items which run something like this: foot-locker-$12; sleeping bag and mattress-$12; 2 blankets-$12; raincoat-$13; watch-$15; underwear and socks-$7; hunting knife-$8.50; and tooth brushes-$4; toothpaste, soap, medicine, etc.-approximately $10. And so it goes. There are many other things such as 2 pair of heavy marine boots and flashlight, too numerous to mention. The watch was something not absolutely necessary, but a luminous dial is almost imperative and there were none available for my Hamilton. The Marine QM had 100 of these Elgin 17-jewel jobs, so I felt it was worth the money.

It appears now that we may be stationed near here for several months yet. That isn't definite, of course. I just missed leaving immediately upon arrival here by the four days proceed time which I had coming and took.

Dodie is being married Saturday—a small wedding at her home. I talked to her tonight on the phone, first time since my only visit with her. She wanted me to come to the wedding to represent the East, and of course, Marine Corps willing, I shall be there. My greens may look a bit shabby and out of place, but I'll shine up the Sam Brown and try to look dignified.

Christmas here didn't seem like much of a Christmas, I will say. It fogged up early here the 24th and rained steadily and hard all Christmas Eve. Pete and Bill and I trudged through the rain down to the bar, bought 4 quarts of champagne, and returned to Bill's room for our own quiet celebration, in solid comfort and the entertainment of the radio. Christmas afternoon, we went into Coronado, bought supplies and adjourned to the Hotel Del Coronado Officer's Club for a milk-punch party. The hotel supplied an enormous punch bowl with a great piece of ice, sugar, and nutmeg. We did the rest.

Jim asked especially to be remembered. He has been intending to write, as have I, to his folks, but time just hasn't permitted. He is going great guns in the squadron—has about thirty hours in the F4U and is crazy about the plane. His skipper was up dog-fighting with the Jap Zero here over the field this afternoon.

It's good to hear that all is well at home, in spite of the cold. I'm glad you braved it to make the wedding. Give my best wishes to grandmother and my deepest regards to Sis. As soon as things are settled, I'll write to both of them.

Best wishes and greetings for the New Year to all, and to you.

Love,

Stuff

The day after Carl wrote to describe the "dog-fighting" in the skies over San Diego, the chief of staff of the Japanese army appeared at the Imperial Palace in Tokyo for an audience with Emperor Hirohito. The purpose of the audience was to receive the emperor's formal approval of a reluctant decision by the Imperial High Command to withdraw the nation's remaining troops from Guadalcanal and effectuate Japan's first military retreat of the Pacific campaign. The emperor admonished General Sugiyama Hajime upon receiving the "regrettable" news but gave his approval to the decision recommended by his commanders, and the planning for the evacuation of the remaining Japanese troops on Guadalcanal began at Rabaul.[9]

The following day in San Diego, Carl was reassigned from Air

Regulatory Squadron Three to the 4th Marine Air Base Defense Wing, and his wait for a permanent assignment in the Pacific theater began to draw to a close.

On January 18 he was reassigned again, this time to Marine Base Defense Group 42. There, he began the final preparations for departure to his next duty station in Hawaii. On January 19 he called New Haven to give his family the news, and his call was followed two days later by the next letter home. The letter was written on the first day of the voyage en route from San Diego to Hawaii. In addition to Carl, the passenger list of the *Robin Wentley* included Harry Hollmeyer, Tom Tomlinson, Drury McCall, and four other Marine pilots who were to become the final members of VMF-214.[10]

In the South Pacific four days before the *Robin Wentley* sailed from San Diego, the Japanese commanders at Rabaul deployed a task force of nine destroyers to Guadalcanal. Following the decision at the Imperial Palace in Tokyo, the warships were to serve as the rear guard for the evacuation of the remaining Japanese forces on the island; in the process, the control of Guadalcanal and its strategic airfields was ceded permanently to Admiral Halsey's South Pacific command.[11]

Received January 21, 1943

Thursday

Dear Mom and Dad,

   If my call Tuesday morning was a rather abrupt, rude awakening to you, it was a great thrill to me—one that should offset any commotion it caused you. I debated some about calling, lest it cause you undue concern to be awakened by a long distance call early in the morning—it was 4:00 A.M. here. I do believe that was the fastest long distance call I've ever completed. San Diego operator called Chicago "through to New York City" and New York City called New Haven. In less than twenty seconds, I heard the old familiar ring of 5-1896.

   I picked a bad time to let my correspondence lapse. We were spending so much time buzzing about, especially at night, that what should have been our waking hours were really sleeping ones. Both of our last two weekends we spent in Los Angeles; we rented a car and spent from Saturday evening until Monday A.M., 2:30 and 3:00 respectively. Weekend before last when Pete and Bill and I journeyed together, we stayed at the Beverly-Wilshire just outside of Hollywood. Saturday night, we took in Cirro's—saw Edgar Bergen, in fact bumped into him on the dance floor—but no other stars. Breakfast at Sardi's Sunday noon was a bit dreary until after the second bottle of beer, when a patron in the next booth began cussing out his wife, which was quite an amazing scene. Sunday afternoon, we sat drinking martinis in the Wilshire cocktail lounge when Pete spied Thomas Mitchell ("Gone with the Wind"—Academy Award for Best Supporting Role, and "Moontide") standing at the bar. He cruised up and cast a friendly arm around his shoulder, and we had a pleasant chat with him. He's exactly as on the screen, bushy eyebrows, stubble beard, piercing glance and all. Earlier in the afternoon, we drove out through Beverly Hills among the palatial homes that are truly unbelievable.

Last weekend, we went back to Los Angeles again and this time rented a so-called bungalow at the fashionable Ambassador Hotel— a living room and bedroom of giant size with excellent bath accommodations. After a big Saturday night (Freddy Martin plays at the Hotel's Coconut Grove), we wakened Sunday morning to milk punches. Peter and I never left the room all day—Pete stayed in his striped blue and white pajamas, and I lounged on the sofa in shorts and skivi shirt. It's hard to imagine more solid comfort than last Sunday afternoon stretched out on the sofa with one cushion under my head, a wool blanket around me, a milk punch and a hot sandwich served beside me, a pipe in the other hand, listening to Brahm's First Symphony—and all with never a care in the world.

I put a call to the Cooper's weekend before last, but they were out for the afternoon. I had no good opportunity to call last weekend.

Before leaving San Diego, I filled out an allotment card which will send home $150 a month. In case of death or capture by the enemy, that allotment will be continued for six months. It will be necessary for you to make application for insurance premiums, which will begin as soon as application is made. You can bank the salary or spend it as you see fit or if the need should arise. I didn't have time to get off a money order to Abbott's before leaving. So I shall attempt to do so at the earliest possibility. Meantime, I can let you know the amount of the balance due and the address if you can, and if you will, send it out of the monthly pay check. I didn't sign over the insurance to Sis, but I'm sure you could take care of that if the need should arise.

It certainly was a relief to shove off finally. I was getting so darn fidgety doing no flying except for those few cub hops that I was unbearable to myself. When you stop to realize that I haven't flown since the 28th of October, except for a scant 8 hours here and there, you can understand my feeling. Every one of us is raring to go. A few hours in the Wildcat or the Corsair, and we'll take anything the Japs have to offer and give about ten times as much in return.

We had really a grand last night in San Diego. Jim and I went to dinner with one of our classmates and his wife who cooked a very good dinner. We returned to Coronado to our favorite bar (called "La Fiesta") to meet Pete and Bill, who had driven down with a truck convoy in the afternoon, and Harry Hollmeyer (Harvard '40) who is sitting across the table from me now. It seemed only fitting that we should join in song at our last meeting—so we did. After our first rendition, the entire assemblage was gravely attentive. Two majors were hollering requests, someone else bought us drinks, lovely women cried bravo, mellow civilians staggered up to blend their voices and belches—and the shore patrol walked in. First thing you know, the chief has joined us too.

I've come to the end of my paper allotment and so will stop for now. The pitch and roll seems to have put most of our compliment in their bunks, so I'll take a stroll on deck. Best of health to you both and courage.

Love,

Stuff

During his first year away from home, the letters periodically describe financial matters remaining back in New Haven, but by the time the *Robin Wentley* sailed from San Diego, most of these had been addressed and only minor financial details remained unresolved. Carl's life insurance

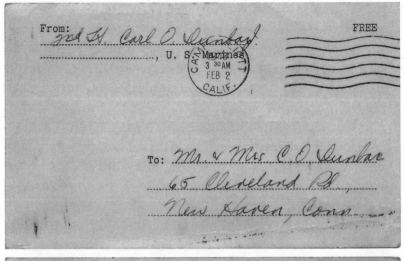

Military postcard to family announcing Carl Dunbar's deployment and his safe arrival in the Pacific theater. (Dunbar family collection.)

arrangements had been made, an allotment card had been completed to divert a portion of his monthly pay to his parents with instructions for handling the funds, and only the bill at Abbott Military Tailors for new uniforms remained unpaid.

The next postcard, filled out by Carl with his new mailing address, was prepared in January on the day of his departure from San Diego and postdated. The limited information it provided concealed his destination, but it accommodated the ability of the family to continue to communicate once he deployed.[12] The card was the final piece of paperwork completed before his departure, but it was not mailed to the family until after the ship ferrying the new pilots to Hawaii had crossed the Pacific and arrived safely at Pearl Harbor.

February 2, 1943

> Dear Mom and Dad,
> I have been transferred overseas and have safely reached my destination.
> Please address all mail for me exactly as follows:
> 2dLt. Carl O. Dunbar, Jr., USMC
> U.S. Marine Corps Unit #765
> c/o Postmaster, San Francisco,
> California
> Stuff

Carl's letter on January 13 was the first written after his arrival at the Marine air base at Ewa on the island of Oahu. The sea voyage on the first ocean leg of his journey to the South Pacific is described in detail in the letter, but again the port of arrival is not revealed. After what he had seen on the beaches at Jacksonville, there was, however, an expression of relief that threats from enemy submarines did not materialize during the voyage.

While descriptive narratives of the events and the local surroundings continue to be featured in his letters as before, the exact locations of the places, events, and missions are not revealed. Some of these details are found in Carl's flight logbook and others are now available in the historical records and accounts of the time, but when the correspondence was written, the security precautions and the censorship restrictions brought on by the war did not allow such details to be described in his letters.

According to his sister, some of Carl's letters from the Pacific contained a code in their opening paragraph that had been devised with his father. As Lora Johnson remembers it, the word combinations, when decoded, allowed Professor Dunbar to decipher the latitude and longitude of Carl's changing locations in the Pacific theater.[13] After more than sixty years, Lora was not able to recall the details of the hidden code, and it is not readily apparent in the letters. I have made no effort to rediscover the code that Carl and his father created because I have had the benefit of the logbook and the historical accounts that were not available to the family in New Haven when the letters arrived.

Once in Hawaii, Carl and the other new pilots reported to the commanding officer of Marine Aircraft Group 21 (MAG-21). They were then assigned to VMF-214, one of the MAG-21 fighter squadrons that had been commissioned seven months earlier.[14] With the arrival of these final eight pilots at the end of January, the twenty-seven-man flight roster for VMF-214 was finally complete.[15] The voyage from San Diego to Hawaii had taken nine days, and the arrival in Hawaii was recalled by Tom Tomlinson, who was one of the pilots traveling with Carl aboard the *Robin Wentley*.

> In no time at all the gangway was down and an old truck appeared to take the pilots away from the wreckage of the naval base to their new home. This was to be the Marine Corps Air Station at Ewa Plantation. It was at the end of a long, two-lane road through pineapple fields and jungle. There was also a narrow-gauge railroad mostly to haul the products of the plantation to the docks. Ewa was also somewhat wrecked from the Japanese attack. Since this was far from an impressive place to begin with, the bullet holes, although plentiful, were not particularly noticeable.[16]

As the final members of VMF-214 assembled at Ewa, Guadalcanal and the area around Henderson Field "was so secure in American eyes that when Secretary of the Navy Frank Knox came to the South Pacific, he was brought to the island by Admiral Nimitz and Admiral Halsey."[17] The remote island battlefield, once the desperate worry of the American Pacific Command, was now to become the new forward staging area for America's Pacific offensive.

For the first time, the Americans had struck back, not in a desperate defensive action like at Midway but in a genuine offensive. At Guadalcanal the American offensive against the enemy had begun, the advance of the Japanese war machine toward Australia had been halted, and the momentum of the war in the Pacific began to shift.[18]

Received March 5, 1943

January 30, 1943
Dear Mom and Dad,

No seasickness! No torpedoes! In spite of the fact that the weather calmed after my last letter, and even though it was warm and sunny on deck, the old terra firma underfoot, and even before that, the sight of land was mighty, mighty good.

We aren't squared away yet. Fortunately, however, our baggage arrived all in tact. And that's something to be thankful for considering the time I put in buying tooth brushes, toothpaste, razor blades, ointment and goodness knows what else. I begin to wonder whether it was all necessary. If food is any indication of how we are to be provided, then we are much better off than we were in the States. That certainly is heartening.

We were greeted yesterday morning as we approached land by a formation of four planes. They appeared from nowhere, or more exactly, from right off the waves, going hell bent for election. When they were almost upon us, they pulled up in perfect slow-rolls, spectacularly one after another. Then they joined up and made strafing runs on us. They were so close when they screamed by that we could have thrown a wad of crumpled paper as far as their wingtips. If they hadn't gone by so fast, we could have read the instrument panels. Made me feel just like a youngster all over again, at his first air meet.

We spent several hours sitting on or standing in the bow of our ship watching the flying fish scatter out of our path. It was incredible to see them glide so leisurely over distances of several hundred yards into the wind. Every now and then, they'd get a fresh start by wiggling the tip of their tails in the water, and go skimming off anew, banking around extra high swells and gliding on the updrafts over the wave crests. Of course, they weren't nearly as graceful as the albatrosses which accompanied us. They are the epitome of ease and grace. Day after day, they glided along behind, in front and around us, with nary a flap of their wings. At times, they seemed to skim the water with their wing-tips. They would disappear often behind the swells; and again you'd find them mast-high overhead. It's a mystery to me how they survive, for they don't seem to come within five hundred miles of shore. Sometimes, just for diversion I guess, they let down their landing flaps, and run on the water, up one side of a wave and down the other. That's why we called them gooney-birds.

I left one Val Pak at San Diego for Jim to mail back. I didn't need it, nor the few clothes which are in it. You'll find my watch in the box, too. The one I bought at the Marine Base is sufficient.

Tom is fine. You'd never guess he was a married man the way he takes to this military life.

Don't worry too much about the mail situation. It doesn't look too dependable for regularity's sake. But I'll keep on writing as often as time permits and you'll probably get my letters all in a bunch. I'm going to close now and read for a few minutes before going to sleep. Tomorrow is my first crack here at the Wildcat; so I feel a good night's rest is a wise move.

Best wishes to you both. I'm with you all the time!

Love,

Stuff

Beginning on their second day at Ewa, the new pilots of VMF-214 returned to the cockpit, not in SNJ trainers or outdated Brewster Buffaloes but in new Grumman F4F-4 Wildcat fighters.[19] The airplanes were combat-ready, but most of the arriving young second lieutenants had little or no flight experience in these planes that they would take into combat, and most had never flown anything as powerful as the F4F.[20] The task for the pilots was to become combat-ready as well, and it took hours of flight time to become acquainted with the peculiarities of their new aircraft.[21] In the days that followed, the squadron commander drilled the pilots in proficiency and tactics and filled their days with training flights.

The Wildcat was a far better airplane than the Brewster Buffalo it replaced. It was the best, most powerful, and most reliable production fighter that had been put into service during the early stages of the war in the Pacific theater. The F4F-4 weaponry included a solid battery of six .50-caliber Colt-Browning machine guns, three in each wing, and it sported a good reflector gun sight.[22] Each of the machine guns was capable of discharging 240 rounds at a muzzle velocity of 2,840 per second, and each round was a half inch wide and weighed more than an ounce.[23]

The tactical training in the new Wildcats was the final, transitional stage for the pilots. This final phase, according to pilot Tom Blackburn, was "to mesh the man and the machine and then to mesh both of them into cohesive units-two-plane sections of section leader and wingman, four-plane divisions of two two-plane sections each, flights of two four-plane divisions each, building to a complete squadron."[24]

When the orientation and transition was complete, according to Blackburn, the squadron was "to be thoroughly proficient in fighter-versus-fighter combat, to be able to defend friendly airfields and flight decks from enemy bombers and fighters, and to escort and protect friendly bombers and torpedo planes charged with attacking enemy ships and ground targets."[25]

As the transition into the high-performance Wildcats got under way, the letters from Hawaii describe Carl's new surroundings and begin to introduce some of the squadron members to the family back home, first among them, Carl's roommate, Harry Hollmeyer.

Received March 5, 1943

Sunday (2/14)

Dear Mom and Dad,

Having lighted and puffed upon one of my Robert Burns panatelas, I feel most comfortable and just in the mood to think of home as I write to you. It bothers me each time I sit down to write and realize that it has been so long since the last time. But again, as usual, I find that several days have passed. At least it lets you know that time is not weighing on our hands.

Your letter dated January 13 arrived the other day with its enclosures. I have been looking and hoping for word from home ever since we arrived, and though this wasn't the most recent mail, it certainly was welcome. I shall return the two letters you requested. Again, I want to urge you not to worry if it is sometimes as much as a month between letters. We are bound to be moving often, and many times, there are no post offices, especially aboard ships; and rarely, if ever, do we carry pigeons.

I dropped in on Tim one day last week. Though I had only twenty minutes to spend with him, it was wonderful to see him again. I am hoping that I can spend tomorrow night visiting with him. We have so much to talk over! Tim has kept a record, and it is well over a year since we have seen each other. Wouldn't you know that we would be only 70 miles apart when he and Mary were wed; and still I didn't get to the wedding! Tim looks well, but he insists that he has lost weight. In the short time we had together, I had no chance to find out what he is doing, but I gather that he is very satisfied, except that he misses Mary so much. That I believe is his main preoccupation, to get her here.

You should see the fight we have to get laundry done these days. The natives are so overtaxed by the demand that they will scarcely accept any more soiled clothes. We buzz off in a jeep, several of us, pile off at one end of the street, and canvass from house to house. It took me exactly one block the first time; and the clothes ought to go back for another washing without being worn. I will admit that we did find a better spot the second try, and the situation was much improved. You should see us trying to hold all the clean clothes in tact bouncing over the primitive roads! Safety belts wouldn't be amiss.

I had quite an unexpected experience week before last when my ship got into an inverted spin at low altitude and I had to hit the silk. I was so upset at losing the plane that the jump was very much of an anti-climax. Didn't even collect any bruises, largely, I guess because of the spot in which I landed—a shoulder-deep, muddy-water swamp. I straddled an old stump and started collecting my chute, but left that job to others who soon appeared on the scene. I doubt whether the weight of the world ever drooped heavier upon my shoulders than it did as I trudged back to the nearest telephone.

I was doing slow-rolls at the time my ship went into a spin. I had already done four successfully. The fifth time around, the ship snapped and went into a spin as I passed the vertical between ¼ and ½ the roll. I immediately corrected for a normal spin, but of course it did no good. I tried three times to correct without response. By that time, I was getting too low to possibly recover, having started the roll at 4,000 feet. So I slid open the hatch, flipped the safety-belt, and—swish! I was sailing through space, clean as a whistle.

The Major and the fellows in the squadron were grand about the thing, which helped a great deal. I went ahead and flew my next hop and another scheduled later in the afternoon. That did a great deal for my morale. Well, I certainly wouldn't hesitate to use my chute in any emergency, but I am going to be a bit more wary of slow-rolls, or my method of executing them.

We raided a sugarcane field this afternoon, and I had my first taste of sugar in the rough. It was rather sickening sweet, but as good candy as anyone could ask. I had just finished a milkshake and perhaps that had something to do with the over sweetness. Often, we fly through the heavy smoke rising off the cane fields, which are burned prior to harvesting, to clear out the saw-toothed leaf blades which make any progress afoot through the fields virtually impossible. The smoke has a sweet fragrance, much like jelly cooking on the stove at home.

Harry has taken several snapshots. (Harry Hollmeyer—my roommate; Harvard '40). They are to be ready tomorrow noon, and if they turn out, I'll send them along. I've been getting a lot of sunshine these past ten days working on the planes. This coral is terribly bright with a tropical sun on it and throws back plenty of sunshine. It's dusty, too.

I plan to send $200.00 to Abbott's tomorrow, which will leave a balance. (I can't find my accounts at the moment and the room is so fouled up I'll let Abbott's send you a balance—it should be about $100.) Whenever my first allotment reaches you, you can pay off the rest of the note, if you will.

Time to say goodnight, and wish both of you every good wish and good health. Write soon.

Love,

Stuff

On the fourth day of familiarization with the F4F-4 Wildcat, Carl became a new member of the "Caterpillar Club" after parachuting safely from the cockpit of his out-of-control fighter. Practicing tactical rolls at an altitude of 4,500 feet in his second orientation flight of the day, he entered an inverted spin, crossed the controls, and put the aircraft into a maneuver from which he was unable to recover. Forced to abandon the plane, he parachuted safely and suffered only minor injuries.[26] Basically unhurt, he returned to the cockpit of another Wildcat the following morning for the first of three flights that he made during the day to practice division tactics with other pilots in the squadron.[27]

With the exception of February 9, the orientation flights took place every day, and on every day but one there were at least two flights for familiarization in the new aircraft. Pilots came to know the plane's flight characteristics, the weaponry it carried, and the two-aircraft section, four-plane division tactical formations that they were expected to use when the squadron entered combat.[28]

By the time the pilots had completed their familiarization with the new Wildcats and Carl had posted his letter on February 14, the American Marines on Guadalcanal had driven the remaining enemy troops from the island.[29]

Received March 5, 1943

Saturday

Dear Mom and Dad,

With my typical thoroughness, I forgot to put air-mail stamps on my last letter. Consequently, this one may pass it up on the way. Perhaps 'tis well, for there is at least one change in what I wrote last.

Dad's letter arrived today in excellent time—and I was awfully glad to get it. It arrived just in time. I might well start off this letter by answering Dad's query about my insurance. The policy is issued through the government and is administered by the Veteran's Administration in Washington, D.C. The policy, I assume, is in Washington. One was never issued to me. The premiums are deducted from my monthly paycheck. The amount of the insurance is $10,000. That total will not be paid in one lump, but in small monthly allotments, and only after you make claim to the Veteran's Administration. That is the only worry you have regarding the insurance. But it is good that you asked me about it, so that I have, I hope, clarified the situation.

One other thing I should mention now is the bill at Abbott's. There have been several unexpected financial drains since I last wrote, and I've found it expedient to send only $100 instead of $200 from here. The total bill is $300.75. So that will leave $200.75 remaining. According to Abbott's schedule, the entire amount was to be paid by 4/3/43. I think the allotment should provide funds in plenty of time.

I had a wonderful evening and morning with Tom this week. I dropped in just in time to join him for baseball practice. (He's the only officer on the station team and has been playing good ball. He hit a home run the day before my visit and made several fielding gems.) After practice and a shower, we sat talking while Tom showed me his wedding pictures. Mary certainly was a beautiful bride! Old Sem Taber looked his usual pluckiness all decked out in tails. The service was held in the evening—a candle-light service, in a chapel that much resembles Marquand. After we had talked of the wedding, we strolled out onto the green slope that overlooks the breakers far below and flopped on the grass while the moon gathered up its reflection. There, Tom told me of the events that had led to the announcement, and we brought each other up to date on our lives since we had last seen each other over a year ago.

We finally ambled into the mess hall and sat down to an excellent pork chop, browned potato, etc. meal, the best I've had since leaving the States. We both ate two full dinners. I spent the night at BOQ, the following morning in Tom's office and then returned to base.

I walked into a Navy PX the other day (met Carter Dye there) and among their record albums found three of Yale Glee Club selections. I couldn't resist. (Also found some "Handsome Dan" pipe tobacco.) Vince Carpenter (our squadron—Yale '42) and I spent several fond minutes over them and were soon joined by Captain Bralar (Yale '40). Incidentally, Vince has been arranging music for us, and we're a very promising quartet. As Dad mentioned, there's nothing like a little close harmony to boost your morale.

Sis is certainly welcome to wear the insignias about which you inquired. Anything else she can find, too. I don't know what came of my intention to get her a Christmas present, but I hope you may have gone ahead with it and can take same out of my allotments when they start coming.

I must close here and head over for chow. Don't cease writing if you shouldn't hear from me for a time. The letters will catch up eventually to the new address outside.

Best wishes and love,
Stuff
Abbott Military Tailors, Inc.
1020 West Pratt Street
Baltimore, Md.

During the final days of preparations for the squadron's departure from Hawaii described in his letter, Carl also provided final instructions to his mother and father concerning his personal affairs. He asked that they make the payment due for his new uniforms from Abbott's, and he described the final purchases of music and pipe tobacco that he had made. He also matter-of-factly provides the procedures for making a claim for his death benefits from the Veterans' Administration in the event that he does not survive the journey.

On the morning of February 21, he penned and posted his final letter from Hawaii with a brief description of the island's landscape and vegetation, but he makes no mention of the Squadron's planned deployment that occurred later in the day.

Received March 8, 1943

February 21, 1943
Dear Mom,

Here are the letters you wanted back. I enjoyed reading both.

I have a whole box full of records and albums to take along with us. The squadron bought a good machine, and so we shall not want for musical diversion beside that which we can provide for ourselves.

We went swimming the other day for my first time here. I was surprised to find the water considerably cooler than at Miami. And it isn't nearly as salty. It's always such a beautiful blue color, framed by the long white breakers along the light strand, that I've been anxious to get in for a swim before this.

I wish that you could see the flowers and verdant vegetation, both of which are so profuse here. Heavy clouds hang over the mountains every day and the water drains down the valleys, so that everything from bottom to the very top is bursting with a crisp green foliage. I know you'll want to visit this part of the world when the war is over. It will just be an overnight trip to practically any place in the world then.

My best regards to all the friends. How is Don making out? And what do the Frasers think about Roy's announcement?

Love to all,

Stuff

The answers to Carl's questions about his friends would come to him farther into the Pacific and south of the equator. On the afternoon of February 21, the pilots of VMF-214 and the other MAG-21 fighter squadrons ferried their aircraft from the base at Ewa to Ford Island at Pearl Harbor.[30] At Ford Island, fifty-four Wildcats were craned onto the flight deck of the transport carrier USS *Nassau*, and late in the afternoon the *Nassau* was unleashed from her moorings and departed from Hawaii for the ten-day sea voyage to the pilot's next duty station.[31]

To get to their destination, the planes and pilots had to traverse several thousand miles of submarine-infested ocean, and the *Nassau* was hardly a seagoing fortress. The Wildcats lashed to her deck were simply cargo and were of no practical use against enemy submarines.[32] The carrier's only real protection against a potential attack from patrolling Japanese U-boats was its escort destroyer, the USS *Sterett*, which carried both detection equipment and depth charges to ward off the threat of an attack.[33]

Three days out of Pearl Harbor, the *Sterett* reported its first sonar

Officers and ground crew of VMF-214 in a stylized formation at Marine Corps Air Station Ewa, February 1943, one week before embarking to the South Pacific aboard the USS *Nassau*. (National Archives.)

USS *Nassau* Auxiliary Aircraft Carrier commissioned on August 20, 1942, and used to transport the aircraft and pilots of VMF-214, VMF-213, and VMF-221 from Pearl Harbor to Espiritu Santo between February and early March of 1943. (National Archives.)

contact and evidence of a possible enemy submarine in the area. On the *Nassau*, "general quarters" were sounded warning the ship to prepare for a possible enemy attack. The captain ordered the carrier to her top speed of eighteen knots and then began a series of twisting, rolling evasive maneuvers that could be felt by all hands. The *Sterett* responded to the threat by dropping three depth charges, their detonations reverberating though the *Nassau*'s hull. After the underwater concussions subsided, the *Sterett* lost sonar contact with the target, allowing both ships to secure from general quarters shortly past noon.

With the threat of the enemy submarine past, "*Nassau*'s crew began preparations for the most boisterous ceremony encountered in naval service. They were going to cross the Line."[34] Four days out of Pearl Harbor, the USS *Nassau* crossed the equator into the South Pacific.[35] The ceremony that followed was described by Carl in his letter written on April 15 after the pilots arrived at their destination.

South of the equator, the *Sterett* registered underwater sonar contacts on two more occasions as the *Nassau* continued into the South Pacific. On each occasion, the destroyer dropped four depth charges on the area of the sonar contact, and each time, no evidence of the underwater menace appeared.[36] The *Sterett*'s last recorded sonar contact appeared on March 1, and the next day, Second Lieutenant Carl Dunbar turned twenty-three years old.[37]

On March 3 and the day after his twenty-third birthday, Carl and the other Marine fighter pilots were catapulted from the flight deck of the *Nassau* into the tropical skies of the South Pacific.[38] Once airborne from the carrier deck, the pilots flew to their new home at the Turtle Bay airfield on Espiritu Santo in the New Hebrides.[39]

5

Fighter One Air Base, Guadalcanal, March 13, 1943–May 28, 1943

Well, at last I've had my baptism of fire. I've looked into the nose and up the tail of a Zero, and I've watched their remarkable maneuverability around and over me. Unhappily, my first shots to be fired at the enemy reflected a bit of pre-game nervousness. I was pumping six guns into the after tail of a Zero which had made a pass at my division leader and zoomed on between, by, and out in front of us. Vince got his sights to bear also, but apparently was a bit excited, too. We don't know that we missed, but the Zero didn't explode. The last we saw, he had rolled over on his back and was heading straight down.

Carl O. Dunbar Jr., April 10, 1943

The chain of Solomon Islands lies more than one thousand miles northeast of Australia, five hundred miles northwest of Espiritu Santo, and several hundred miles northeast of New Guinea. The island chain moves from north to south at an easterly slant, and above its northern terminus is the Bismarck Archipelago and its largest island, New Britain. On New Britain for more than a year preceding the arrival of VMF-214, the Japanese had built their South Pacific military command center at Rabaul.[1] From the fortress at Rabaul the Japanese expanded their military presence south into the Solomon chain, constructing major installations on the islands of Bougainville and New Georgia and adding supporting satellite installations on Shortland Island, Rendova, Choiseul,

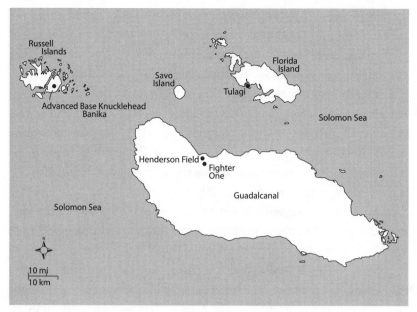

Map 3. Guadalcanal and the Southern Solomon Islands.

Santa Isabel, Vella Lavella, Kolombangara, the Russell Islands, and on Tulagi adjacent to Guadalcanal.[2]

With the control of Guadalcanal in February of 1943, the Allies also occupied the port and seaplane base at Tulagi and secured the Russell Islands off the northwest coast of Guadalcanal.[3] From the runways of Henderson Field and the adjacent islands, the Allies now dominated the airspace over the islands in the southern portion of the Solomon Island archipelago. Ahead lay a hard and treacherous island-hopping journey north toward Bougainville and Rabaul. In sequence, the key battles for the islands after Guadalcanal were fought to possess the strategic installations bordering New Georgia Sound—the airfield at Munda on New Georgia Island, the Vila Airfield on Kolombangara, the Barakoma airfield on Vella Lavella, the installations at Rekata Bay on Santa Isabel, and the northern most airfields and installations on Bougainville.

Before and after World War II, the Solomon Islands were little more than an isolated, remote, and little-known archipelago. Noted World War II author Dan van der Vat encapsulated the irrelevant remoteness of the Allied base of operations in his book *Pacific Campaign*. "Guadalcanal," wrote van der Vat, "[was] a singularly obscure fleck of mud on one of the remotest parts of the earth's surface."[4] After less than two weeks of preparation on Espiritu Santo, it was to this "obscure fleck of mud" that the squadron deployed to enter the battle in the Pacific theater.

Ten letters from Carl Dunbar to his family were written during VMF-214's first combat tour in the Solomon Islands. Some of the letters provide insight into the emotions of entering battle in the skies over these islands in the southern Pacific. Others speak of the pilots' living quarters, the conditions in the squadron's camp at Fighter One, the pilot's leisure hours, and the harmonies of the "quartet."

Some of the letters written during this period continue the observations and narratives about the natural surroundings encountered by the Marine aviators. The observations are of the island jungles, the beaches, the coral reefs and tropical fish, and the native families that occupied the islands. But in none of the letters are the places named, the locations identified, or the missions described. In his letter of April 10, 1943, he describes his first aerial combat encounter against the Japanese and his "baptism of fire," and in the letter on April 15, he recalls the ceremonies that accompanied the crossing of the equator.[5] While his letter on April 10 makes no claim of downing an enemy plane, the New Haven newspaper reported that Carl was "credited with the probable downing of a Zero while breaking up a formation of Japanese planes which raided the Russell Islands" northwest of Guadalcanal.[6]

The logbook entries provide some information about the mission sorties that has been omitted from the letters, and postwar history now reveals other details of the missions and locations of the squadron at the times when the letters were written. To help put Carl's letters into the context of the progressing Battle of the Solomons, the narrative relies on the logbook mission entries, relevant passages from Bruce Gamble's history of the squadron, and the personal recollections of four of the other members of the squadron: Vince Carpenter, Henry Miller, Tom Tomlinson, and O. K. Williams.[7]

After leaving the carrier flight deck of the USS *Nassau* on March 3, the squadron reassembled on Espiritu Santo, referred to in Carl's logbook by its code name, "Button."[8] The squadron remained on the island for eight more days, acclimating to the new surroundings, making flights to refresh themselves in the tactics to be used in combat, and preparing for their move forward to the airfield known as Fighter One on Guadalcanal.[9]

The first letter from this part of the journey was written on March 9 while VMF-214 was still at the Turtle Bay airfield on Espiritu Santo.

Received March 18, 1943

March 9, 1943

Dear Mom and Dad,

Surprise! Two letters from home today. Wonder whether we couldn't afford to exchange a little of our respective weather. It just goes to prove the old rhyme about "whether it's cold or whether it's hot, etc." I suppose I'd be wishing for what we have here if I could trade places with you. At any rate, there wouldn't be any worry about fuel oil for heat.

Every day is a new experience. A little acclimation is all it takes. Right now, we're still in the process of getting used to living in mud—mud like only a true Kansan, I'm sure, could appreciate. I'm still hoping the rain will hold off long enough for my clothes to dry out. I wore the skin off several knuckles yesterday washing them. If the writing is a trifle shaky, it's because I'm lying on my side under the mosquito netting. I got tired of swatting mosquitoes, and I'm still rather malaria-conscious.

I must mention one of the amusing sidelights of this problem of supply. Occasionally, through oversight or hold-up in transportation, some commodity doesn't arrive at the right place on time. Such was the case yesterday with our Scott's Tissue. That becomes rather crucial when there aren't any old newspapers or Sears catalogs around! Well, it just happened that I had brought along two rolls of that precious article, one of which I gave to the Major—with his sincere blessing. Word of my prize soon got around, and for the rest of the afternoon and evening, a steady stream (forgive my slight exaggeration!) of pained faces wended their way to our tent to plead their cases before this ration board. "Noblesse oblige" or something like that.

After my last letter about money to Abbott's, I wasn't able to get any money order blanks. So the $100 remains in my wallet. Now I find great pressure brought to bear by squadron mates without funds who have great longing (together with my own) to join the exclusive Officers Club. This necessitates a substantial deposit among other things. What with the almost total inaccessibility of money order blanks at this time and indefinitely into the future, plus this heart felt pressure, I feel obliged to leave the bill in your hands to be paid as the government allotments roll in. Hope the government can do better than I have.

We went down to the old coral swimming hole the other afternoon. It's about fifteen feet deep and twenty to thirty feet across. There's a channel out into the surf which is navigable, too. The water is crystal-clear and just under body temperature. There are all sorts of beautifully colored tropical fish, the most striking, a small brilliant blue one with pink ridges on its fins. If you can imagine a brilliant hue of the bluest blue in the labradorite on the side table, that is about the color. There's a little dove that walks around our tent occasionally with velvet green wings. I won't even try to describe the jungle vegetation. It's too imposing.

I'll stop here, as my arm is about asleep. My best wishes to all at home. I hope both of you are taking good care to stay healthy.
Love to you both—
Stuff

On the squadron's last evening at Turtle Bay on March 12, Carl dined with two other squadron pilots in the transient officers' mess.[10] The following morning, the squadron made the 3 1½ one and a half-hour flight from Espiritu Santo in their Grumman Wildcats to the forward base at the Fighter One on Guadalcanal.[11] In the nearly seven months since the Marine invasion force had first come ashore, little on Guadalcanal had changed. As the squadron settled into their rudimentary accommodations, squadron commander George Britt described the operational environment that greeted the pilots after their arrival. It was, according to Britt, "primitive by any standard and fraught with hazards—unpredictable weather with unreliable forecasting, no navigational aids of any kind, 4:30 a.m. join-ups in the blackest sky imaginable, sleepless nights caused by Washing Machine Charlie's nightly visits, and aircraft maintenance made difficult by parts shortages and dust, dust, dust."[12]

From the primitive conditions at Fighter One the squadron combat missions began. They were flown in tactical four-plane divisions, each consisting of two, two-plane sections.[13] On the third day after arriving, Carl's division, now commanded by Vince Carpenter, flew its initial mission of the tour, providing air cover for the movement of Navy destroyers up the Slot northwest of Guadalcanal. The division's first flight over the "no-man's-land" of the Slot was completed without incident and without enemy contact.[14] The following day, two squadron divisions, including Carl's, were in the air again to support a long-range search-and-rescue mission for a downed pilot in enemy territory near Segi on the northern coast of New Georgia 150 miles northwest of Guadalcanal.[15] In Carl's logbook the mission is described simply as a "Dumbo escort (Segi NG)."

The "Dumbo" moniker was the pilots' shorthand reference to the ungainly looking Consolidated PBY-5A Catalina seaplanes used for the air–sea rescue missions and the seaplanes' resemblance to Disney's big-eared flying elephant of the same name. These twin-engine Catalina flying boats, originally described by Carl to his family in the letters from Jacksonville, were very slow and extremely vulnerable, but their crews, escorted by planes from VMF-214 and other fighter squadrons, nevertheless routinely flew straight into the teeth of enemy territory to complete their rescue missions and recover downed pilots.[16]

The mission on March 18 was to be the first of three Dumbo escorts for Carl's division during VMF-214's first combat tour, but unlike the other two, this first rescue mission ended in disappointment and tragedy. After a lengthy search deep into the island outposts near New Georgia, the crew of the PBY was not able to locate or recover the missing pilot. For the squadron, it also marked the mission where the first of their own pilots was lost. In his logbook entry following the Dumbo mission entry, Carl notes that the group "lost Steed."[17] In Bruce Gamble's account of the mission, he reported that "just east of the Russell Islands the last man in the formation dropped out. Bill Steed, on his first flight since arriving in the South Pacific, inexplicably rolled over, spun in, and vanished beneath the waves."[18] Bill Stead was the first pilot lost, but before the end of their assigned time in combat, five more members of the squadron would die in the cockpit and would not make the return journey home.

Received March 29, 1943

March 18, 1943

Dear Mom and Dad,

Seems like we never get settled without getting unsettled again. Consequently, my letter-writing schedule never could be called a schedule, I guess, for up to now we've been jumping hither and thither too fast. The mud I was telling you about in my last letter has become dust, and I have no hesitation about saying I prefer the mud. The mud didn't usually creep above your knees, but the dust—!

Eventually, maybe we will have snow. There wasn't anything particularly pleasant about our Squantum E-base weather for operating conditions, but at least there weren't any flies or mosquitoes. The nets keep most of the mosquitoes out, but it doesn't keep their drills from coming through. Just let a knee or elbow or hand lie against it, and bingo, there's a solid mass of welts in the morning.

I've heard several programs from the States out here, as well as Jap, German, Russian and English broadcasts. Fibber and Molly were on the other night when I was listening. Also heard some Ivy League basketball scores. What about hockey? I see that the Yanks have already begun training at West Point, so I suppose "dem Bums" have hit New Haven. I just wonder how many of the old faces will be reporting.

It would certainly be good to hear from home. We all must have mail chasing us about somewhere. Just when it will catch up with us, no one can say. However, it will be equally welcome whenever it arrives, and it will bring us up to date on affairs at home. I hope Sis has found time to write a note so I'll know how things are going at Poughkeepsie. It's hard to believe that this is almost the end of Sophomore year. I saw a show couple of weeks ago called Ice Follies

Review. It was a second-rate picture, but the skaters were the same that performed in November at the Ice Follies which Sis and I saw. Rather a strange, but interesting coincidence.

The wobbly writing on this sheet (it seems there's always some reason I can find) is due to a partially crippled right hand garnered at the end of this morning's flight. I let the landing-gear crank get away from me, and it really cracked into the back of my hand. Doc doesn't think any bones are broken, but he isn't absolutely sure. Time will tell.

I hope the food situation at home is better than it appeared at San Diego. It's not bad here. All best wishes for you both. Good health, above all. I'll write again soon. You, too.

Love,

Stuff

The "partially crippled right hand garnered at the end of the morning's flight" was an occupational hazard for the F4F-4 pilots, and Carl's injury followed a routine "cleanslate" patrol over Tulagi on the day the letter was written.[19]

The retraction mechanism for the main landing gear of the Wildcat was a chain attached to a metal handle that the pilot was obliged to manually turn approximately twenty-seven times to retract the gear.[20] Once the Wildcat was airborne, it was necessary for the pilot to switch hands and take the stick in the left hand while using the right hand to raise the landing gear. Flipping the little locking lever above the metal crank, the full turns to heave the wheels home got under way, and losing the grip on the crank during the process allowed the handle to spin violently in reverse. The same violent spin was an option if the crank was lost when the landing gear was being let down, and many unwary Wildcat pilots experienced severely bruised right wrists, and sometimes broken ones, when the crank got loose.[21]

At Fighter One, the Squadron pilots lived in tents pitched in between orderly rows of towering coconut palms adjacent to the airfield runway, and the tents provided only rudimentary refuge from the rains that appeared almost daily. The tropical precipitation made for a constant supply of mud and ensured an endless supply of flies and mosquitoes;

according to Tom Tomlinson, "these miserable insects gave malaria to about 90 percent of the command despite the daily ingestion of the bitter Atabrine tablets."[22]

When the rains dissipated, the tropical heat quickly turned the mud to dust, leaving the pilots sweaty and grimy in their rustic living environment between their missions in the Wildcats. It was a phenomenon that Carl shared in his letters—in the first, describing that he was "living in mud" and "hoping the rain (would) hold off long enough for . . . clothes to dry out," and then wishing for relief from the ubiquitous "dust" in the next. The strange weather phenomenon that contributed to these conditions was explained by Melvin Levet, who served as a weather officer in the Solomons with the Army's 13th Air Force.

"Over any island mass," said Levet, "it was typical to have thunderstorms almost any afternoon. When the sun goes down they clear up. It was so hot, however, that the water evaporated with tremendous speed. So it could be dusty one minute and then you'd drive down the road in a jeep and run into mud the next minute, and five minutes later it was dry and dusty again—all depending on the drainage. The mud and dust was tough on operations."[23]

The weather, rudimentary accommodations, and difficult operating conditions were not all the challenges the pilots faced. "The food was atrocious," remembered Vince Carpenter. "It was Spam, Spam, Spam, Spam, and then there was canned horse meat from Argentina put into the cans in 1916. There was never any ice. We did laundry and shaved in our helmets. We turned yellow from the Atabrine tablets. We all lost weight, and we looked cadaverous in the squadron picture that was taken on Fighter One."[24]

Although the southern islands in the Solomon chain were secure from enemy ground forces in the early months of 1943, the threat of enemy air raids remained a constant concern as the squadron acclimated to the difficult operations in the tropical mud and dust. After their arrival on Guadalcanal, the squadron planes were constantly in the air during daylight hours to patrol the skies and to repel the air raids that originated on the Japanese held islands to the northwest. As regional commanders turned their attention to the challenge of interdicting Japanese facilities in the central Solomons, squadron divisions were also assigned escort duty for bombing raids against these airfields and against the movement of enemy troops and supplies in the islands further up the chain.[25]

According to squadron pilot Tomlinson, "the patrols were all necessary due to the primitive warning system" of potential Japanese air attacks, and in Tomlinson's recollection

> the work was unremitting, and when not flying patrols, the strikes were scheduled. These included escorts for dive-bombers and torpedo planes rigged with glide bombs up "the Slot" to the Japanese airfields at Munda and Kolombangara. These strikes often called for flak suppression. This entailed diving in front of the dive-bombers to try and take out the antiaircraft fire. On other strikes the fighters would make aggressive sweeps by themselves and strafe assigned targets. The fighter squadrons were here to work, and work they did. The one routine that never varied was the patrols.[26]

Following the incident with the landing gear that bruised his hand, and before his next letter, Carl flew two more patrols. Following a dawn patrol on March 20, his division took part in a second mission later in the day to escort a flight of dive bombers on a strike against the enemy airfield at Munda on the southern coast of New Georgia amidst heavy antiaircraft fire.[27] On March 22 his logbook records no flight time and a day of rest.

Received April 5, 1943

Monday 22
Dear Mom and Dad,
    The ready-tent is not the most conducive spot to letter-writing. I imagine you must wonder sometimes just what is going through my mind. There is such a crossfire of chatter with a lot of comical ribbing and bantering that it's difficult to maintain much continuity of thought. However, it's easier for me who can let you know what's going on than for those who are penning the sweet-scented billets—doux of amour propre.

The biggest complaint these days is an extremely tender spot of repose. Three and four hours at a clip sitting on a hard-chute pack and held in position by a safety-belt and shoulder straps has its effects. There's no one who doesn't complain of the same affliction, in spite of the fact that several of us are admirably equipped to withstand the gaff. The only time we forget the malady is when someone thinks he sights an enemy aircraft or an anti-aircraft burst nearby. When you get right down to it, that isn't much of a complaint, is it?

Harry had a brainstorm the other day and made himself a sling shot. Expressly, it was manufactured for the purpose of knocking down the scarlet and green parrots and also the white ones. I started one yesterday and completed it this morning. Several other weapons have made their appearance around the tent, and much of the time, you'll find a bunch of school boys tormenting each other with threats and flying pebbles.

I wish it were possible to write more of what we're doing. However, it isn't advisable for the sake of security. Suffice it to say that our duties are rather routine, though interesting. They do lack the glamour of the Major Smith—Captain Foss era.

Washing is going to be a good deal simpler henceforth, I believe. Heretofore, the water has been well-drawn and consequently hard. You know how much lather that works up. Now we've access to a wonderful, swift-moving cold river with soft water and water a-plenty. It certainly is a treat both for the easier washing and a cool dip after a hard, hot day.

We're all beginning to hope that there's some mail not far off. And that should mean word from you. I hope that the lean mail from this end won't be too disappointing. I hope, too, that you won't find it necessary to reply in kind.

All for now. Best of health to you both. Enjoy the spring weather for me when it arrives.

Love,

Stuff

The routine of constant patrols came with a consistent pattern. In the morning the assigned pilots were shaken out of their cots at about 4:30,

Carl Dunbar in the cockpit in full flight gear, "sitting on a hard-chute pack and held in position by a safety-belt and shoulder straps," ready for missions lasting "three and four hours at a clip." (Dunbar family collection.)

given breakfast at the mess tent, and carried by truck to the waiting planes on the air strip at Fighter One.[28] "The Wildcats would be coughing to life, and the plane captain would help the pilot with his shoulder harness and hand him the yellow sheet to sign, accepting the machine as ready for flight," remembered Tom Tomlinson.[29] Once in the air, the discomfort of the cockpit "sitting on a hard-chute pack" recounted by Carl in his letter was simply another part of the pilot's routine.

Carl flew seven sorties in seven days following his letter home on March 22.[30] Six were routine patrols—four over the installations on Guadalcanal and two others over the Russell Islands approximately fifty-five miles northwest of the base at Fighter One, all without encountering enemy aircraft.[31] The seventh mission of the week took two four-plane divisions, including Carl's, north on a strafing raid against the airfield at Munda Point. The logbook records that the pilots encountered "fairly heavy" antiaircraft fire during the mission, but they succeeded in emptying the guns of their Wildcats against the enemy installations without losing any aircraft.[32] Attacks against the installations on Munda and on the other island installations northwest of Guadalcanal

Squadron pilot Al Jensen in the cockpit of his Wildcat with two Japanese victory flags. Jensen would be credited with a total of seven aerial victories over the Solomons and for destroying two dozen enemy planes on the ground at Kahili airfield on Bougainville during the squadron's second tour, an action for which he was awarded the Navy Cross. (Dunbar family collection.)

were part of the new phase in the Battle of the Solomon Islands, one in which VMF-214 and other Marine fighter squadrons were to figure prominently. Winning the rest of the Solomons ultimately required the neutralization of the Japanese strongholds to the north, and 560 miles of heavily defended enemy islands stood as a row of sentinels en route.

New Georgia and Bougainville were two of the largest sentinel islands, and they were guarded by heavily protected airfields on smaller adjacent islands.[33] During the squadron's first tour, the Japanese launched continuous bombing raids against Henderson Field and Fighter One from the bases on New Georgia and Bougainville.[34] Accounts of these raids appear in Carl's letters, including descriptions of the nighttime raids that disrupted sleep and kept the Marine pilots on edge.[35] These night sorties were frequently carried out by a lone bomber, using an unsynchronized propeller pitch to make more noise. The sound of the unsynchronized motors of the twin-engine bomber dubbed it "Washing

Machine Charlie," and it became the permanent moniker for the night-time enemy raiders.[36]

The Japanese air raids were sporadic in March, according to the letters, but the frequency and intensity soon changed. In April the Imperial Japanese Headquarters had formulated a plan to retaliate against the Allied bases in the south by attacking the ship anchorage at Tulagi, the airfields on Guadalcanal, and the installations on the Russell Islands with a powerful air assault.

To personally oversee the details of the plan, Admiral Yamamoto traveled to the Japanese base at Rabaul where more than 185 combat aircraft from the 11th Air Fleet of the Japanese navy were already housed. After his arrival, Yamamoto called in even more carrier-based planes to the island, and Rabaul's airfields swelled to some 350 combat aircraft, more than 180 of them fighters.[37] From Rabaul, Bougainville, and New Georgia, Yamamoto was determined to scourge the Allied bases.[38]

As the number of combat aircraft increased, the attacks from the Japanese became more frequent, the time in the air became more intense for the pilots of VMF-214, and the time on the ground made them even more familiar with the muddy foxholes that protected them during the enemy air raids.[39]

Received April 16, 1943

Monday 30th

Dear Mom and Dad,

I feel pretty much relaxed this evening after a day off. We did some washing this morning—had hot water from a gas-burner and a 5-gallon can for the first time since I've been doing my own laundry. Each week my clothes get a shade darker. It's getting so I hate to pull an unworn pair of shorts out of the bag because the contrast is so shocking. Like everything else, when you work into a condition gradually, it doesn't seem so bad—until you are shocked back to normalcy. It was so with the smells around the mess-hall, the continual perspiring, the dust, and eating utensils that are never clean.

This has been a marvelous day, just like a perfect day late in June at home. Brilliant blue sky overhead, clouds hanging over the mountains to the south and a fairly good breeze. I went without a shirt all day except at mealtime and gathered a couple of pink shoulders. There isn't much opportunity to bask in the sun down here and continued sweating causes what tan you do get to disappear rapidly. My nose, as usual, continues to peal and blisters with monotonous regularity.

At last I have had word from home—a double letter from both of you. That's the first mail we've had since Ewa. No need to say I was very pleased to hear from home! The letter you wrote from Poughkeepsie, Mom, started memories winging back, but the situation as it exists today is so foreign to those memories that it refused to countenance them long. I agree with your enthusiasm about the verse you sent along, Dad. I was repeating it to myself again last night before I dropped off to sleep. I fear that my mind or my thoughts never run to far away channels when I am flying. Once upon a time, maybe, but not here. The eternal alert, constantly sweeping the horizon, then overhead, then behind—then a fleeting glance at the instruments—oil pressure 90, oil temp 80, fuel pressure 15—they're all O.K. Generator putting out, cylinder head temp 160, R.P.M.'s not dropping off. Then back to the eternal vigilance again and straining to hear a far-off radio communication, sweeping the horizon, a glance in the rear-view mirror and a check overhead and behind over the other section. On one of the sweeps across the instrument panel,—fuel pressure is down, fluctuating. Instantly, I tighten up and watch it closer. Ten thousand feet doesn't seem like much with the field a hundred miles away and only blue Pacific and jungle islands below. Water landings are routine, and I have life-jacket, rubber-boat, and plenty of provisions on my back—but I'm tense anyway. Switch on the emergency pump, and pressure returns to normal. Spot a plane in the distance, and you jump to alert with a greater start, ready to shift prop pitch, gas mixture, full throttle, release wing-tanks, switch on gun sight. And all the time you are flying wing on your section leader. So you can see just about how confined and uninspiring the thoughts are while I'm flying.

I've come to know foxholes fairly well these days. And I can get into shirt, pants and a pair of shoes out of a sound sleep as fast as the next man. Strangely enough, this talk of foxhole casualties isn't the biggest joke in the world. There's many a bruise garnered in the shuffle for shelter. Many people refuse to leave their bunks until the well-known, unsynchronized hum becomes audible. Then the anti-aircraft fire commences and people begin to scramble. Everyone pauses at the foxhole entrance to watch the incoming bombers bearing straight in and as plain as daylight in the beam of the searchlights. It wasn't until we heard the swish of the dropping bombs the other night that we ducked into the shelter. Well, it was a long time coming, and I sometimes wondered whether I ever would get in the scrap, but this is it!

It seemed to me that Roy's bride is very attractive. I can't blame him for getting married, being stationed where he is. It's pretty tough to see so many happy young couples with their own homes in such beautiful surroundings all around you and not be strongly influenced. Especially when life seems rather precarious at times. I wish you'd remember me to Mr. and Mrs. Fraser and tell them I was happy to hear about Roy. I know he didn't make any mistake—he's looked them all over. I must write and send him my congratulations.

No word from Bill or Jim yet, though I expect to hear when the mail schedule settles down. (Bill's address at home was 12 Nepaug Street—I've forgotten Jim's.) Mom, you mentioned something recently about wondering whether Jim was still where I left him. I believe there was something in the paper that made you wonder. Guess I must have missed the article, and I can't figure just what you could have seen. Let me know if it was anything important.

Harris had to leave his pictures behind to be developed and they haven't come through yet. When and if they do, I'll send them along. Right now I'm even less photogenic than usual, My attempt at growing a goatee isn't entirely successful, although it's coming along. There's no question about the color being red, but the goatee lacks fullness in the middle.

We had fried chicken for lunch this noon—and believe me, it was a treat! A whole half-chicken, dressed and frozen in the U.S. and fried in deep-fat with a crisp brown coating. It sure was good and a rare diversion from the old standby, corned-beef and spam. We had fresh apples one day last week. Aside from the wild limes which we mix with brandy and bourbon, that's the only fresh fruit in sometime. There are plenty of bananas in the vicinity, but we just haven't had time to hunt them up. And no one seems much interested in waiting for them to hang around and ripen.

I hope you are both taking care of your health. Spring ought to be a pretty good tonic as well as a relief. How I hate to miss my second in a row! Hope there will be more mail soon.

Love,

Stuff

Sleep became a precious commodity as the enemy bombing raids intensified and regularly interrupted the night with forays from bases in the north.[40] Still, the sorties for the Marine pilots continued. In the eleven days between the letters posted on March 13 and April 10, Carl's division flew twelve missions. Two days after posting his letter on April 10, Carl took part in two more sorties.

The first mission was to provide air cover for a task force of Navy surface ships moving troops and supplies up the Slot. The second mission was a scramble by four divisions of VMF-214, joined by other Army and Navy squadrons, to intercept "a swarm of fifty-eight enemy planes, mostly A6M Zeros along with a few D3A Vals (that) approached from the northwest to sweep Allied fighters based on the Russells and Guadalcanal."[41] The Marine fighter pilots gave better than they got in their first major aerial combat against the Japanese, and Carl's logbook entry notes that twenty-one of the twenty-six Japanese aircraft encountered by the Allied fighters were "downed."[42]

The other missions flown between the two letters home consisted of two sorties to provide task force cover for surface ships moving north from the anchorage at Tulagi, three more provided air support and flak suppression for dive-bombing missions in the central islands, and the remaining three were routine local patrol flights.[43]

After returning from the local patrol on April 7, the squadron's planes were hastily refueled and the pilots sent back into the air for their second major encounter with Japanese raiders. Carl's division, other planes of VMF-214, and two other Marine squadrons were "scrambled" to intercept more than one hundred incoming Japanese airplanes at twenty-six thousand feet, near the limit of the performance ceiling of the Wildcats.[44] Carl's division commander, Vince Carpenter, recalled the high altitude encounter with the Japanese Zeros in an interview with Bruce Gamble.

Four of the Zeros peeled off and came for us. Those Zeros were better at high altitude because they were lighter, and we were really at the max altitude for the F4F. We had a lot of throttle on, and were burning fuel like mad once we dropped those wing tanks. Our first pass was head-on, but we were sort of squishing through the air. When we passed each other, they went over the top of us. We threw ourselves around into a turn—they did too—and started back after them. With that, everybody split up, and that was the beginning of the big fight. I got on the tail of a Zero. He held his altitude for a minute and I took a good long shot at him. He turned over on his back and smoked, then pulled down in a dive.[45]

After the "probable" Zero victory in the high altitude dogfight, Carpenter encountered one of the returning bombers at low level and "flamed the aircraft," watching it break up and crash into the sea.[46] When results for the opposing forces in the aerial combat were compiled, the three Marine squadrons responding to the "scramble" received credit for downing ten enemy planes without losing a single pilot.[47] Some of the enemy bombers being escorted by the Zeros did make it through the defenders, however, and were able to reach the harbor at Tulagi. The raiders were able to sink an American tanker, a Navy destroyer, and one smaller ship, but the widespread destruction planned by the Imperial Japanese Headquarters and Admiral Yamamoto on April 7 did not occur. At the end of the day, dominance of the airspace over the southern Solomon Islands remained with the Allies.[48]

In one of his rare conversations with me about his time in combat, Carl did relate that his closest brush with a Zero occurred during a "scramble," and it was a closeness that he was unaware of when the event actually occurred. Once back on the ground at Fighter One, a member of his aircraft's ground crew pointed to a single bullet hole in

Pilots of VMF-214, "yellow-skinned from Atabrine" and "cadaverous" from weight loss, posed in front of the squadron ready tent at Fighter One. The squadron's first ten enemy "victories" are memorialized with Japanese flags on the propeller blades to the right of O. K. Williams and Harry Hollmeyer. *Front row, left to right*: Petit, Dunbar, Sigel, Williams, Carpenter, Bernard, Hazelwood, Hollmeyer, Blakeslee, Deetz, and Taylor. *Back Row*: Miller, McCall, Kraft, Fidler, Pace, Scarborough, Britt, Rankin, Ellis, O'Dell, Burnett, Lanphier, Tomlinson, Cavanagh, Jensen, and Moak. (Courtesy of Vince Carpenter.)

At the edge of the jungle adjacent to Fighter One, Tom Tomlinson and Vince Carpenter inspect the remains of a Japanese bomber ("Washing Machine Charlie") shot down during a raid against the airfields on Guadalcanal. (Dunbar family collection.)

the headrest of his cockpit seat. The enemy machine gun bullet had entered inches above where his head had been, but it had gone unnoticed during the heat of the aerial dogfight.

Received April 23, 1943

Saturday 10

Dear Mom and Dad,

The mailman has been very good the past two weeks—two large bunches of letters. I really feel almost caught up to date now, for the last letter was postmarked 3/24. Would you believe it if I admit that I can scarcely picture thawing snow and the harbingers of spring! After perspiring so long and continuously and missing most of two winters in a row, I almost need a formal introduction to spring, which is my favorite time of the year.

I was very interested in reading the copy of your broadcast, Dad. No wonder the printer was flooded with requests. I found the article intensely interesting and especially valuable because it looks beyond the daily AP reports on advances and losses. People never could glean the picture of Russia your broadcast portrayed if they mulled over the newspaper and radio accounts. Personally, I am very gratified to see people looking forward to future certainty and planning as the reaction to your broadcast indicates. I can certainly be proud that my Dad is among the pioneers of post-war reconstruction.

Well, at last I've had my baptism of fire. I've looked into the nose and up the tail of a Zero, and I've watched their remarkable maneuverability around and over me. Unhappily, my first shots to be fired at the enemy reflected a bit of pre-game nervousness. I was pumping six guns into the after tail of a Zero which had made a pass at my division leader and zoomed on between, by, and out in front of us. Vince got his sights to bear also, but apparently was a bit excited, too. We don't know that we missed, but the Zero didn't explode. The last we saw, he had rolled over on his back and was heading straight down. After that we had much too much else to watch and look out for. The squadron as a whole did excellently in its first day of combat. No losses and a very respectable number of enemy planes shot down. No doubt you have heard the totals for the forces participating. If not, they will be announced soon. Interestingly enough, the fighting we did was probably out of sight of the ground for altitude.

You asked about the Alumni Magazines. I regret to say that as yet, I haven't received any of them. However, I feel certain they will turn up one of these days. I hope so, because they always make good reading from cover to cover.

I wish that my camera was along and also a good supply of Kodachrome film. Just the other day, we were wishing that we could convey the beauty that we see every day. Description would never do these Pacific scenes justice. In spite of the constant vigilance of combat flying, I can't help occasionally indulging in admiration for the setting. The intense blues and greens and whites, through all their shadings, defy any painter. The jungle is so dense and green, rising abruptly as it does out of the blue sea. The sea itself pays homage in delicate blue tints of the shallower water that laps the white coral beaches. The serenity of the islands is not in the least disturbed by a native hut or village partially hidden among the palms, or by an occasional solitary dugout, jet black as its native boatman silhouetted on the rippled blue below. You can take it from me, the romance of the tropical islands is at least as real as any writer ever portrayed it.

I have to run along now. Give my regards to the friends at home. I will try to get off a few letters, but retiring hours are early as well as the rising hours. Take a good number of breaths of spring air for me and get lots of sunshine. Love to you both and the best of health.

Stuff

On one of the final missions before he wrote again, Carl's division was assigned to provide escort for a second Dumbo mission to Segi in search of a missing pilot lost in a raid earlier in the day. Unlike the first Dumbo recovery effort three weeks earlier, the mission objective on April 15 was successful, and the downed pilot was recovered without incident.[49]

Received May 3, 1943

Thursday 15th

Dear Mom and Dad,

More mail from home with news of good spring weather, which seems to be finding difficulty deciding whether or not to stay.

Had a letter from Sis, too, the first in a long while. It was very good. Also a letter from Jim who was still in the States at that writing. No word from Bill or Tom.

You wrote recently, Mom, of Frank Turner. I think I may be able to look him up soon. Will let you know, however. The announcement of Ruthie's engagement was not entirely a surprise, although it certainly was a disappointment. I hate to see Ruthie go. Will you ask Mrs. Smith whether Seaver's address is still the same. I haven't written because I felt sure it would have changed. I'd like to drop him a line. Incidentally, if I had any idea where to look for Bud Root, I would, but I don't. And what about Steve?

You asked some time ago about the meaning of my address letters. They are no secret. "V" stands for heavier-than-air-craft, as distinguished from dirigibles, etc., which would be "Z"; "M" stands for Marine; "F" for fighting. Put them together and you have Marine Fighting Squadron 214, Marine Air Group 21. That is us and the VMF-214, and we are part of MAG 21.

Early retiring hours are the main cause of little spare time for letter-writing, except for times like these during the day at squadron. However, there are a couple of hours each evening that are hard to pass up for correspondence or anything else. Just before dark, usually, everyone gathers around outside the Major's tent, bringing stools, cups and canteens. We sit around the fire sipping bourbon or scotch or plain lime juice and water, telling stories, talking over our day's experiences and generally shooting the breeze. Usually, too, we do a little singing. The quartet sings a couple of numbers and then we lapse into the old familiar routine of Sweet Adeline, Way Down Yonder in the Cornfield, Tell Me Why, and on into the night. You can readily see why those nightly get-togethers are hard to pass up.

We've spent several evenings lately practicing and learning a few new songs by kerosene lamp to add to our all too meager repertoire. There are plenty of sour notes, but once we get a song down, it sounds pretty fair. Up to now, we have so few songs that we know well that we can't entertain for more than a couple of minutes. So while the assembled gathering calls for more, we are forced to withdraw and adjourn to our lighted tent and practice to ourselves.

It won't likely mean anything to you if I say it, but I am a Shellback. It all happened when we crossed the Equator, which is a much more severe trial than I ever expected. There is a thorough initiation of all Pollywogs (those who have not previously crossed) at the hands of hardy Shellbacks (those who have). For the enlisted men, it began the day before we crossed the line; for us the day itself. A solemn court was held the night before in the wardroom where the cases of the Pollywogs were considered. Numerous assignments to duty were meted out such as iceberg watchers, watchers for King Neptune, navigators and a myriad of other jobs. The iceberg watchers donned heavy winter flight gear, mittens and boots, and with a pair of binoculars made of the interiors of Scott tissue rolls, reported no icebergs in sight and then proclaimed loudly, "I want to be a Shellback!" Our Colonel was taking sun sights on deck at a map held aloft by our Major with one of the pilots for a horizon. Two other Majors marched about the deck tooting horns and chortling the old refrain, "I want to be a Shellback!" Platoons and squads were marched and paraded "ad ridiculum." More ridiculous costumes than I can ever remember were gamboling and cavorting about the deck. The royal barbers went about shearing off what hair they could find, cutting V's and all sorts of weird designs on all heads alike. A long line of Shellbacks armed with inch-rope inside canvas holsters tested the fortitude of all Pollywogs. Then Neptune Rex and his royal court came aboard and offending Pollywogs were brought before him to meet the royal barber, or dentist with his devilish-tasting concoctions, and be anointed with machine oil. There was so much going on all at once and in such crazy fashion that no one could possibly see or watch everything. It was exactly like a three ring circus. I can't possibly paint the picture, but I can refer you to a book called "Queen of the Flattops" by Stanley Johnston, which has an excellent description of the event. You might be interested in reading that part if not all the book.

I don't know whether copies would reach me, though some seem to get through, but I'd like to get a subscription to Time magazine. I wonder whether you could look into the possibility and subscribe for me if it seems reasonably sure of getting to me. Reading material here is rather scarce and whatever does come is thumbed until it falls apart. We do have a small library, phonograph and records, but either we haven't caught up with them yet, or they haven't caught up with us.

Well, I wish that I could be back to hear the robins and the song sparrows. The parrots here are a mighty poor substitute. The scarlet and green coloring is brilliant enough, but the noise that comes out shouldn't happen to a dog. They don't even stop at night, for the big bats get into the roosts and raise havoc.

All the best of health and good fortune. Regards to all.

Love,

Stuff

Carl's letter looks back briefly to recall the celebration aboard the USS *Nassau* when the carrier crossed the equator into the southern hemisphere more than a month earlier, and he explains to the family the meaning of the squadron's numerical designation. He also describes the pilots' evening hours of leisure at Fighter One and introduces the "squadron quartet."

The quartet formed under the watchful eye of Vince Carpenter during the idle hours at Ewa and refined its harmonies on the long sea voyage from Hawaii to Espiritu Santo. Carpenter had taken blank music sheets with him from Hawaii, and as the voyage of the *Nassau* progressed toward the South Pacific, he created musical scores and organized the practice sessions for the group until the voices harmonized to his satisfaction.[50]

Each evening after arriving at Fighter One, weather permitting, the squadron commander, Major Britt, hosted a gasoline stove campfire in front of his tent in the grove of coconut palms adjacent to the airfield, and according to historian Bruce Gamble, the quartet obligingly performed.[51]

The fires, quickly extinguished in the event of an air raid, were an essential contribution to the men's wellness. Beginning with their training period at Ewa, Britt noticed growing bonds among the young pilots, later writing, "A certain squadron personality began to develop, characterized by pride in the attainment of increased flight proficiency, congeniality, humor, and high morale." Among the many reasons for the success of these gatherings, the most visible was . . . (the) talented quartet.

Among the singers, only Vic Scarborough lacked Ivy League roots. Carl Dunbar and Vince Carpenter were from Yale, and Henry W. Hollmeyer, of Boston, was Harvard through and through. . . . Hollmeyer's contribution ran the gamut of bawdy pub songs, such as "Three Old Ladies in the Lavatory," "Roll Your Leg Over," "The Sexual Life of a Camel," and more, but the quartet's favorite number was a complex jazz rendition of "Old Black Magic." Carpenter had scored the arrangement during the voyage aboard the *Nassau* and tutored the group until the men achieved spine-tingling harmony. The song became a campfire staple.[52]

Earlier on the day that Carl posted his letter describing the quartet to his family, one of the squadron's Wildcats, piloted by Charlie Lanphier, developed an oil line break, and the engine shut down following a mission against the Japanese seaplane base at Rekata Bay, 130 miles northwest of Guadalcanal. Lanphier made a water landing adjacent to the island behind the enemy lines and was able to make it safely to shore.[53] The following morning Carl joined seven other members of VMF-214 to provide the Dumbo escort for the search and recovery of their missing pilot. For the second time in less than a week, the rescue mission was a success. Lanphier was recovered in good health, and Carl's logbook entry simply notes "Dumbo Escort-Found Chuck."[54]

Two days after Lanphier's rescue, Carl's four-plane division was one of two from the squadron that participated in a successful raid against the Japanese airfield at Munda, providing the escort for a flight of twelve Navy dive bombers assigned to the raid.[55] On each of the next four days, Carl's missions combined flights to provide air cover for Navy surface ships and routine local patrols in the airspace over Guadalcanal and the adjacent Russell Islands.[56]

Received May 24, 1943

AIR MAIL
Saturday—29th
Dear Mom and Dad,

I've just had a surprise visit from Jack Quinlin and Bill Myers who were classmates of mine in flight school. Mom, you met Jack at Miami. He's a Boston chap, went to Wesleyan and has been with us ever since Squantum. His dive-bombing squadron has been here for some time and I never knew that they were here. In fact, we've been escorting them. So we were probably dodging the same bullets and shells. For Jacko, I learn that Bill is now flying dive-bombers; and Jim had not moved up to mid-March. Now I have hopes of seeing both Jim and Bill out here. What a day that will be! Gradually, our living quarters are beginning to take real shape. I suppose it's about time for us to move. Last time we had just laid an excellent floor and made some furniture when orders came. We have two large tables now, one around the ridge pole, and this upon which I'm writing—a tremendous wooden packing-case. Harry found some wool blankets, one for a tablecloth and a home-made lounging chair complete with mattress. The tent sides are stretched straight out from the eaves, giving us a good deal more room, light and air. We have three kerosene lights, one fashioned from a hand-grenade with a piece of quarter-inch rope for a wick, and a paper mache Haig & Haig bottle cover for a base; the other two are cigarette cans with a hole punched in the top for wicks. Our row of used bottles houses our spare gasoline and kerosene while it lends dignity to our establishment. I've managed to get a fairly good laundry system working, and clothes turn out most as white as new. I even bleach them with water-chlorinating capsules. We finally found our squadron radio and phonograph this week. It is being repaired, and meanwhile, we have a hand-crank job that, for all its shortcomings, is being played to death. Oh yes, we got some more of our scotch and bourbon, so life is almost complete—cigars, cigarettes, candy occasionally, cocktails, radio and bacon fry's or fudge parties at night. Sounds like a college-girl, doesn't it.

I thought this afternoon, being my day off, I'd trek out into the jungle to have a look at the orchids. One of the men directed me to the spot where there apparently are a good number of them. However, I shall have to wait 'til next time now, after Jack's visit and laundry. I thought some, too, of trying to send back seeds, but from what I understand, growing orchids takes seven years of tedious care.

Your birthday card came this week. I got a big kick out it. There were letters, too, from all three of you. Sis must have spent the better part of vacation poring over hers. Apparently, V-mail travels almost as fast as air-mail, though it's a bit of a bother addressing twice and trying to get everything you have to say on one sheet. If we don't get hold of some stationary soon, however, I shall be obliged to write via V-mail. In that case, I'll just continue my letter from one envelope to the next.

I read an interesting article in (the) March 22nd Saturday Evening Post on Russia, her position in the world picture and her aims at the peace table. The author, Demarce Bess, concluded with the assertion that Russia's position and intentions regarding world policy, as well as toward the neighboring Slav countries, is well-defined and logically just; whereas, it is the United States policy, which is no policy at all but a dreamer's panacea, that needs clarification and definition. Well put, I thought. Wonder whether you happened to run across the article, Dad. Also in the same issue was a lecture on "How to be Shipwrecked Though Healthy." Some of the boys in the squadron attended the classes held on the subject back at Pearl. I read the practical suggestions with great interest. They certainly are applicable. I can picture being isolated for a considerable time—it certainly is possible here—yet feel very little physical discomfort. One would never lack for food, and on the smaller islands where there is practically no fresh water, stagnant at any rate, mosquitoes would not be a problem. There is no dysentery and we've been "shot" for everything else. (Incidentally, I've only taken two

antiseptics since leaving the States; so you can judge for yourself.)
See what you think of living the life of a shipwreck.

I wonder, Mom, whether you'd call Mrs. Stuhlman and get Bill's
address, which apparently has been changed. I found Jim's home
address. It's 79 Forest Street, Kearny.

I can't picture it Spring at home, but the thought gladdens my
heart. I picture a sizeable victory garden and some real eating as a
consequence. It's not without effort, I know, but I'll bet you both
will get a kick out of eating and canning your own vegetables. If
you'd put in outdoor plumbing, you'd be back again a few years,
wouldn't you?

Lots of warm sunshine and good health.

Love,

Stuff

The remaining missions in the two weeks that followed Carl's letter did
not involve further aerial confrontations with the enemy, and, with two
exceptions, the duties were limited to local patrols over the Russell Islands and Guadalcanal. The exceptions to patrol duty were task force
escort sorties providing cover for Navy surface ships on May 12 and 13.

There was no flight time entered in the logbook for the following day;
it was time used to hike the island and explore the area surrounding
the airfield. May 14 was also VMF-214's last day in the rustic tent quarters in the grove of coconut palms on Guadalcanal, and it concluded the
squadron's first tour over the front lines in the Solomon Islands.[57]

Received May 24, 1943

Wed 14th

Dear Mom and Dad,

I fear that more time than I like to think has slipped by since
my last letter. I started a letter last Saturday, but never finished it,
largely, I believe, because there was so little to write.

Carp and I took an eight-mile hike our last day off, the main
objective, a look at some orchids. However, we didn't get far
enough. So all we got was a good bit of exercise and a look at some

real tropical jungle. We found some native grapefruits, though they were too tart to be very edible, perhaps because they had fallen from the tree prematurely. We also found a grove of papayas and had a try at them. But neither of us was very hungry.

Unfortunately, we didn't come across any banana palms for which we were keeping a sharp eye.

The going a good part of the way was plenty soggy after a three day stretch of heavy rain. One day in particular flooded our camp area almost beyond recognition. We were used to water flowing about an inch deep across the tent floor, but not a torrent. The water was about 18-inches deep in one side of the Doc's tent next door. Shoes floated out and away and practically all walking was as precarious as on a frozen lake. Much of the mud still remains here in the camp area, but the roads are dusty as mid-summer at home. So we get both ends of the candle burnt in our faces.

I heard from Bill just after my last letter to you. He's still in the States after being transferred to dive-bombing and thence to torpedo-bombers. Carter Dye arrived recently, but he was up on a hop the only time I got over to see him.

Somehow, our mail has become fouled up and we haven't seen any for over ten days. Before that, we were getting letters every four or five days. Nine to ten days was the best on letters from home. My address has changed slightly, officially that is, but I still write it the same. Actually, it should be "1st Lt. C.O.D., Jr., etc."

Did I write about the strange coincidence of the brothers, one in our squadron and one flying for the other, meeting here after a year of separation? When you think of all the possibilities, it's truly amazing. Tom, the Army brother, has distinguished himself singly out here, as you may be hearing one of these days, and we found great pleasure in hearing him describe the day's adventure around our campfire. He has set a tremendous example for brother Charlie, for all of us in fact.

I'll close here and wait for more of interest to write which there should be by next letter. Best wishes to you and all.

Love,

Stuff

The coincidence of the reunion of brothers—Chuck Lanphier of VMF-214, who had been rescued three days earlier after the raid on Rekata Bay, and his brother Tom Lanphier, an Army P-38 pilot—is shared by Carl in his letter to the family with "great pleasure." And the accounts by Tom of his "day's adventure" have survived the night around the squadron's campfire on April 18 and are widely remembered in the historical accounts of the squadron's first combat tour.[58] The details could not be told by those who heard it that evening, and Carl's letter does not do so.[59] The passing reference to Charlie and Tom, however, implies that "one of these days" the nature of Tom's "adventure" might be known back at home, and these words by Carl proved prophetic indeed.

In the weeks leading up to VMF-214's evening campfire, American naval intelligence officers learned that Admiral Yamamoto was making his first trip to Rabaul, intending to personally direct the combat operations in the Solomon Islands.[60] Once at Rabaul, Yamamoto decided to inspect the forward bases on Bougainville, and reports of this decision were also intercepted by American intelligence. Based on these reports, Admiral Nimitz approved a long-range mission against Yamamoto's party as it approached Bougainville.[61] According to Vince Carpenter, it was a mission that officers at VMF-214 had initially been briefed to fly, but the range of the Squadron Wildcats was too limited.[62] The mission was assigned to the long-range P-38 Lightnings from the Army's 339th Squadron based on Guadalcanal, and one of the pilots was Tom Lanphier.[63]

Around the squadron's evening campfire the quartet sang as usual, but the news of day was Tom Lanphier's account of the mission over Bougainville. His words told that the P-38 pilots had succeeded in their mission and had downed two Japanese Betty bombers that carried Yamamoto and his staff.[64]

What Carl could not reveal in his letter at the time history now records as a mission where bullets from Lanphier's P-38 fatally damaged the aircraft transporting the admiral. Yamamoto and the other officers aboard the bomber died in a subsequent crash into the Bougainville jungle, and the long-range attack by the pilots from Guadalcanal, in the words of military historian Eric Bergerund, became "the most famous fighter mission of World War II."[65]

Jeep on Fighter One flight line with pilots returning from the day's mission. *Left to right*: Ledge Hazelwood, O. K. Williams, George Sigel, Tom Tomlinson, assigned driver, "Smiley" Burnett, Vince Carpenter, and Howie O'Dell. (Dunbar family collection.)

Pilot and quartet member Harry "the Horse" Hollmeyer with his Wildcat on the flight line at Fighter One. (Dunbar family collection.)

Left to right: Squadron pilots George Sigel, Charlie Lanphier (recovered in a "Dumbo" mission escorted by VMF-214), and Henry Miller, squadron executive officer, at Fighter One in front of the squadron Wildcat nicknamed "Miss Carriage." (Dunbar family collection.)

The final two letters from the squadron's first tour are dated May 16 and 22; they were written after the pilots arrived back in the New Hebrides and before they flew on to Sydney, Australia, to continue their rest and recuperation. The first letter was written on the island of Espiritu Santo, where the pilots of VMF-214 had initially embarked after their voyage from Hawaii. The second letter was posted from the smaller island of Efate, 140 miles southeast of Espiritu Santo, where another camp had been established for pilots resting between combat assignments.[66]

Received May 31, 1943

5/16

Dear Mom and Dad,

The warm sea breeze is drying the ink almost as fast as I write. What a wonderful feeling to have nothing to do for a day but lie in the sun, drink ice-cold beer for the first time in four months and admire the tropic seas for their beauty. I saw a velvet-green dove yesterday and made eyes at the brightest blue fish swimming leisurely about in our coral pool. It's grand! And the best is yet to come.

I got talking with the fellow bunking next to me last night. He looked so familiar that I remarked about it. He went to Brown, which didn't click; but he spent a good deal of time in New Haven with two of my classmates. To Brown, I spoke of Peter Prudden. Well, George turned out to be Pete's roommate at Brown, thereby making the world that much smaller. Pete is married, lucky fellow!

We had a great celebration night before last. As usual, everyone gathered about seven o'clock around the Major's tent. We had five gallons of ice-cream to begin with, which was a rare treat. Then we had grapefruit juice, ice and water for mixers. Our group Colonel arrived and Major requested a performance from the quartet. Well, that started things off. From there, we went into all the drinking songs anyone had ever heard of. As the evening wore on and got damper, the singing got louder and worse. Harry wrote a fitting finish to the evening with a tremendous bonfire, to which he added various caliber ammunition.

We went swimming just now. The water is just about perfect and clear as a bell. These blue fish I wrote you about seem to be just as curious to look at us as we are to see them, and they gather around our noses, perfectly tame. I'm sitting about twenty feet from their coral pool, and there are a number of little lizards about eight inches long running about, cocking their heads up to look at me occasionally. They must be relatives of the little 4 and 5 inchers that hide in our mosquito-netting and catch the mosquitoes.

This could be a saltwater scene at home. The coral is worn and darkened so it looks like a New England rocky shore. I'm between the water and the shore, where the breakers are rolling up on the outer coral fringe, sitting on a big square rock. Between me and the beach, the rocks grow smaller and rounder until they grade into sand, where Ledge and Vince are sunning themselves. The beach is semicircular, forming a small cove. It isn't very wide, perhaps twenty feet. Beyond the sand, a broad-leafed creeper with pink blossoms that resemble sweet peas covers the ground. It even grows under the bushes that rise behind. They have slick leaves like rhododendron and fragrant white blossoms. Behind these, the jungle trees grow thick; but strangely enough, there's a sprinkling of trees that must be in the pine family. They have long graceful needles that weave to and fro on the breeze. Their bark is crinkly and they have little cones. They fringe the strand a little below this cove and remind me more than anything else, perhaps, of home. I don't have to tell you about the smell of the salt spray and the crash of the breakers, nor the clear blue tropical water. I only wish I could pass on the beauty that is here. But, I know you will have to see it for yourselves, as I believe you will one of these days.

I think I'll go join the fellows in another dip. The sun is getting pretty warm and I'm not sure how much I can take. We haven't been hiding from the sun, but we haven't basked in it regularly either.

Best wishes to you both. Dabble your fingers in the ground for me. Hope the mail gets straightened out soon.

Love,

Stuff

The "great celebration night before last" described by Carl in his letter took place during the pilots' final evening on Guadalcanal, and it was described by Bruce Gamble in his history of the Squadron.[67] It was "a tremendous party," according to Gamble's account. "The remaining bottles of liquor were unstopped and the quartet was in full voice."[68] The party began the days of relaxation that followed for the pilots, first on Espiritu Santo and Efate and then in Sydney.

Once arriving on Espiritu Santo, the pilots retrieved their uniforms and other personal items from storage that were needed for their time in Australia, and then they turned their attention to the leisure options available at Turtle Bay.[69] Some of these Carl shares in his previous letter, and similar descriptions of the time on Espiritu Santo appear in the diary of Squadron member and fellow pilot Henry Miller.

"Before lunch," wrote Miller, "we had an excellent swim in the imperial tub—a deep crevice in the coral, alive with light blue and striped fish. Our impression of this spot is totally different from our previous visit—it is greatly relieving to have no duties but to swim, eat good food, etc. After lunch I did some laundry and, finally, darned six pairs of wool socks. Everyone was airing everything."[70]

After three days on Espiritu Santo, the pilots boarded a DC-3 transport and flew on to the island of Efate in the Vanuatu archipelago to continue their leave. "After Guadalcanal," remembered Tom Tomlinson of Efate, "the 'livin' was easy' and there were no duties except relaxing. The water was crystal clear and the breeze helped with the flies and the heat. Nearly every day the natives in their outrigger canoes would come into the lagoon and run them up on the beach to trade."[71]

In Carl's next letter, he too describes the topical waters and the daily encounters with native islanders remembered by Tomlinson.

Received June 7, 1943

5/22

Dear Mom and Dad,

Another beach, this one sandy and for the past few days nothing but sun, saltwater, fun and rest. The swimming is well-nigh perfect, not everywhere along the beach because of the coral boulders, but in the channel the bottom is sandy, the water is warm and not too salty. The coral shelf dips very gradually out to the reef, some three hundred yards out, I judge. There, of course, the bottom drops out. Dave and I were out in a rubber boat day before yesterday beyond the reef. And when we were returning, a big breaker upset us right over the reef. We fell out of opposite sides of the boat, both oars went in different directions and we lost the pump. For a few seconds, the surf threw us about on the coral crazily. Eventually, we got a footing and recovered all gear, the pump not until yesterday's low tide. There are three islands north of here that stick up like signal beacons, old volcanic cores they must be, rising sheer from the water, poking up to almost two thousand feet. The jungle is much less dense than we have been seeing. There's a great deal of the pandanus, bread-fruit, tree everywhere.

The natives, for the most part, live on an island about three miles directly across from me here on the beach. The island is several miles long, how long I can't be sure, as it extends away from me. It rises somewhat less than 1,000 feet and is well-rounded. This side of the slope and much of the top appears to be tall grass, though it may be low underbrush. The natives live in six villages about the perimeter of the island. They sail over here in their outrigger canoes to trade or sell bananas, oranges, beads, sugarcane, chickens, etc. Four to six of the family usually come in the canoe along with various dogs and whatever they have to sell. The sail is an orthodox gaff-rig.

The natives are very friendly. Some of them speak a fair amount of English, most of them understand a few simple words and expressions. We were sitting with a group of them the other afternoon asking their words for various parts of the body, etc., and laboring between ourselves over the spelling, when one youngster objected violently to one of our attempts and offered a corrected version. He said the word to himself and then spelled it according to syllables in excellent grammatical fashion. From him, we learned that besides the British missionary who pays regular visits, there is a native school teacher who went to school at Espiritu Santo and then returned to teach the natives. We weren't able to find out how to put the language together, if there is anything more to it than the association of words. You can imagine the difficulty of trying to ask the natives that question. The words themselves are not difficult to pronounce, except for a throaty quality on some like the word "to eat"—nanegane, where the first "n" sounds much like "gn." Just to show you some other words, only a few of which I remember at present: hands—ngro; feet—nadua; head—nape; hair—nalulu; ears—nalinge; nose—los; watch—houra; sun—alo; friend—tadai; boat—rarua; sail—alae (to sail—navase); good morning—molibog wia; good-bye—ido. It doesn't seem too hard.

Because of the broad coral shelf, most of the shells get battered or broken before they reach the beach. However, we have had an interesting time turning up rocks at low tide, and under them, we have found a goodly number of live shell-animals, as well as any number of surprises. The small clumps of coral that grow everywhere are colored almost unbelievably—pink, purple, red, green, blue and combinations of brown and blue, green and pink, etc. There are all sorts of sea anemones and sea urchins. The most striking to me was jet black with long, two-inch jet black spines. The only other color at all was a hairline of shiny metallic blue on the body itself. We turned up a couple of small octopi yesterday. They are the model of a funny-paper ghost when they swim.

My best regards to everyone at home. What duty did Don Hudson get?

Take care of your health!

Love,

Stuff

The small South Pacific island of Efate where this last letter was written cannot be found on contemporary maps as it was known in 1943. Thirty-five years after the end of World War II, in 1980, the islanders of Efate achieved independence from the British and the island nation was renamed the Republic of Vanuatu.[72]

The pilots of VMF-214 lounged for a week in Efate. Their days were spent on the beach, relaxing, swimming, and shelling. They hiked to the native villages, learned bits of the native language, visited the copra plantations on the island, and indulged in restful siestas.[73] In the evenings they enjoyed good meals, watched movies, and talked of Sydney.[74]

"In its first eight weeks of combat (a new single tour record), VMF-214 claimed ten Japanese aircraft while losing only two planes and no pilots to the enemy," according to historian Bruce Gamble. "Operationally, its losses were somewhat heavier. Bill Steed was officially listed as missing but obviously died on the third day of the tour, and a half-dozen aircraft had been lost to mishaps."[75]

The squadron's Grumman Wildcat fighter planes had generally performed well, however, and they had earned their spurs in the mud, dust, and constant humidity of Guadalcanal.[76] Carl and the Carpenter division flew forty-eight missions in their Wildcats during the squadron's

Pilot and quartet member Vic Scarborough had a "hard landing" on April 7, 1943, after an encounter with a Japanese Zero. The damage from the Zero's 20 mm explosive rounds is visible behind the left side of the cockpit of Scarborough's Wildcat. Scarborough would return the favor with five confirmed aerial victories during the squadron's two tours. The white star centered in a dark blue circle and set against a blue-gray surface was the standard color scheme for all the squadron's Wildcats. (Dunbar family collection.)

Carl Dunbar, Major O'Neil, Harry Hollmeyer, and Ledge Hazelwood at the Turtle Bay base in Espiritu Santo following squadron's first combat tour in May 1943. The pilots had aired out their uniforms and were preparing for R & R in Australia. (Dunbar family collection.)

Carl Dunbar and Ledge Hazelwood aboard the DC-3 military transport (R4D) flight from Efate to Sydney for R & R, May 26, 1943. (Dunbar family collection.)

initial eight-week tour, contributing to Allied efforts to turn back the Japanese expansion in the South Pacific.[77]

Slowly, the tide had begun to turn in the Battle of the Solomon Islands.[78] On May 26 the pilots from VMF-214 boarded DC-3 military transports for Sydney and the distractions of a well-deserved rest before returning to their second tour of combat duty.[79]

6

Advance Base Knucklehead, Banika in the Russell Islands, June 6, 1943–August 14, 1943

> *We're doing a good deal of flying these days, but that ship of ours is a dream. It practically flies itself, and when you want to get someplace or away from someplace in a hurry, it's unbelievable what an advance throttle will do!*
>
> Carl O. Dunbar Jr., August 3, 1943

While the pilots of VMF-214 were on leave and preparing for their return to combat duty, Admiral Halsey and his commanders began to refine and implement an island-hopping strategy intended to take the war north across the equator to the shores of Japan.[1] From the airfields on Guadalcanal and the nearby Russell Islands, the first objectives of the new strategy focused on Japanese installations in the central Solomon Islands at Munda Point, Segi, Vila Airfield, Rekata Bay, Ringi Cove, Barakoma Airfield, and Kahili Airfield. All were facilities constructed as a line of defense for the main Japanese bases on Bougainville and Rabaul.[2]

At these locations on the main island of New Georgia and on the other large central islands of Vella Lavella, Rendova, Choiseul, Santa Isabel, and Kolombangara, the Japanese had fortified their airfields and military outposts.[3] To man the outposts with troops and resupply them with food, ammunition, and other necessities, the Imperial Army relied chiefly on regular trips from Rabaul and Bougainville by armored transport barges and other small coastal vessels.[4]

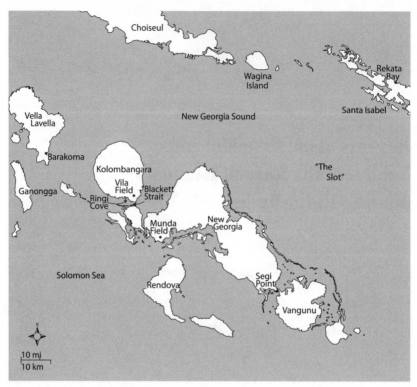

Map 4. New Georgia island group, Central Solomon Islands

Reliance on these coastal supply vessels was a legacy from the battle for Guadalcanal when many of the larger Japanese transports and surface warships were lost or severely damaged under skies dominated by American land-based fighters and bombers. The barges and other coastal transports were cheaper, they were abundant, and they were more difficult for Allied pilots to detect as they lay beached along tree-shrouded shorelines during the daylight.[5] By the time the VMF-214 pilots returned to combat, the coastal supply vessels had become new targets of opportunity, and squadron missions included periodic fighter sweeps around the central islands to keep a sharp eye for the barges and other small seaworthy transports.[6]

After returning from Australia on June 4, the squadron spent eleven more days at the rest camp on the island of Efate, and on June 15 they returned to the Turtle Bay airfield on Espiritu Santo. The pilots remained at Turtle Bay until June 29, 1943, preparing with new aircraft for their second tour in combat.[7]

Carl wrote fourteen letters between June 6, 1943, and September 18, 1943, following the squadron's return from Sydney. His letters on June 6 and 12 were written from Efate. The first letter describes the "ten wonderful days in civilization" in Sydney, and the second talks about the island surroundings on Efate. His letter on June 20 was written from Espiritu Santo after VMF-214 had begun its preparations for a return to combat, and the remaining correspondence provides his accounts of the time spent during the squadron's second tour of duty in the Solomon Islands.

Received July 8, 1943

Sunday 6th

Dear Mom and Dad,

We are just back from ten wonderful days in civilization—days which I'm sure have never been equaled for sustained activity and enjoyment. We arrived for our leave, worn out and bedraggled after an all-night plane trip in zero weather (where we were flying), piled our gear into a truck and roared away down the left-hand side of the road to the American Red Cross Officers Club. It was unbelievable passing factories, women with dresses and attractive features, automobiles and trucks with charcoal burners fore or aft or great gas bags on top. We piled into the dining-room for breakfast of steak, eggs, bacon, tomatoes, milk, toast and honey; then a great, long hot bath and clean clothes. The greens smelled of mothballs and the blouse was too wrinkled to wear after five months in a Val-Pak. We headed for town—gawking at flower shops, stores and traffic. Haircut, shave and shampoo were exotic—what a treat!

The bar of the hotel was next in order. Soon, most of the squadron had congregated to celebrate and listen to the stories of the bar maids while all kinds of individuals came and went. We met some Australian commandos just back from the front who proved to be fast friends and the finest men I've ever met. An elderly gentleman, a retired barrister we found and a veteran of the last war, took us in tow, and throughout our stay, proved a great friend and helper.

Every night was party night at one of two nightclubs. The bands were good, but the liquor situation could have been better. The domestic whiskey is impossible, besides being rationed, although the champagne is excellent. That was our mainstay, although our drinking was governed largely by the availability. When beer gave out in the afternoon, we drank whiskey; when whiskey gave out, we drank brandy; and so on through the gin and the rest. No one seemed to be floored, in spite of the changing diet. I did change uniforms late one evening with my commando friend, but except for that, I was only garrulous and more so as evenings wore on.

Arthur Paton, our barrister friend, arranged for us to fete the entire chorus of the Tivoli Ballet our second evening. John Fidler, with Arthur and myself, met the girls at the stage door. While we waited, Arthur recited Hamlet to the empty house, while Barf and I did a buck and wing entrance onto the stage. The maids never looked up from their cleaning at either. The girls were very lovely and a pack of fun. We saw a great deal of them during our stay. In fact, two of them are wearing gold wings as a result of our stay.

Eight of us rented a house on 11 Carlysle Road. That became the war-cry for winding up all of our evenings and for the whole of some. We had an excellent private stock, ice-box facilities and milk. We would all gather in the spacious living room around the fireplace fire to drink and sing far into the morning. There were never less than eight couples, and I feel quite sure that everyone in the squadron was at the house sometime during the stay. Our gatherings around the fire were very cosmopolitan—ourselves, the chorines, commandos, taxi-drivers, civilians. I got to know one taxi-driver very well; we had good opportunity, inasmuch as we hired them by the day. He was an ex-Lieutenant in the Signal Corps who had lost a leg early in the war. At our request, he joined the party and turned out to be a grand addition with his excellent baritone voice and repertoire. He sang opera before the war. So our singing that night included everything from Landlord Fill the Flowing Bowl to Gilbert and Sullivan and the Alleluia Chorus. That particular party wound up at six in the morning.

Our squadron party was a tremendous affair of great gaiety. We had a table for sixty at the nightclub. The quartet was scheduled to entertain during intermission, but fortunately everyone was saved for Carpenter was laid up in bed with a cold. Anyhow, everyone was pretty gay and they claim I always sing flat when I've been drinking.

Four of us got interested in golfing and spent our last four days at the best golf course in the city, which was open to us. We had an awful time trying to figure out our bets in threepence, sixpence, bob and quids, what with bingle-bangle-bungle, match play and all. The golf wasn't much, but I've never laughed harder in my life. I doubt whether we ever played more than ten holes in a day (a day went from 11 to 4)—we didn't get up earlier, and it was too cold later in the afternoon to play. We never minded the cold for the warm showers were delicious and the beer and scotch warmed us inwardly. We hurried nightly from the golf club to Tattersall's Club downtown, where our evenings were always successfully begun. They had endless imported English scotch in each of the four bars and two dining rooms. It was a tremendous establishment, five stories high, with swimming pool and all. It was swimming there that Captain Miller met a friend who used to swim for Harvard, a former member of the Australian Olympic team. You may remember the name Kendall from Yale-Harvard meets of '37 and '38. Bill invited us to his home, and we spent two grand evenings with he and his wife and three lovely friends who they invited. I found Bill's sister-in-law a very attractive girl and grieved long that it was so late in the leave that I met her. However, I shall not lose contact with her. Let us hope I can say more than that.

I can't do justice to the hospitality which was extended to us. It seems the U.S. Marines can do no wrong, especially the fliers. Our hosts appeared to be greatly indebted for our past service. There are very few able-bodied natives not actively engaged in the armed services, and so we are doubly welcome to the young people. We have the glamour, the money and the reputation which, as Harry points out, Hollywood has created for us. There were times when I felt we were resented by some, but on the whole, I was tremendously impressed with the friendship extended us. I think we returned some of the pleasure, enough so that we would surely be welcome back.

We spent one Sunday afternoon at the Baytown Sport Centre—an organization something like our Boy's Clubs. They had a tremendous bowl, with bleachers on one side and a rolling slope opposite. There were countless bicycle races on the grass track and trotting races on the dirt track. Inside on the rugby field, acrobats and clowns performed to general satisfaction. We had ice cream cones and watched the show with great interest and excitement.

As you can well imagine, the pace of our stay was telling after a very few days. Faces at breakfast grew gradually paler and movements early in the day were generally slower. However, by afternoon and with a quick pick-me-up, faces beamed and eyes lit up with all their former energy. It was a grand relaxation for us, just what we needed, as well as a lasting experience. Perhaps best of all, we feel now not so far away from everything. Coming out here as we did made the South Pacific seem like the end of world—8,000 miles from home. Now we feel that within a day, we can reach civilization which is our own and for which we are fighting. And it adds some new strength and courage to have that friendship and civilization so nearby.

I shall close for tonight. Perchance in the morning, there will be more to add. I have written too hastily to give you a fair picture of the past ten days, I know, but at least it will give you an idea. Meantime, best wishes for good health to all, and
Love,
Stuff

P.S. Spent two hours with Will Sanborn yesterday; found out Jim is married and that I'll probably be running into Barry.
The squadron's return to Efate was a three-hour flight from Sydney. During the early years of the Pacific war, the island served as a significant staging area and supply depot for the theater.[8] For the returning

pilots, their days on Efate were spent in the continued pursuit of leisure activities—swimming, ball playing, exploring, and relaxing.

Noticeable in the subtleties of Carl's letters are the changes in the living conditions that greeted the pilots when they returned from Australia. Allied supply lines had strengthened steadily, and the staging areas on Efate and Espiritu Santo were vibrant and expanded installations.[9] In addition to supplies and equipment found there to support the expanding campaign in the Solomon Islands, the bases in the New Hebrides also had amenities to support the military personnel in residence. The accommodations for the pilots were no longer tents, there were magazines and periodicals from home, nightly movies were shown, and the pilots had music, radio broadcasts, and other conveniences to occupy their leisure hours.[10]

Carl was angered by one of the articles he read in an available magazine, and his displeasure is expressed in his next letter from Efate. The article in *Time* described a strike by coal miners led by United Mine Workers of America president John L. Lewis, and Carl's sentiments were widely shared among the military personnel.[11] The impacts of an earlier coal strike ordained by Lewis had cost two hundred thousand miners a week's wages and had cost the defense program an estimated thirty thousand tons of steel, enough to construct thirty Navy destroyers or three thousand light tanks.[12] News of a new strike presented "a bitter hard week for President Roosevelt; and a week of shame, dismay and helpless wrath for the U.S. people."[13]

Concern over the coal strike was little more than a passing distraction from the business at hand, however, and the pilots in the squadron readied to move forward to Espiritu Santo. The evening gatherings of camaraderie that began around the campfires on Guadalcanal continued on Efate, and, during the squadron's last evening before returning to Turtle Bay, the featured beverage at the gathering was Carl's concoction of "milk punch." The punch contributed to what Henry Miller described in his diary as a "spontaneous grand farewell."[14] The milk punch and celebration were also remembered decades later by Tom Tomlinson in his accounts of the squadron published in 2004.

"Before leaving Efate," wrote Tomlinson, "there was the matter of the milk punch. Some creative souls found a use for the powdered milk, powdered eggs, and powdered anything else available. In fact, the only non-powdered ingredient was the booze. The resulting celebration rivaled an outbreak of the plague and was a fitting conclusion to the carefree life of the vacationing fighter pilots."[15]

The next letter was written two days before the "milk punch" evening, and the surroundings described in the letter are on the island of Efate where the celebration took place.

Received July 7, 1943

Saturday 12th

Dear Mom and Dad,

It's a bit windy up here in the control tower where I'm standing duty this afternoon. The sky is grey with low, scuddy overcast, which rolls over the hill beside the strip closing down and then lifting intermittently. Really a rather unpleasant day, at least for what weather here usually is at this time of year. There hasn't been any of the sunshine in which we bathed so luxuriously two weeks ago. For five solid days, we dressed only in shorts (sometimes not even them) and a pair of tennis shoes, and we spent the whole day lying in the sun, swimming, reading, or for my part, turning over stones and boulders at low tide, seeking shellfish with "cats-eyes." Such peace and contentment and relaxation!

In spite of clouds with occasional and fairly regular showers or drizzles, the weather has been warm and we've done a good deal of swimming. Day before yesterday, I had the use of an underwater mask, a round plate-glass window about five inches across with rubber sides to fit against the face and keep water out. It opened up a veritable underwater fairyland. I was in the water well over an hour (and could have stayed longer except for chow) peering at the life below, beside and about me. Every kind of fish from two inches to two feet long, and every kind of coloration you can imagine. The water is crystal clear to any depth—it's fascinating to gaze down to the bottom and find life so peaceful, yet so full of life. The bigger fish are rather tame so that I could almost reach out and touch them.

And they moved leisurely enough that I could follow them with my feeble underwater strokes. The smaller fish in shallower water scurried for their favorite crannies in the coral at my approach, but as I watched quietly, they gradually returned to their feeding and curiously skirted about me. One pair of little white fish with big black eyes were busy digging a home beneath a coral rock. They disappeared one at a time and reappeared to blow out a mouth full of sand in front of their den.

Coloration is so gaudy and extreme among the shellfish, as well as the fish, that one can hardly believe they are real. There were the weirdest sea urchins, all shapes and colors, brilliant blue starfish, as well as red ones, dazzling snail-like shells with jet black, orange, purple, blue spots, highly polished shells that glisten in the sun. The coral itself is an easy match for the most fantastic shells. The "cats-eyes" are protective caps for a certain variety of large snails. What ordinarily is a brown, flat cover on our snails at home when they withdraw into their shells, on this variety is a shell-like formation, oval and convex, with usually greenish-blue center grading into orange and/or brown and finally white. Then there's another variety that has a baby-blue cap. I collected quite a number of both along with big batches of shells. Someone walked off with all my shells while we were gone. But perhaps I'll get around to making something out of the "cats-eyes."[16]

Someone got hold of a May 10 Time magazine which I was perusing last night. I was so burned up over the coal strike situation that I could scarcely sleep after reading about it. I suppose Time is wont to over-darken the picture at home, but on the whole, the impression wasn't very encouraging. Everybody out here seems to be convinced that someone in the know should carry through a program; in fact, people at home seem to be convinced of the same. And yet, no one has or will take the power to push through some kind of a program. Everyone takes a fling at the thing, each in his turn, until someone is dissatisfied and then he gets the boot. Now, it seems even the President has to bow to that traitor Lewis, who claims to represent another dissatisfied minority. Maybe the process that's going on now is the only way to coordinate the civilian and the military effort, but it sure looks terrible on paper. I guess there's a reason for that, too, inasmuch as the only way for the trodden, too, to get out from underneath is to scream like mad. And that's what we get in print, the screaming, which no doubt paints a far blacker picture than actually exists. However, I know well that the situation could really be improved.

My legs are so stiff from our softball game this morning that I waddle around in a shuffle. We have another game in the morning, not within the squadron, but versus another outfit. I hate to think of the creaking backs and sore arms tomorrow. What a team we'll make.

The nostalgia of our stay in Sydney grows daily more bewitching. There's a certain contingent which slips off quietly each night to a quiet office, and there, pine sweet words aimed in the direction of Australia. There are a couple of others who look moon-eyed and sigh heavily every time a sentimental ballad is played on the phonograph or at the movies. Poor fellows! So many servicemen will be in their shoes before they make the trip once again. I hope the impressions on their "amours proprel" was as deep as they seem to feel. I'd like to go back myself—to play golf!

I haven't done a very good job of keeping up my correspondence with Sis. However, I think I'll wait until we get the batch of mail that is due us for the past six weeks before I write her, in case there's a letter from her. Warmest regards, anyhow to her. I'll have to try and remember whether this is the beginning of junior year or two months from now. The new system has me puzzled. Just as long as she doesn't get the idea from some embryonic aviator or Navy ensign about getting married all at once, I think we'll get along pretty well.

Enough for now. I'll light up a pipe and take a survey of the situation down below. Give my best to friends at home. And both of you take care of your health! Good luck and
Love,
Stuff

Two days after his letter, Carl and the other members of VMF-214 returned by transport to Espiritu Santo, and two days later the pilots began orientation with the new and more modern fighters they would fly during their second tour of combat. It was the fighter that Carl had seen and admired during his layover in San Diego—the Chance-Vought F4U-1 Corsair, the aircraft that history now identifies most readily with the squadron.[17] In comparison to the Wildcats that the pilots had flown during their first tour, the Corsair used a complex hydraulic system to operate the cowl flaps, wing flaps, wing-fold mechanism, and the landing gear. (There was no more concern about losing the metal hand crank and damaging wrists and forearms.) The Corsair was heavier, and when filled with fuel and ammunition, it had a two-ton advantage over the Wildcat. "And the Corsair simply looked more stable," in the words of Bruce Gamble. "The Wildcat sat on spindly, narrow-tracked landing gear; the Corsair was planted firmly on hydraulically operated gear extending from the elbows of its unique wings."[18]

Orientation to the Corsair began with engine handbooks and manuals, lectures on the plane's mechanics and engineering, and organizational assignments for the pilots. On the evening of June 17, the squadron gathered for a "song-and-beer" farewell for two of their members being reassigned, and the next day the first group of pilots made their orientation flights in the F4U-1.[19] Two days later Carl and the remaining pilots made their initial flights in the aircraft.[20]

The Corsair, easily recognizable by its distinctive, inverted gull-wing architecture, had a huge radial two-thousand-horsepower engine, and it was the first true four-hundred-mile-an-hour fighter of the war.[21] The F4U-1 swung a fourteen-foot propeller that the inverted gull-wing construction permitted to clear the ground, and the Corsair's cockpit was located fourteen feet back behind the propeller, giving the aircraft a sleek and menacing appearance.[22] The aircraft was fast, its flight characteristics embodied excellent maneuverability, and it bristled with six .50-caliber machine guns.[23]

While the pilots were learning the characteristics of the new aircraft, they also enjoyed the tropical surroundings of Espiritu Santo, picking up where they had left off during the middle of May on their way to

Sydney. They enjoyed comfortable quarters, swam in the "imperial tub" (and were reintroduced to the "little blue fish"), and almost nightly enjoyed the recordings of radio programs and movies recently received from home.[24]

Inside the U.S. South Pacific command, as the pilots readied themselves at Turtle Bay, Admiral Halsey was implementing plans for the next step in the island-hopping campaign into the central Solomon Islands. "Halsey's planned road to Tokyo passed through New Georgia, then Bougainville, and finally Rabaul, and each had to be taken in sequence."[25] The beginning of the offensive strategy called for a campaign of combined forces against New Georgia.[26] VMF-214 would soon move forward to take part in the battle from a new base of operations in the Russell Islands northwest of Guadalcanal.[27]

Received July 6, 1943

Sunday 20

Dear Mom and Dad,

Back with those little blue fish again, those about which I wrote some time ago. We've been in the process of getting settled again. There are five of us in a tiny cabin, so full of gear, nick-knacks, etc., that it's practically obligatory to lie down rather than sit. I find it hard to believe five men could lug around so much gear—there's a grass skirt hanging on one wall, flight gear, headphones, pistols, throat "mike," raincoats, Marine green uniforms, cigarettes, candy and all sorts of dirty clothes hanging on others. I mustn't forget to mention the lovely pictures which adorn wall and bureau top alike. There are two bureaus (homemade) with three partitions—all full—writing paper, tobacco, ink, sewing kits, books, etc. Besides those, we have a center table covered with magazines, while its shelf is likewise packed. I've a shelf above my bunk with toilet articles and a dozen pipes among other things. Under every bunk, every bit of space is filled with suitcases, grips, bedrolls, sea-bags, shoes, and here and there, a stray beer bottle—(empty of course). Everyone of our footlockers is covered with gear. I'm sitting on an empty cartridge box, tending the phonograph which is giving forth the

Firestone Hour. I managed to get hold of the machine yesterday, along with a big box of transcriptions made of actual broadcasts at home. It takes 15 minutes to play both sides. We've enjoyed the recordings all day immensely.

At last, I am realizing the fruits of that visit Dad and I took with Mr. Hudson. It has taken a long time for us, hasn't it? This is my first hop this morning (in a Corsair), so I'm not in much position to judge. But it's a sweetheart!

There were sizeable stacks of mail for all upon our arrival here. I managed to ration myself to a certain extent. At least, I saved part of my mail until the second day. I read with great interest the development of your V-garden. I fancy you'll be able to supply the whole neighborhood with canned vegetables if the crop is good. Sorry I can't report on the V-mail—air mail speeds, but mail was so mixed up that I can't be sure this time. Fourteen days is about the best time for air mail coming this way. I question whether that can be beat, but if you care to try the experiment again, I'll watch for it. There were letters, besides those from home, from Russ Fritz, Grandmother D., Sis, Mr. Dearmont, the Church, the Government, etc. I had dropped V-mail notes to Russ and Mr. Dearmont, scarcely expecting replies to either. Russ is now at O.C.S. in Miami. Mr. Dearmont wrote a wonderful letter—gave me a complete picture of their family. He mentioned that he had been considering writing you to get my address.

Bumped into two more classmates the other day—I don't believe you know either. They tell me I'm apt to bump into Barry any day. The January Alumni Magazine came with the batch of mail we got. It was interesting to read of so many classmates' engagements. I found names in the graduating class of December that I recall when I was a senior and they were freshmen. Amazing the way some of them developed.

We have a very choice spot here in the camp area. As usual, beneath the palms. We're on top of a gentle slope which overlooks a sheltered bay with a large island in the background. The water is shallow and has a beautiful light blue hue. There's always a breeze off the water to cool our cabin, while others in the camp are nearly unbearable at midday. We're far enough from the center of things to have quiet at night. The shower and the head are right below us, and there's a water spigot just outside the door.

Dad, you asked about the weather. It's warm and rather humid most of the time. Nights are cool enough to sleep in a sleeping bag or under a blanket, in spite of the fact that you can't wear a shirt and keep it dry for ten minutes at mid-day. Flying conditions were excellent, while we were most concerned with them, but since our trip to civilization, weather's been generally stinko. It had rained for a fort night prior to arrival in Sydney. However, things are getting very much better. The general conditions that prevail in this area so close to the doldrums are pretty routine. Most of the air is unstable due to rising currents at the Equator. Consequently, tremendous thunder-heads, cumulonimbus formations, small fronts, are almost always prevalent. Sometimes, you can fly over the cumulus clouds, sometimes you are forced down to sea level, oft-times you go around. Naturally, the air is bumpy at almost all altitudes, except in the upper oxygen-mask levels. Visibility is not always excellent because of the cloud formations. The Japs appeared over the top of cirrus clouds the day they attacked us. Needless to say, some of the sunsets and sunrises are very spectacular with the varied and gargantuan cloud formations.

It has been difficult to maintain a coordinated train of thought, as you've undoubtedly noticed, what with changing records, arguing over who'd go after the beer, exchanging quips, etc. I'll try again in more peaceful and solitary surroundings.

I'll say goodnight and wish you all the best. It's good to know that you are both so busy and well. Regards to yours and my friends. Thank Mrs. Stockwell for her letter and enclosures. Hope to hear from you soon!

Love,

Stuff

Others who flew and fought in the Solomon Islands remembered the weather and conditions much as Carl describes them to his father in the letter. "It was never dry," recalled fighter pilot Robert Croft. "They had a wet season and a rainy season. The moisture was either being sucked up by evaporation or landing on your head. And it was extremely hot all the time."[28]

Carl's second orientation flight in the F4U-1 came on June 23, but rain and weather canceled and delayed flights scheduled for two of the next three days.[29] On June 29 the logbook records that Carl and the other pilots moved forward with their Corsairs to Guadalcanal, and the following day the squadron flew from Guadalcanal on to their permanent base of operations at Banika in the Russell Islands.[30] Carl's flight to Guadalcanal—around the thunderheads, small fronts, and cumulonimbus clouds—was entered as a four-hour "ferry hop" in his logbook, and it is described in his letter of July 2, 1943.[31]

On the evening after the letter was written, the pilots commemorated the first anniversary of VMF-214 with an organized fish fry and an evening of songs led by the quartet.[32] The day before the squadron arrived at Banika, Admiral Halsey's forces began their land offensive in the New Georgia island group in the central Solomons.[33] Amphibious forces landed first on the east coast of the island of Rendova across the Diamond Narrow southwest of Munda Point on New Georgia.[34] The invasion was supported by air cover from Guadalcanal and the Russell Islands.[35] From Rendova, the strategic objective of the Allied invasion force and its supporting air cover was to capture the enemy airfield at Munda. Two days after the squadron's arrival at Banika, Allied ground forces began their march toward Munda Point.[36]

The assault on Rendova and then on New Georgia in July 1943 had an uncanny resemblance to Guadalcanal. The eight thousand Japanese defenders knew that the Allied objective was the airfield, and they created a fortified defensive perimeter around the base. The battle, which lasted for more than five weeks, was almost as violent on the ground as Guadalcanal had been, and the Allied commanders leading the invasion force requested and received continuous air support throughout the battle.[37] Initially the objective of the American fighter pilots was to protect the invasion force and its resupply lines from intense Japanese air attacks. Later the pilots from Banika and Henderson Field were tasked with preventing warships and barge traffic from resupplying the enemy troops defending Munda.

Received July 24, 1943

July 2

Dear Mom and Dad,

I'm just about a month behind on mail from home. Last letter was postmarked May 30. The postmaster seems to have a grudge against us, else he's tied up in such a knot of confusion, he can't get straightened out. I've a feeling you're already past strawberry time at home and well on the way to roasting ears. Recently, we've had fresh carrots and new potatoes out of someone's V-garden, but how I'd like some strawberry shortcake and fresh corn! I imagine your carrots, radishes and onions have already found their way to your table.

We're just back from a thousand mile ferry hop, half that distance each way. It was a very uneventful journey successfully carried through. I had no airspeed indicator going, that is, it didn't work, and you can believe me, I really greased that plane on hot. We flew a scouting line coming back, looking for survivors of a DC crash the previous day. We found no sign of them, but subsequently all were picked up. We certainly saw lots of ocean on that trip!

A couple of boys in the squadron were fishing night before last within a stone's throw of our cabin. They caught a sizeable tuna and a four-foot barracuda. So tonight, we are going to have a fish fry. Artie Shaw and his band are scheduled here tonight, which should set the stage for a good party. It is a squadron anniversary.

Had I received your letters before instead of after returning from Sydney, I would have looked up Luther Weigle. I spent a day at his location, lapping up chocolate milkshakes and trying to buy some "1st Looie's bars."

There are numerous cocoanut plantations on this island, as there are on most. This is the first good opportunity I've had, however, to see the copra ovens. "Sechoir" is the French name for them. The names are posted in French because most of the plantations are run by Frenchmen. One of the plantation owners runs a laundry. The lady in charge of receiving and dispensing the laundry speaks no

English. Her French is more perfect than I've ever heard before, just like a classroom text-book grammar.

These "sechoirs" are long, open-sided structures much like the brick kiln sheds in North Haven. These have tin roofs. The cocoanut is spread thinly on trays surrounded by a cement catwalk. Under these and below ground level, wood fires are kept smoldering. The cocoanut turns brown as it dries and emits a strange, rather unpleasant odor. Harvesting of the nuts and operation of the sechoirs is done largely by Tongonese, who look like dwarfed Japs. I think everyone mistrusts them. In fact, I understand there's an open season on them after six o'clock in the evening on any military reservation. They don't look intelligent enough to be effective as spies, but you can never tell.

I burned out the crystal pick-up on our record player the other day thereby ingratiating myself to one and all in this tent. I'm going to try and get it replaced, but I doubt that will be possible. I wonder whether you could airmail me a package as big as a magnetic pick-up arm. Even if it takes a couple of months, we could certainly use one—a magnetic pick-up. (Crystal deteriorates, that's why we need a magnetic pick-up.) See what you can do.

Hope to hear from you soon. Anyhow, it's good to know you are both well and busy. Best wishes and all good health!
Love,
Stuff

The Russell Islands are located northwest of Guadalcanal's western cape, Cape Esperance, and the islands and their numerous coconut plantations were bloodlessly seized in mid-February after being abandoned by the Japanese.[38] Once in possession of the Allies, Navy Seabees were assigned to quickly construct a fighter strip—Advance Base Knucklehead—on Banika, one of the two main islands in the group.[39] The new American facilities at Banika were positioned fifty-five miles northwest of the squadron's prior airfield at Fighter One on Guadalcanal, and the base was about the same distance from the next Allied objective on New Georgia.[40] Arriving on Banika, the squadron pilots spent the first two and half weeks of July preparing to rejoin the fray, engaging in familiarization flights, aerial tactics, and gunnery practice in the new Corsairs.[41] Seven letters were written from the Russell Islands, beginning with the correspondence on July 2, 1943. The narratives in the letters reveal little of the missions entered in the logbook, but each provides insightful descriptions of the sights on Banika surrounding the airfield. A description of the airfield is also found in passages from Tom Tomlinson's account of the squadron's second tour:

> In the Russell Islands, consisting of two main islands, MAG (Marine Air Group) 21's colonel and staff had built a wonderful fighter camp on Banika. Banika will always be remembered as having the whitest coral airstrip in memory. This strip crossed the whole small island in a narrow cut in the stately coconut palms from Sunlight Channel to the deep blue ocean at the east end. The pilots of each four-plane division had their own Dallas hut provided with screening to keep the mosquitoes at bay. The grass under the stately rows of coconut palms had the appearance of having been mowed and gave the area a parklike feeling.[42]

On Banika, VMF-214 did not suffer the incessant Japanese air attacks that the pilots had encountered during their first tour on Guadalcanal from "Washing Machine Charlie" and other enemy aircraft based on Bougainville and Rabaul. Instead the pilots trained, patrolled, and later launched regular assaults on enemy targets in the central islands from the Knucklehead base. Once back at the base, harassing air strikes by the enemy was rare.[43]

Received July 26, 1943

July 11

Dear Mom and Dad,

I've been awaiting your next letter rather anxiously to learn whether Dad's dizziness has disappeared. I didn't like the sound of that bump on the head at all. Certainly hope there has been much improvement. Maybe someone ought to put out an official order making it mandatory for anyone in need of bathroom facilities in the middle of the night to crawl on all fours. If that doesn't work, collect that old football helmet from the attic and keep it beside the bed.

The description of your garden crop sounded delicious. I can scarcely picture the vegetables ready for the table; it's been such a short time since I first heard about the project, and now, bingo, here the fruits of your efforts are on the table. How are the other gardens producing? I'll bet neither of you will relish the return to canned foods after eating fresh-picked vegetables. One of these days, perhaps we'll have a big enough greenhouse of our own to produce tomatoes and a few other things the year round.

I'm looking hard for Jim and Bill these days. Rumor has it that they are either in the vicinity or due any day. You know they gave me a couple of fifths of Johnny Walker Black Label before I left San Diego. Well, I've saved it for the day when we are all three, or at least two of us, get together. We shall celebrate the reunion in style anyway.

I had a pleasant surprise in a letter from Jeanne last week. She had just returned from a two and a half week vacation in Pensacola with Bill. It was good to hear from her; it was better still to know that the rather unsavory memory of our parting last November is forgotten and our friendship is secure, as it should be. I don't know quite what the trouble was then, but something certainly was wrong. I thought we would always enjoy an evening together, whatever our heart interests were. Perhaps my being two and a half hours late because of a cocktail party had something to do with it. I suppose it could have been construed as an intentional indignity, which it wasn't. Anyhow, friendship is as it should be again. That's the important thing.

Mail from Sydney has been very sluggish. A few of the fellows have heard from friends there. I haven't. What word there has been is very encouraging. VMF-214 has not been forgotten there, and I don't think there's much question about the reception that awaits us if we get there again. There are plenty of open arms—not that there weren't plenty the first trip. But this time, there's some affection besides.

We've had flowers in the cabin this past week. I picked two

different kinds, one from a tree, and the other from a ground plant, and they are still blossoming fragrantly and profusely. They both have a very delicate fragrance—cross between gardenias and lilies of the valley. The ground plant flower faces downward like a bell, about half a dozen blossoms at the top of a stem like narcissi. They are white and look considerably like a daffodil, with a slightly shorter horn. Six stamens protrude from the fringe of the horn, and where they protrude, the fringe has a delicate greenish color. The other blooms which grow on a large tree that reminds you somewhat of a magnolia tree are my favorites. They last for over a week a piece. A great many blossoms cluster on a finger of branches at the end of a limb. There are no leaves on these flowery fingers. When open, the flowers are a little larger than a half-dollar, gardenia white in texture at the outer tips shading to a rich yellow at the throat. There are five petals curved delicately inward at the edges. The buds are delicately pink outside before they open. I have looked for seeds, but there seem to be none.

John and I got very domestic yesterday afternoon and went to work on our lawn with the implements that are supplied—a double-edged cutter (swung like a golf club) and a rake. We found beneath the tall coarse grass and weeds a good stand of fine creeping bent. It undoubtedly was introduced by the plantation owner who probably had his house in this vicinity. We have about the best looking grounds in the area now and without question, the most blistered hands.

I received the pages from the Alumni Weekly. Many thanks. Recently, I have visited with several of the fellows who were mentioned as being in this area. Tough luck for Billy Barnes, wasn't it?

I'll sign off for now and get a letter off to Grandmother. Best wishes to all at home. Take care of yourselves and let me know what is going on.

Love,
Stuff

By July 15, Carl had made sixteen flights in the F4U-1 and accumulated almost twenty hours of flight time in the Corsair.[44] Three days after his next letter home, VMF-214 was deemed combat-ready and their initial missions began. In his first mission in the new plane, Carl joined other pilots from the squadron providing air cover for a stranded naval vessel, the seaplane tender USS *Chincoteague* that had been paralyzed and intermittently attacked by Japanese bombers near Vanikoro Island west of the Russells.[45] The pilots from VMF-214 maintained a day-long series of overlapping patrols above the stricken vessel until it could be taken under tow by a naval destroyer and removed to safety.[46] While providing their protective cover, the squadron was credited with downing one Japanese bomber and the "probable" destruction of a second.[47]

Received August 2, 1943

July 15

Dear Mom and Dad,

For a change, we are lounging in solid comfort today, with the sun hidden behind a high overcast and a cool breeze blowing off the water. You could scarcely ask for more pleasant weather.

We need it though! Another squadron party last night in honor of one of us who is leaving would have made a hot sun most unwelcome. We gathered driftwood and kindling and built a campfire just outside our cabin so we could sit in a circle around the embers, as in the days I used to write about. We had an ample supply of beer. As usual, the quartet was called upon to sing; some poems were recited; Harry read a condensed account of our earlier days in action and also a choice bit entitled "The Battle of Sydney;" toasts were offered; and finally we ended the evening with the usual gamut of community songs, many unique with our squadron, and last "Auld Lang Syne." It was a grand evening.

Dale Fisher was over and spent the night with us last week. He's a survivor. We sat up quite late talking and drinking, and next morning, I took him up for a hop.

I understand that another of us was inducted into the "Caterpillar Club" this morning. I don't know much about it except that it was Harry and that he is all right. That makes three of us under the same roof. That's quite a percentage isn't it, three out of five? As if that isn't enough, I think there's more than an even chance that we may have another married man in our midst one of these days. At the rate letters are arriving from Sydney and if the moon-eyed expressions are any indication, poor John will never get another trip to civilization without being snared. I get a big kick out of watching him as he reads the sugar reports. Invariably, he brings them back to the cabin, undresses but for shorts and flops on his cot. You watch him smile, blush, and finally with a cry of delight, roll over and bury his face in the bedding roll. For hours after the letters, he walks around on a cloud, smiling and hearing only about half of what you say to him. Doesn't that sound like the last stages to you?

18th (15th continued)

We went "erstering" this morning, three of us. Spent half the morning in the sun, paddling in a rubber boat, swimming, and wading from island to island. We saw countless numbers of tropical fish in coral pools, several new ones to me. The parrotfish was most spectacular; gets its name from the red and green coloring like our oft-heard parakeets. The oysters are flattened out on large rocks and ledges in great abundance. You pry the upper shell away with bayonet, or chisel and hammer, and cut the muscle holding him to the lower shell. I took a brief excursion through the island jungle and marveled at the flowering trees and abundant edible nuts and fruit. I didn't happen to run into any of the wild game which some of the fellows have been bagging recently—wild chickens and doves. There seemed to be a million fiddler crabs running in and out of their holes—shiny "jet black" little fellows with bright green markings on their shells and a big red claw which shaded to pink at the top.

We had oyster stew this afternoon about 4:30—and it was darned good, a bit too salty, but not bad. Cooked it in a bucket over a blow-torch, evaporated milk, salt, pepper and butter.

I was driving Bill Mann home the other night (he was one of our gang at Jacksonville) after a visit and got myself a ticket for driving with only one light. Picture that, if you can! Bill was just passing through. He had definite word of Jim. I should be seeing him almost anytime now. It's just a matter of one of us getting where the other is.

Well, I'll finish up here and so get this letter in the mail. You can see I've had a little trouble so far, for there isn't a great deal to say.

I do hope all is well at home. Mail has been rather fouled up so I'm not exactly up to date. Best of health and good fortune to all of you.

Love,

Stuff

Carl's tentmate, Harry Hollmeyer, was the squadron pilot who joined the "Caterpillar Club" on the morning the letter was written. The engine on his Corsair failed and caught fire during a high-altitude gunnery exercise, forcing him to bailout before the plane smashed into the sea. He landed safely in the waters adjacent to another portion of Banika away from the Knucklehead base, and he was brought to the home of one of the island's French plantation owners where he was later recovered by a rescue boat from the airfield.[48]

In the week that followed, the squadron missions included sorties to help provide the protective umbrella over the invasion force on the island of Rendova, bomber escorts for strikes against enemy positions around Munda Point on New Georgia, and strafing missions against well-defended Japanese strongholds on both islands.[49]

In his next letter Carl introduces some of the members of VMF-214 to his mother and father, he shares the monikers by which they were known among their fellow pilots, and he explains the role he has flown as the wing-man for Vince Carpenter's division since arriving in the South Pacific. It was, according to Carpenter, "a very proud division." Carpenter had adapted a distinctive "break-up" maneuver for the four planes when they returned from a mission that he had learned from the Australian and New Zealand Army Corps (ANZAC) pilots, and it became the division's trademark during their time in the Solomons. "They'd dive over the field head to tail in close formation," remembered Carpenter, "and the leader would suddenly pull up sharply with everyone else doing the same split seconds later. The division would explode straight up this way and then curve down into the landing approaches. Everyone knew when Carpenter's division was returning home. We were pretty proud of our trademark."[50]

July 25

Dear Mom and Dad,

You are both taking very good care of me! Besides your letters, which have been coming cheerfully rather regularly at last, there were two copies of Time yesterday—June 7th and 19th. I appreciate your prompt attention of my request. And I am always anxious to hear from home—that goes without saying.

Mom, your letter of July 10 arrived today. We are certainly proud of our submariners, especially those like Eddie who deserve special commendation. I imagine it was Stan Livingston who carried news of me. We had an excellent chat one afternoon. I must write to the new "Looie J.G." Our last letters crossed paths about three weeks ago. I didn't know whether or not I could safely address it Lt. (j.g.) then, so I didn't. From the record Tom's boys are compiling, I'd say he's doing a top-notch job. Lucky fellow to be returning home! The news about Libby is most gratifying. I know how proud Mr. Schuller must be. If anyone deserves a break, it's Libby.

I think your remarks about the relative attraction of Australian and American girls were very wise. I agree entirely. No one should jump over the big brink at a time like this. It isn't at all fair to any girl; and it isn't fair to the man himself. We all know that a person gets lonesome living like this and when someone sweetly feminine sympathizes and presents herself attractively, well you just have to get hold of yourself. I'd never consider making a decision until I'd been home under normal conditions, even if I thought I'd found the right girl. And I don't think any such thing. I've got lots of ideas in the back of my head for the future and they certainly don't include a wife for some time. Margaret is a very intelligent girl and attractive. Her father is a chief justice and the family rates tops socially. So it's understandable why I like her, why I'm keeping a correspondence and hoping to see her next trip. No Marine flyer has to resort to marriage for feminine companionship anyway; all he has to do is cast a searching eye about and his desires will soon be met. It's rather a strange thing to get used to at first.

Have I never clarified my position in the squadron? I've flown the same position from the first. It was inevitable that we who arrived late would be wing-men, and it is best so in light of relative experience. I asked to fly on Vince Carpenter (Yale '42) and fortunately was granted my request. He's our division leader. That makes me No. 2 man in the 4-man division. Ours is practically the only division which has remained unchanged from the outset. We're proud and happy in it, and quite naturally are convinced that it is the best division in the squadron. The section leader has been a roommate since we first arrived out here. That makes the whole set-up that much closer knit. Five of us have roomed together during our entire stay here—Hollmeyer (Harvard '40), Hazelwood (Princeton '42), McCall (U. of Cal), and Fidler (Wisconsin's Monmouth College). I didn't mention the first names for you scarcely ever hear them. Instead, you'd hear something like this in the order listed above. "Hey, Horse!" for "Harry the Horse" Hollmeyer, also known as "Hairbreadth Harry" or "Harry the Hairless." It's always "House" or "Hazel" or "Hazel-House" for Ledge Hazelwood. I believe you'll be hearing from his folks. He's a mighty fine guy, full of the old Ned. "Mac" is a natural for Drury McCall, although you'll sometimes here McCall-berg. It's not appropriate or significant, but it tickles our fancy. "Barf" for John Fidler is a household expression which he gained at Ewa one night when he had drunk "not wisely, but too well." He answers, too, to "Long John." The photo he brought from Sydney is inscribed "To Long John, with all my Love." He has never, nor will he, hear the end of that. Altogether, it's a madhouse. The whole squadron is a mad, happy family, but our own tent is a well-nigh perfect cross-section. We are told occasionally that our squadron has made an excellent impression wherever it has gone. I believe we can feel sincerely proud, for if the life within is any indication of the impression without, it would be hard to beat. We have been very fortunate to have had two wonderful men as our leaders—Majors Britt and Ellis. Their example has been the mold which fashioned our squadron.

I must surely have told you that I am Assistant Ordinance

Officer of the squadron. Carpenter is the Ordinance Officer. My responsibilities are far less imposing than the title suggests.

I have a great deal to write about our home here, but rather than try to put everything in one letter, I'll close this one here and write another about it. We have a big day ahead of us tomorrow which needs a full night of rest, too. So for now, I'll send best wishes and wish you best health. Take care of yourselves and let me know how things are. Good night!

Love,

Stuff

During the final week of July, the squadron's missions continued to concentrate on the central islands in the New Georgia group as Allied ground forces pressed on to capture and secure the airfield at Munda.[51] Other sorties were flown against the well-fortified enemy complex at Kahili. At the southern tip of Bougainville, Kahili was a primary base for Japanese air operations in the Solomons and the location for major staging facilities to resupply enemy positions in the central islands.[52]

It was also during the final week of July that the pilots settled on a name and insignia for their squadron. As July became August, the pilots of VMF-214 became the "Swashbucklers." Harry Hollmeyer is credited with the design of the squadron's new insignia that linked the distinctive gull-winged Corsair with the pirate swashbucklers of a different century. The design he created in orange and black used a head-on front view of the bent gull-wings of the F4U-1, and in place of the plane's engine cowling, a grimacing skull appeared. The design bore the Latin motto *Semper vincere*—"Always to Conquer"—and the insignia became the permanent symbol for the pilots who flew the first two combat tours as Marine Fighting Squadron VMF-214.[53]

In the final days of July the Swashbucklers were "scrambled" for the first time during their second tour on July 28. They took off from the Knucklehead base to meet incoming enemy planes that were reported to be headed for Banika, but the enemy bombers either turned away or had a different target, and Carl's logbook reports that no contacts were made with the enemy over the Russell Islands on that day.[54]

On the same day in Washington, D.C., President Roosevelt addressed

Swashbuckler squadron patch, designed by Harry Hollmeyer while the pilots were in Australia. (Dunbar family collection.)

the nation in an evening "fireside chat" and spoke about America's progress in the global conflict, including the efforts in the South Pacific. The president's broadcast was also heard by the pilots on Banika when they returned from their mission of the day, and in Carl's next letter, he remembers other "fireside chats" and identifies personally with the words of the president in this one. To Carl, the words from the president spoke of him, his fellow Marine pilots, and the other members of the Allied forces engaged in the new island-hopping offensive intended to push the Japanese out of the South Pacific:

> In the Pacific, we are pushing the Japs around from the Aleutians to New Guinea. The continuous and energetic prosecution of the war of attrition will drive the Japs from their over-extended line running from Burma . . . to eastern New Guinea and the Solomons. And we have good reason to believe that their shipping and their air power cannot support such outposts. Our naval and land and air strength in the Pacific is constantly growing. And if the Japanese are basing their future plans for the Pacific on a long period in which they will be permitted to consolidate and exploit their

conquered resources, they had better start revising their plans now. I give that to them merely as a helpful suggestion.[55]

Carl wrote next after the squadron had completed another mission over enemy positions in the central islands, this one to escort bombers targeting the Barakoma airfield on Vella Lavella northwest of the main island of New Georgia.[56] As July ended, his logbook entries totaled 35.5 hours of flight time in the Corsair and included eight combat sorties over the central islands in the Solomon group.[57]

Now familiar with their F4U-1 aircraft, the squadron pilots expected their flight hours in August to multiply and all of their time in the air to be flown in anticipation of enemy contact.[58]

Received August 10, 1943

July 30

Dear Mom and Dad,

I pictured you sitting in the living room day before yesterday evening listening to the President's address, the one for which we hastened our lunch yesterday. I remember so well evenings which seem eons ago when we sat listening to the same voice, Dad, bent close to the speaker, elbows on knees or chin in hand. This address struck me as very reassuring. Sometimes when I see press releases on the South Pacific or hear us referred to as yesterday, I have to cock my head and question myself "Is he talking about us?" I say it's reassuring because all the loose-ends we pick up here and there get coordinated, and the total picture presents a more optimistic outlook than what you see every day.

If heat and work have taken weight off of me—I'm not sure they have, but you expect it—I'm going to replace the loss with interest, given a few weeks. When we're on the ground, I eat about every two hours, sometimes more frequently. Our "South Pacific Club" I wrote Sis about really dishes out the food. I even overheard a couple of the mess-men exchanging recipes for cake. The coffee is so good that I seem to be developing a real taste for it. The chocolate malt still rates first, however. On top of the luxurious eating, we're getting a real share of exercise for a change. The punching bag is going most of the time, the ping-pong table all of the time, and the badminton court probably will be when it's completed. This is the nearest thing to a Marine summer camp I've ever seen.

There was a letter today from Mrs. Northrup, which was very gracious and interesting. Will you express my appreciation and best wishes next time you see her?

I've been having the time of my life days off working in the carpenter shop. It's fully equipped with all the best electric tools. The boys just turn me loose and I go around pushing buttons with reckless abandon. I've made a case for clean clothes, helped with a center table, and a rack for our transcriptions. Barf has built a liquor chest. I started out to make an adjustable chair, but that project didn't turn out so well.

A couple of the fellows went off alligator and duck hunting this morning. I'm going to try and get in on the next trip. They tell me alligator steaks are very tasty, and I'm willing to give them a try. The barracuda steaks were good, as reported, so perhaps these will be, too.

I seem to have run down. So it's time to close. Best wishes to all at home and some cooling breezes for your heat. Good health and Love,

Stuff

August brought the expected intensity and frequency to the mission assignments for VMF-214 as the Allied ground forces closed in on the airfield at Munda Point.[59] Many of the squadron sorties were an integrated part of the Allied offensive in the central islands around New Georgia, and other missions took them farther north on raids against the installations on Bougainville supporting the enemy positions in the central islands.[60]

On August 1 two four-plane divisions, including Carpenter's with Carl on wing, flew cover for a dozen SBD Dauntless dive bombers and the same number of TBF Avenger torpedo bombers in a raid against Kahili on Bougainville. The Dauntless and Avenger bombers struck with precision and destroyed four out of the five Japanese ships anchored off the end of the airfield in the face of intense antiaircraft fire.[61] Several Zeros shadowed the formation on the return flight, but the Marine fighter pilots stayed close to the bombers to protect their safe return south. Carl's logbook notes the sighting of the Zeros but indicates that there was no engagement with the enemy fighters.[62] Later in the day Carpenter's division returned to the air as part of the umbrella of air cover over the American invasion force fighting its way toward Munda Point.[63]

The mission sorties of the Allied air assets on the first day of August were described in a contemporaneous report filed by Associated Press correspondent Arthur Burgess from "somewhere in the South Pacific." Burgess' account of the day appeared two weeks later in the daily newspapers back in the United States.

> Demonstrating America's growing air might in the Solomons as many as 100 fighter planes were aloft at one time today as victory after victory was piled up in dogfights with the Japanese.
>
> Three fights ranged from Japanese-held Kahili Airfield on Bougainville, South across Vella Lavella, to New Georgia and Rendova. During them the enemy lost a total of 34 planes. Only two of our planes were lost and their pilots were believed saved.
>
> Japanese plane losses in the Solomons since February are estimated unofficially to approximate 1000.
>
> At an advanced base I watched one of our fighter pilots dive on a Japanese bomber, give him a burst, turn, come back and deliver a second burst as the enemy started a flaming plunge into the ocean. In air battles which started over southern Vella Lavella and spread south over Ganongga Island (southwest of Vella Lavella), Marine, Army and Navy fighters took on all comers. Marine Corsairs over Ganongga tangled with about 40 Zeros and an undetermined number of dive bombers at low altitude, shooting down ten Zeros and three bombers.[64]

Carl's mission assignment on the following day was to escort a flight of B-25 Mitchell bombers on a raid against the Vila airfield on Kolombangara adjacent to New Georgia. Unlike the mission over Bougainville, however, no Japanese fighters materialized to interfere with the mission.[65]

Between the Swashbuckler's daytime missions against Bougainville and Kolombangara on August 1 and 2, a flotilla of fifteen U.S. Navy torpedo boats began a night patrol south of Kolombangara to interdict barges and other vessels supplying the enemy positions in the central islands.[66] The torpedo boats began their patrol on the afternoon of August 1, and two hours after midnight in the waters south of Kolombangara one of the boats was struck and cut in half by the Japanese escort destroyer *Amagiri* as it returned from its resupply mission.

Considered simply another footnote in the Battle of the Solomon Islands at the time it occurred, decades later, the sinking of PT-109 became one of the most remembered events of the conflict in the central islands. Following its violent collision with *Amagiri*, the commander and crew of the PT boat found themselves adrift in the dark waters of Blackett Strait. The young commander of the boat, Lieutenant (junior grade) John F. Kennedy, gathered the surviving crew, helped them to swim safely to a nearby uninhabited island, and later facilitated their rescue by inscribing a message for help into the husk of a coconut.[67]

The coconut, later recovered by Kennedy and saved, was prominently displayed in the Oval Office of the White House while he served as the thirty-fifth president of the United States.[68] As Kennedy ascended to the nation's presidency in 1960, the first of his generation to do so, the little-remembered event in the central islands south of Kolombangara returned the battles fought in these remote reaches of the South Pacific to the contemporary consciousness of the country.

In the diversions from the hours and days of combat in the late summer of 1943, Carl's thoughts were on the well-being of the family and the effects of the war back at home. These included frequent questions about the progress of the family's victory garden, which Carl mentions in six of his letters during the squadron's second tour. As the war entered its second summer, victory gardens, or "V-gardens," appeared in residential yards and cooperative plots around the county, and New Haven was no exception.

On the fringes of the campus at Yale University, a sizeable plot was plowed up in what had been the football practice fields and game-day parking area, and the university administration permitted faculty members to reserve space in the plot for their individual gardens.[69] The V-gardens, like those in New Haven, provided vegetables, herbs, and fruits for the dinner tables of family and friends in all parts of the country, and the gardens took the pressure off the public food supply brought on by the global war.

Received August 12, 1943

August 3

Dear Mom and Dad,

I am just beginning to realize what a herculean task the victory garden is imposing on you, now that reports of your early harvests are coming in. I know that the weeds and the crops won't wait. So don't worry if there isn't time to farm and write both. There will be plenty of rainy days anyhow.

We're doing a good deal of flying these days, but that ship of ours is a dream. It practically flies itself, and when you want to get someplace or away from someplace in a hurry, it's unbelievable what an advance in the throttle will do! (And I don't mean just increase the cylinder head temperature.) I still suffer from the pilots occupational disease of parachutitis, but that's one of those things that will have to wait for remedy until the new model of the human body comes out. I believe it was Tom who used to speak of "bearding the lion in his den." Well, I've a pretty good idea what he was talking about now. The lion seemed to turn a little mousey on us.

I shall be utterly spoiled for further life in the rough. Hamburgers every hour on the hour is enough to soften any man. But a laundry (with one day service) is even more insidious. I find, however, although I'm one of the laundry's most confirmed patrons, that I became rather particular while I was doing my own laundry. At least then, I knew just how dirty my clothes were after a washing. And by a few deft strokes of the bristle brush, I could bring the questionable article within the allowable tolerance. If ever I have to plan a departure from the States again, there will be four essentials I shall bring with me and nothing more: a washing machine, a Hallicrafter's shortwave radio, a small refrigerator, and a good stock of wines and liquor. A man could fight a damned comfortable war so equipped.

We have done fairly well at the carpenter shop this past week. The chateau is full of our modern art, which I can easily and safely forecast as future heirlooms because they are so securely nailed down. The two chairs and our table are not guaranteed their historic niche; they probably won't stand up long enough and they are bound to go out whence they came in, when we move out—by the door. The liquor cabinet (with lock) has an undecided future. It appears slightly too heavy to remain with us for all its handsomeness. But getting down the shelves and the open-faced bureaus! Those are the real permanent fixtures. What gems! The record-rack is one of our most imposing decorations. It hangs over the transcription unit on the wall, displaying amply our forty-seven discs. The grooves are numbered carefully and each record is catalogued by program and by selections on the program. I wish I could just overlook the candy-hoist which hangs precariously like a sword of Damocles over my head. So far, it has proven just as ant-repellant as unsightly. One could scarcely say more for its effectiveness. I wonder sometimes what the long term effect of all this interior decorating will be on the tastes for a home of my own.

I saw Carter Dye the other day for only a few swift minutes, but long enough to find him hearty and jubilant as ever. Ours was a highly precarious rendezvous at the edge of a runway where a stream of heavily-laden aircraft were taking off. Carter made a mad dash across the runway between planes and we shouted and talked and prepared to take evasive action throughout our few minutes together. Mrs. Northrup will probably remember Bill Coagland. I bumped into him day before yesterday on a lime-hunting expedition.

The lime trees we found apparently were planted on the grounds of some planteur's estate. The dwellings have since been removed; only the cement foundations remain. There were several tremendous trees of questionable variety, beside the lime trees. There were also three large trees full of the flowers I wrote about before, the yellow-throated, velvet-white, four-pedaled, intensely fragrant blossoms. I know I have never walked into such perfumed air before. The fragrance came down from the tree and up from the ground and the fallen petals. It blew far down the slope on the breeze and scarcely diminished in intensity. I looked high and low for seeds, but once again there appeared to be none. The flower-stems withered and fell off. I wish I could find a way to get seeds of the tree to you for it is my favorite flower in all this area.

It's time to make a delivery at the laundry and also pay a visit to the great equalizer. So I must say good-bye for the present. Every best wish to all of you.

Love,

Stuff

The missions from Advance Base Knucklehead on Banika were longer for the Marine pilots of VMF-214 than those they had flown from Fighter One on Guadalcanal in the spring. Each sortie required between 2.5 and 3.5 hours, and the time for each mission was nearly twice what it had been during their first tour. On many days, the pilots flew more than one mission a day, resulting in as much as 6 hours of flight time in their Corsairs.[70] And while the parachute and equipment worn by pilots for the long hours of flight created discomfort in the cockpit, the performance characteristics of the Corsair surpassed those of the Wildcat.[71] Carl reports in his correspondence that the new F4U-1 aircraft was "a dream."

The Swashbuckler pilots did not fly every day, and the pilots alternated their time in the new aircraft. When not on flight duty, the pilots' time off on Banika was spent in accommodations and surroundings much different than the mud and dust encountered on Guadalcanal. Off-duty days allowed for the opportunity to explore the island or to simply relax. There were laundry facilities for the Marines, and the airfield at Banika had its own "hamburger hut."

Carl makes a brief reference to the hamburger hut and "hamburgers every hour" in his letter, but the "hut" and its source of fresh beef were described in more detail by fellow pilot Tom Tomlinson in his account of VMF-214's time on Banika:

The oasis of civilization had the famous hamburger hut. In a world of execrable cuisine ranging from infamous Spam to powdered anything, this was indeed remarkable. It was made possible by the same instrument that kept the grass so neatly maintained. This was a herd of cows from the former plantation whose proprietors had fled as the Japanese approached. A certain number of these cows were said to sacrifice their lives to the falling shrapnel from the antiaircraft fire during air raids. What charges the former owners would have levied had they witnessed the deployment of the sharpshooters during these attacks is unknown.[72]

Amenities at the airfield were not the only difference from the first tour when the pilots' sorties were often to defend their own island base. The mission objectives were now offensive actions. The targets included enemy positions on New Georgia, where ground troops were closing in on the airfield at Munda Point, and installations on Kolombangara and Vella Lavella that represented the next progressive steps towards the island of Bougainville.[73] Each presented another opportunity to further isolate the enemy stronghold at Rabaul on New Britain.[74]

Two days after Carl's letter on August 3 the airfield on Munda Point fell to the Allies, finally abandoned after a series of raids had so savaged the installation that the enemy considered it no longer viable.[75] But the Japanese did not abandon New Georgia entirely. From new positions in the island's interior, sporadic shelling from enemy artillery continued to inflict damage on the Allies for more than a month after the perimeter of the airfield had been secured.[76] The Japanese did not readily concede the skies over the central islands either. In August the aerial contests were hotter and dogfights more frequent than any previously experienced by the squadron.[77]

After the fall of the airfield at Munda, the next two island objectives of the Allies were Kolombangara and Vella Lavella. The installations on these islands were important parts of the defensive line that was intended to delay the Allied advance toward Bougainville.[78]

Kolombangara, roughly circular in shape and twenty-five miles in diameter, lay adjacent to the northwest coast of New Georgia. The island's twin extinct volcanoes reached skyward more than five thousand feet and provided the island with a distinctive landscape. The Japanese had deployed a sizable land garrison of more than twelve thousand troops to Kolombangara and built an airfield on the island's south shore at Vila on Ringi Cove.[79]

Even before the fall of Munda, Admiral Halsey had decided to bypass Kolombangara and isolate the large Japanese garrison on the island by cutting off its food, supplies, and reinforcements.[80] The aerial missions against the enemy installations at Vila and Ringi Cove were intended primarily to support the Admiral's isolation strategy and prevent the forces on Kolombangara from interfering with the next planned island-hop to Vella Lavella.

On Vella Lavella, the focal point of the Allied offensive was the Japanese complex on the southwest coast of the island at Barakoma. The facilities there consisted of a fighter airfield and a barge staging area, both supplied by coastal vessels from Bougainville.[81] If the Allies could control Vella Lavella, the base at Barakoma presented a land-based airfield capable of launching fighter attacks directly against Bougainville.[82]

The day after the Munda Point was captured, Navy Seabees moved in to begin reconstruction of the airfield. On the same day, two Swashbucklers divisions, including Vince Carpenter's, launched from the Knucklehead base to escort a P-38 photo plane while it took reconnaissance pictures of the installations on Shortland Island off the south coast of Bougainville.[83] During the mission, the fighters hugged the waves no more than fifty to two hundred feet above the surface, then turned southeast and made a half circle before racing at high speed for the photo run of the island. As the Corsairs approached, the sky was suddenly full of three different types of Japanese fighters, throwing the Swashbucklers into an intense dogfight.[84]

In the first sweep, the division led by Smiley Burnett accounted for five downed enemy aircraft with no damage to their Corsairs. Carpenter's division followed, but the enemy planes were better prepared, and they badly damaged John Fidler's Corsair and shot down the one piloted by Bill Blakeslee.[85] Vince Carpenter and Carl Dunbar's Corsairs were also damaged, but both planes were able to return safely to Banika. The results from the dogfight were five downed enemy aircraft, but the squadron had lost two aircraft of its own along with one of its pilots.

Carl's logbook entry for the mission dryly states that he "failed to get any" of the enemy aircraft during the fight.[86] Months later he

Seabees arrive at denuded Munda Point after the airfield is taken by the Allies on August 5, 1943. (National Archives.)

described the aerial encounter in a newspaper interview after returning to the United States. "We dived low over the water trying to get away from them," Carl recalled, "but they stayed close behind. We practically were wave-hopping. I looked over my shoulder and saw a string of water spouts where the bullets were hitting. I got out of it with only a few holes in each wing. One of our planes was not so lucky. He hit the water."[87]

Two days off for the division followed the dogfight over Shortland Island, and then Carl and the division were aloft again to escort a flight of B-25 Mitchell bombers in search of enemy shipping off Kolombangara. The logbook entry records that no enemy aircraft interfered with the mission objective.[88] On August 13 the division was again in the air to escort a flight of B-25s, this time against the complex at Barakoma on Vella Lavella.[89] The following day Carl's division rotated off the flight line and enjoyed a day of rest.

7 ✗ ✗ ✗ ✗ ✗ ✗ ✗

Airfield at Munda Point, New Georgia Island, August 15, 1943–August 31, 1943

> *We did have some pretty good hunting on the strafing hops.*
> *That's the fighter pilot's apple-pie-a-la-mode!*
>
> Carl O. Dunbar Jr., September 7, 1943

After Allied forces seized control of the airfield at Munda Point on August 5, Navy Seabees moved quickly to repair the field and make it operational for the bigger and heavier American fighters.[1] While Carl and the other pilots in his division were enjoying their day off on August 14, the work by the Seabees had progressed sufficiently so that by the end of the day the airstrip was ready to accommodate the F4U-1 Corsairs.

In his next letter, penned during the evening hours on August 14, Carl's thoughts were not on the progress being made at Munda. Instead, as a baseball fan and former high school and college catcher, he fretted over the downhill slide of the Brooklyn Dodgers ("Dem Bums") in the National League pennant race and the sliding batting average of Dodger first baseman Dolph Camilli, who had lead Brooklyn to a long-awaited pennant flag in the summer of 1941 before the war began.[2] The next morning Carl's priorities returned to the island of New Georgia.

Seabees in the process of extending the runway and repairing the airfield at Munda Point on August 12, 1943, three days before the arrival of the Carpenter division of VMF-214. (National Archives.)

Received August 27, 1943

Aug. 14

Dear Mom and Dad,

I do believe summer is on the way here. We've had several days (over a week) of typical doldrum weather—low clouds, rain, fronts and squalls, the type of flying weather you don't dream about. Now this morning while it's still early, the heat is oppressive in spite of nothing but shorts and shoes for clothing.

We started out for a big fishing and hunting expedition yesterday aboard a thirty-foot launch, armed with carbine, double-barreled shotgun, and deep-sea fishing tackle. Just after we were well started, the motor conked and refused to start again. Result: we gradually drifted toward the coral-studded shore and finally bumped the deck a few times before we managed to hook the two small anchors to hold us twenty feet out of danger. There we waited for three hours to be rescued and towed home. All we caught was sunburn and blisters—the latter from rowing to pull the launch out of trouble. There were two sailors aboard both of whom were really seasick.

I wrote you about Tom's expression of "bearding the lion." Well, our reception wasn't quite so mousey the second time around. I haven't heard from Tom in sometime. Wonder if he isn't back home now or on his way.

"Dem bums" sure have hit the skids. I wasn't in on the news when they first started down-hill, but since we've been here I get the scores of both leagues and the standings every day. I don't see any other way to explain the disintegration except to blame the manager and the owner. Camilli isn't one to drop off to .244 without a reason. And you can be sure something is out of line when they take stand-by after stand-by and put him on the block. Well, it gives Brooklyn something to holler about, anyhow, so people won't forget it still exists.

I marvel anew at your V-garden success. If I could just be there to enjoy the fresh vegetables with you! Have the other gardens been doing as well? What was the trouble with the canning that caused the beans to spoil? I hope that won't make it impossible for you to can other things and so eat well this winter.

Dad's letter about the radio pick-up had already explained the difficulties of rationing and size. I'll wait now and pick up one in Sydney next trip. There haven't been any imports or manufacture of parts there, but I found one dealer who had three, the only ones available at all. He sold me one and I think he'll part with another for this cause. I think the dealer at home was being a bit hyper-conscientious. But perhaps it's a little different when things can be traced on paper. As for the size, we'll make any kind of arm do, either by rebuilding it, or the machine, or both. Seldom if ever are the right things available out here for maintenance and repair. Repair-men and mechanics are wizards of improvisation, or we wouldn't be flying. I'm much indebted to you both for trying to get our part. Our manual arm has been very satisfactory and we've not missed a thing by not having an electrical pick-up. So don't be uneasy about not being able to buy one. Chances are it would have been delayed interminably in the mail, anyway.

Speaking of the quartet, we haven't done much singing recently. There are several reasons, among them fewer parties, no regular evening congregations, movies every night, and people are usually pretty well tired out at night. If we make it in tact to Sydney again, I'll surely see we have recordings made and send one along.

Captain Bound must have been batting in another league. Top cover for Dugout Doug, perhaps.

The mail from Sydney arrives occasionally. In fact, the last letter was rather ominous, in light of your feelings. The letter head was: Judge's Chambers, Supreme Court, Sydney. Margaret had borrowed some of her Dad's stationery. I guess I told you he's a Chief Justice. Once more I urge you not to take the Sydney girls too seriously, although I appreciate and enjoy your opinions and observations— and concur. I think you have both secured a spot in the pundit's niche.

The home front seems not to be outdone by the military for zone numbers. The mail had seemed to be getting through, but N.H.15 it shall be. While I put that on the outside, best wishes and health to you both. Regards to all.

Love,

Stuff

On August 15 the Carpenter division joined two other divisions from the Swashbucklers and left the relative comfort of the Russell Islands. The pilots and their Corsairs moved forward from Advance Base Knucklehead on Banika to the airfield at Munda Point where members of the Swashbucklers took up permanent station for the balance of August.[3] Two hours after their arrival the pilots were back in the air providing protection over Munda and the northwest sector of the island of New Georgia while landing craft carried the 25th U.S. Army Division to their initial amphibious landing on Vella Lavella to the north.[4]

A bomber escort mission followed for the division on their second day at Munda.[5] After the mission Carl penned his next letter from New

Airfield complex at Munda Point after the Seabees' work was completed. (National Archives.)

First Corsair arrives at Munda Point on August 15, 1943, to take up forward combat station on New Georgia Island in the Central Solomons. (National Archives.)

Georgia on "air mail" stationery that had been left behind by the Japanese when the facility at Munda Point was captured by the Allies.

Received September 9, 1943

August 16, 1943

Dear Mom and Dad,

Something new and different in Marine Corps stationery! I was tempted to try writing as the sheet was intended to be used, but you can readily see the chore of writing as well as of reading such an attempt. Wonder what the transit time is for Jap air-mail. Apparently, there is such a thing.

Early summer continues waxing hotter. The laundry will attest to that fact. Two changes of clothes a day would be appropriate if they were accessible. We do the next best thing and sit around in shorts. That's fairly comfortable. When we don full-length flight suits, the heat really begins to bear down. For the flight suit is only the beginning. Shoulder holster, life-jacket, gloves and parachute add some more to the discomfort. On the deck, we sweat and sputter, only to shake and shiver on high patrols. You might say we're pretty hard to satisfy, but I felt plenty uncomfortable from the cold yesterday. Winter flight gear would have been welcome! There doesn't seem to be much change in temperature inside the cockpit until close to 14,000 feet. Then the change seems rather marked. When you sit at twice that altitude for two hours as we did yesterday, you really know it's cold outside.

We're just back from a good hour trip by carry-all around the island. Safety belts weren't, but should have been, installed for the trip. I doubt whether we traveled more than eight miles horizontally, but vertically from rut to bump and back, we must have trebled that. Chalkie remarked that he'd "never seen country that looked so much alike." Grammatically, it didn't make much sense, but it was close to the truth. Some of us will certainly dream about coconut trees tonight or else the myriads of fallen coconuts which lie in various stages of germination on the ground. There's a tremendous lack of inspiration about coconut groves. In fact, they're monotonous as anything, but a barren desert could be. But for all that, they are treacherous! Just let yourself be lulled into complacency by the monotony and blooie!—down crashes a coconut from forty feet above, beside, before or behind or, unhappy day, on top of poor Dilbert! If it isn't a coconut, it's a frond—they are shed continually and fall without warning, ten feet of rattling leaves with a heavy butt-end. Woe unto him who seeks shade or back brace beneath the coconut palm!

We had a good opportunity to test our instinctive reaction to gunfire the other day walking down the side of the landing strip. One of the .50 caliber batteries was test-firing, it so happened over our heads from behind. At first we thought, someone had made a landing approach without turning off his gun switches and had pulled the trigger unintentionally—that happens occasionally. With one accord, we threw ourselves flat on the deck—the coral scratched my legs a bit. I began to revile myself for not having dived over the twenty foot embankment to my left. I was just about to make a dash for it, when the firing stopped. That probably saved me some broken bones, well some deep bruises at any rate. I thought the reactions on the whole were pretty good. So were the vituperations!

The fellows have just shoved off for noon chow. So I'd better close here and head for the mess hall myself, and then the barber. This ought to give you a pretty good indication of where and how things are going.

I am glad you folks and Ledge's family were able to get together, especially with Anne starting at Poughkeepsie this fall. I read an account which she wrote of the launching of the S.S. Emma Willard for which she was sponsor. Judging from that, I'd say she was very able.

The very best to all of you. Since I can't be there to enjoy the fresh vegetables with you, I'll try and be a little "corny" on the side:

If increased girth
With the market dearth
Suggests a birth

I chuckle with mirth
At your plot of earth.

Love,
Stuff

After acknowledging his family's get together with the family of fellow Swashbuckler Ledge Hazelwood and news that Ledge's sister, Anne, would be joining Carl's sister, Lora, at Vassar in the fall, Carl closes his letter from Munda Point with a short parting limerick about the family's victory garden.[6] He then returned to the realities on New Georgia that were not mentioned in his letter.

"Munda was an inhospitable place—hot, humid, barren from shelling, and for a time, smelled of the aftermath of battle from the Marine assault [to take the airfield]."[7] The conditions that the Swashbucklers encountered on the ground when they arrived were appalling. The living conditions there were the worst that the squadron had experienced during their time in the South Pacific.[8] Decaying bodies of enemy soldiers lay scattered among the debris, conditions were unsanitary, and the pilots had to scrounge for everything, including a place to sleep.[9] In addition, the Japanese soldiers who remained on the island in the adjacent jungle shelled the airstrip with artillery in daylight hours, and enemy bombing raids disrupted the field during the night.[10]

These conditions endured by the pilots during their time at Munda were shared by Carl with his family, but they were later described by Bruce Gamble:

> In some ways, the push through the New Georgia jungle had been even more vicious than that on Guadalcanal. The Japanese had defended it fiercely from reinforced coconut-log pill-boxes dug in like so many chiggers,' and the surrounding vegetation had been blasted by many tons of bombs and artillery. Unlike the Russells' picturesque scenes, Munda offered only ugly devastation— ground-up earth, denuded trees, unburied enemy bodies. And the island was not secure. Although a perimeter of ground Marines defended the airfield, Japanese troops still occupied the high

ground and kept the strip under sporadic artillery fire. Dubbed "Pistol Pete" and "Millimeter Mike," the guns lobbed shells onto the strip and camp area during the day. Washing Machine Charlie took over by night.[11]

After two days and two nights at Munda Point, Carl and most of the other Swashbucklers flying the initial missions from the airstrip on New Georgia returned to Banika, replaced by three other divisions from the squadron. Four days later, however, the Carpenter division returned to the airfield, and Munda became the division's base of operations for the remaining days of August.[12] The next letter home was written after Carl and his division returned to Munda Point, but the descriptions of his visit to the "secluded island," the fishing, and the encounter with the native population recount the off-time during his four days back in the Russell Islands.

Received September 18, 1943

Aug. 24

Dear Mom and Dad,

Last day off we spent visiting the natives on their own secluded island, on the way to and from which we had a couple of elegant deep-sea fishing rigs trolling feather jigs over the stern. Our visit was somewhat of a revelation as it was a surprise to me.

Our start was rather inauspicious. We had planned to use the clinker-built dingy and outboard motor. The latter, however, failed us miserably. It would function perfectly for about thirty seconds and then would conk completely, the carburetor dry as dust. Consequently, we spent a good many minutes making 360-degree turns, sweating over the starter rope, and reviling our temperamental Evinrude. Eventually, we returned to the dock—that's what they call the vicinity of shoreline where you run the bow up on sharp coral and disembark. There, after some masterful diplomacy on the part of Lts. Bernard and Bier, we acquired a Navy whaleboat with diesel engine for the rest of the day.

Trolling was unsuccessful on the outbound trip. We followed the gulls, diving over schools of large fish that were breaking water, without success. The fish would disappear as we approached, only to reappear some half-mile in the direction we had just departed. We didn't mind a great deal; it was enough to be basking in the sun, rolling over the blue swells and surveying the many coconut-palm-studded islands and those with heavy jungle growth. This was the epitome of peace and relaxation.

We drew close to the native island and up the channel between it and the neighboring "planteur's" island. On the one hand were the thatched roofs of boat-houses and several warehouses nestled under an expansive, overhanging tree. Its branches stretched across the narrow, white-sandy beach and overspread the rippling water. To the left, on the other hand, midst the coconut grove were numerous red-tin-roofed houses with yellow and white wooden sides. They were storehouses and work sheds for the planteur himself. There was one small white house raised on stilts and overhanging the water. That, we were told, was the plantation sick-bay. All the buildings were vacant and looked in bad state of repair. The Japs had rummaged through most of them, and their planes and ours had strafed them with airplane machine-gun fire.

Finally, we put ashore—had to wade over the coral for the last twenty feet. There were two native men to greet us. Their English was coherent enough. They were about to go diving for "cats-eyes." We were all set to go along when the earlier divers appeared returning, and our hosts decided not to set out. Instead, we wound our way through heavy jungle growth to Lancelot's (the more lugubrious of the two) dwelling. He had moved from the village, when war came, to this wave undercut coral cliff. It offered him protection from bombs and falling shrapnel from anti-aircraft guns. He had built the four sides of thatch, finely-woven; coral formed the roof. The door was a cloth flap through which we did not pass. I heard, but did not see, his wife who remained inside. There were two other males sitting outside the abode, both quite silent, one with metal-rimmed glasses, youngish, the other a granddad with graying hair. The former was dressed in skivie shirt and khaki shorts; the latter in loin-cloth. Both were smoking English-made clay pipes. The ground before the dwelling was swept clean. We sat on a bench between trees to talk. Lancelot did not once put down his small can of powdered lime, into which he dipped a wooden paddle that was his spoon. The lime, he explained, was essential to a good beetle-nut chew; the green spice-leaf he held was equally important. Constantly, we found, the natives chew away on the beetle nut. It discolors their teeth and lips in weird oranges and browns. Lancelot's youngest stole his way out of the flap door and eyed us mysteriously. He was a pathetic sight. His face was covered with tropical ulcers, "yows" so-called, which are hideous even in memory. His upper lip was practically non-existent.

We re-embarked and putted down the channel to the village. A boatload of the returning divers hitched a ride behind us. I expected their dugout to capsize, but it never seemed to waver. Their canoes are a beautiful piece of construction. Out of one log, of course, but fashioned with white man's tools—plane and chisel. They have a rounded V cross-section, not much free-board and very narrow. Actually, they are practically a racing shell. Their sides are not more that a quarter of an inch thick and the canoes are perfectly balanced.

The village was the biggest surprise of all. The paths were straight and covered with white sand, freshly swept each day. They were lined with coral stones outside of which pink lilies were planted in a solid row. The dirt around them was swept each day, too. The village itself was a square, or rather a rectangle, approximately eight houses to a side and three on one end. There was a green in the center and white sand before the houses. The whole place was immaculate. Each house had wooden sides and a front porch. The doors were wooden-paneled and had latches. On one porch was a bamboo lounging chair, obviously of foreign construction. Tacked to the front of one house were two phonetic charts. I didn't go in the church. One family seemed to be complete on our arrival, the rest were here and there. The father was young—looking for his half-dozen children. The youngest was being nursed on the one operating dug of his wife while we were there (the other one seemed to be dried up). I fell in love with two others of his children, ages about seven and eight I judge. One was a tow-head, cute as you'll hope to find. The hair was probably dyed, as it seems to be a favorite custom here. The other's skin was also rather light. Both of them looked so bright and acted so unaffected and friendly that my heart was won at once. They wrote or printed their names, and when I started to explain that my mother lived far away, Lagono replied, "In the United States!" I was trying to find seeds of the pink lily along the path; all the seeds were still green. I explained to them what I wanted. They surveyed for a moment, conversed rapidly in their own tongue and then replied that I could not plant the seeds. I must wait until the weather was more hot (when they would be ripe). Instead, I must dig up the bulb, which they proceeded to do and plant it, which they demonstrated. (I have the bulbs which I may try to send if they appear not to dry up or rot.) I gave them each a stick of gum and some of the others gave them trinkets. All the women were smoking pipes. The men seemed to prefer cigarettes. Everyone, except the babies, wore skirts.

I asked Peter, the father, where they went when the shrapnel started falling, making appropriate gestures to get my point across. His answer was complete and convincing: "Foxhole!" And he pointed to a well-constructed, convenient retreat.

We had taken along numerous trinkets to trade. These had little attraction, however, for the most part. Either the natives already had earrings and baubles, or they were aware of their low value, or there were other things they wanted more. Gaudy cloth is highly desirable to them, especially red. They asked for bread and biscuits and meat. Actually, we didn't give these particular natives enough credit for their degree of intelligence and civilization. I am quite sure we will not bump into as high or higher intelligence again.

On the way home, Bernie had his line over the stern. He hooked one as we were hitting full speed, and for a few minutes, it gave him quite a tussle. As the hooked fish approached the boat, I could see the dark shadow of a shark following it up. A few seconds more and we'd have had no barracuda steaks for dinner next evening. Not only did a shark follow the catch up, but also a whole school, apparently of fellow barracuda. The fish was about two feet long, very sleek and similar to a mackerel in appearance. The steaks were delicious.

We have a very strenuous week starting tomorrow, one which will undoubtedly be devoid of the amenities of life, so if I am unable to find time to write or the proper materials, you will understand that it is because of heavy schedule and primitive conditions.

Best wishes to both of you. This has been a rather impersonal letter, I fear, but I have been thinking of you nevertheless. Best to all.
Love,
Stuff

No combat missions are described in the letter written on August 24, but before it was posted, two more sorties were flown by the Carpenter division—the first was flown from Banika and the second from Munda Point, the airfield Carl described for his parents as "primitive" and "devoid of the amenities of life." The first mission was a strafing attack against Rekata Bay on Santa Isabel east of New Georgia from the Knucklehead base at Banika.[13] Two days later from Munda, Carl and the division were assigned to escort a flight of B-24 Liberator heavy bombers making a strike against Kahili on Bougainville.

Engine trouble encountered by several aircraft, including Carl's, during the strike against Bougainville forced an early return of the Corsairs to New Georgia.[14] Back at Munda Point, the division was off for two days while the F4U-1 engines were being repaired and readied for a return to combat.[15] The battle for the central islands in the Solomons was at its peak during the final days in August of 1943, and on August 25 Carl and the division provided cover for twenty-four torpedo bombers and dive-bombers engaged in strikes against enemy targets at Ringi Cove on Kolombangara.[16] In his second mission of the day, Carl was back at high altitude as part of a three-hour patrol to provide protective cover over the airfield at Munda.[17] The mission sorties on the next two days were directed against Japanese positions on Vella Lavella to support the Allied invasion force that had landed on the island ten days earlier, and on the twenty-eighth of August the mission was to provide task force cover for naval vessels moving forward to reinforce and resupply the invasion.[18]

Above: Corsair in a rudimentary coral rock revetment in the "inhospitable" surroundings of the airfield at Munda Point. For the pilots, Munda was "devoid of the amenities of life." (Courtesy of Jim Laurier and Jack Fellows.)

Left: Carl in front of Corsair. (Dunbar family collection.)

In addition to the escort duties and support for the ground forces in the central islands, interdiction raids became a more frequent part of the Swashbucklers' repertoire, and strafing raids against enemy airfields and interisland barge traffic regularly brought the enemy under the Corsairs' guns.[19] On August 29, Carpenter took his division aloft on a mission over the coast of Kolombangara to find and strafe several suspected coastal installations. Southwest of the island in the waters of the Blackett Strait approximately ten miles east of where the PT-109 had been sunk earlier in the month, the Swashbucklers located and destroyed a Japanese junk and an enemy resupply barge, sinkings that were later confirmed by an Allied coast-watcher.[20]

The mission on August 29 was interpreted in a painting by artist Jim Laurier in 2004, and with the reproduction of his work in the official publication of the Naval Aviation Museum Foundation, Laurier described what he had captured on canvass.

> On the morning of 29 August 1943, First Lieutenant Carl Dunbar, USMC, of VMF-214 took off from Munda in an F4U-1 Corsair, BuNo 02372, and flew toward Japanese resupply targets at Kolombangara. Friendly coastwatchers had indicated the presence of some Japanese barges and surface vessels in Ringi Cove. As part of a flight of four Corsairs, Dunbar flew on Vince Carpenter's wing that clear day and, as they approached Kolombangara, they could see some barges in and around Ringi Cove. These vessels had been busy resupplying Japanese-held Vila Airfield during the night and had not left the area by daybreak, leaving themselves exposed to air attack. As the Corsairs swept in low for a firing pass, antiaircraft positions opened up on them, but the aircraft suffered little damage as their speed made them difficult targets for Japanese gunners. Dunbar's and Carpenter's marksmanship proved accurate, sinking a barge and a junk on the first strafing run.[21]

Two final missions on August 30 concluded Carl's second combat tour, and both—a dawn patrol and a patrol over L.C.S. landing craft—were to provide protective cover for the Allied invasion force approaching Barakoma Harbor on the island of Vella Lavella.[22]

The following morning Carl piloted his Corsair from Munda Point back to Advance Base Knucklehead in the Russell Islands.[23] On September 1 the surviving members of VMF-214's first two combat tours gathered for photographs with their aircraft.[24] At the day's end the Swashbucklers renewed their evening ritual with a party that lasted well into the night and featured the last reported performance by the quartet.[25]

The next day the squadron pilots boarded DC-3 transports and departed Banika for Guadalcanal. On the following day the Swashbucklers flew on to Espiritu Santo and began their second scheduled assignment for rest and recuperation.[26]

Bruce Gamble described the last days on Munda Point in his historical account of the squadron. His account is similar to the surviving memories of other Swashbucklers who flew from the New Georgia airfield in August of 1943:

The Swashbucklers soldiered on through the last days of August, participants in a giant aerial slugfest between two weary heavyweights. With New Georgia as center ring, Japan and the Allies stood toe to toe, trading blows. The Allied hammer fell during daylight as they relentlessly pounded Bougainville's airfields with bomber strikes. The Japanese came after dark, hitting Munda, the Russells, and Guadalcanal almost nightly with sleep-depriving raids. The enemy bombers did not have to come all the way to the Allied bases or release their munitions to cause disruption; it was enough to tickle the radar warning systems and set off air-raid sirens. Many a night the Swashbucklers were rousted from their cots and into sweltering dugouts only to learn after an hour or so that the alarm had been false. There is no way to tell for certain if the alarms were real until the bombs fell, which was often enough to make the men heed every warning.

Sorely did they miss sleep. The schedule had them flying from before dawn until after dark, and between flights they passed the time among the rot, filth, and stench of Munda's devastated landscape. It was Guadalcanal all over again, only worse. In addition to horrid living conditions and sleepless nights, combat tension ran high. There was a good chance they would encounter tenacious enemy pilots on practically every flight, and now there were more strafing missions, each fraught with the particular risks.[27]

After nights spent in muddy foxholes harassed by Japanese artillery and suffering fever and chills from malaria, Tom Tomlinson recalled years later that the "brief life on Munda left its own scars."[28] Henry Miller's diary also recorded the confused conditions during the pilots' first days at Munda Point, and he, too, remembered the muddy foxholes and the decaying bodies of enemy soldiers.[29]

In his next letter from Espiritu Santo on September 7, Carl recalled the conditions encountered during the final days and difficult times at

Swashbuckler pilots in front of a Corsair at Advance Base Knucklehead in the Russell Islands on the final day (September 1, 1943) of the second tour. A week later, the planes were taken over by the replacement pilots commanded by Major Boyington. *Front row, left to right*: Taylor, Tomlinson, Deetz, Hunter, Curran, O'Dell. *Second row*: Hernan, Hazelwood, Moak, Bernard, Williams, Jensen, Dunbar. *Third row*: Cavanaugh, Synar, Hatch, Miller, Burnett, Bookman, Eisele, Carpenter. *Rear row*: Petit, McCall, Hollmeyer, Sigel, Scarborough, Knipping, Fidler, Rankin. (Dunbar family collection.)

Munda. The graphic details are not present in the letter to his family, but the tenor of his words mirror the conditions that were described by Gamble, Tomlinson, and Miller, who remembered the days and nights on New Georgia as a time of fatigue, erratic sleep, and filled with the intensity of combat. From these conditions at Munda Point and from the airfield on Banika, Carl's logbook entries for the Swashbuckler's second combat tour record a total of 82 hours of flight time and 28 combat missions in the Vought F4U-1 Corsair.[30] At the end of their time on New Georgia and with their second tour complete, the pilots all looked forward to much needed rest.

Received September 20, 1943

Sept. 7

Dear Mom and Dad,

I shall seek to clear away the cobwebs from my brain long enough to let you know we are well and safe and resting, though I can scarcely hope to say more. Fatigue and inertia dull my imagination as well as my industry! The past few days I have taken to sleeping during the day, which as you know is quite a novelty for me. It was always Tom who took the naps. Even without rain, which for two days has fallen almost steadily, I shouldn't have found energy for much of any exercise. For the first time in a long time I'm content just to lie down and trust that my body is recuperating.

The week I anticipated in my last letter was strenuous, not so much from aerial combat, which was sadly missing as from long hours of duty, constant alert and somewhat erratic sleep. Artillery fire at your feet isn't conducive to sweet dreams. We were up and active long before dawn, and seldom did we return to camp until well after dark. We had no electric lights, and for the greater part of our stay, no showers. We dressed and undressed in the dark, and out of expediency and sheer fatigue, usually went direct from dinner to bed. The rain fell heavily, if intermittently, day and night, leaving roads and camp area a veritable sea of mud. Happily, there were practically no mosquitoes. Only innumerable, swarming, pestiferous flies during the daylight hours.

The cobwebs I was brushing away are left over from last night's revelry with its boisterousness and frequent allusions to days at Jacksonville and San Diego. At last, Bill and Harry and Hazel and Bung were together again. This was not the first night, but it was the first one when we had felt up to more than a short snort.

Along with your clipping from the Register came a veritable flood of clippings to other members of the squadron. There was no end to our merriment. The press is obviously Hollywood crazy, but I guess the American people have to have the same sort of thing shoveled at them off as well as on the screen. My part in the particular engagement was far from glamorous—Zeroes piled in on us from high above (I watched them come), and we were right on the water. My wingtips practically fanned the spume in the heat of the invasion action. And over either shoulder, I could see lines of bullet splashes on the ocean, chasing me but far behind. Only two bullets found their way to my wings. Unfortunately, I didn't have time or opportunity to return the fire. If we ever get a break, and I guess we will one of these days, I won't have to keep repeating that worn-out phrase "I didn't get a shot at 'em!" We did have some pretty good hunting on the strafing hops. That's the fighter pilot's apple-pie-a-la-mode!

Forgive me if I write so briefly now. I shall be having more time and lots of sunshine to tell you more—and I'll feel more garrulous.

Every best wish to both of you. Keep your health!

Love,

Stuff

A copy of the news clipping referred to in Carl's correspondence was among the items that were kept by his mother with the letters and other documents from his journey to the South Pacific. The item appeared in the *New Haven Register*, and it was filed by combat correspondent Staff Sergeant Pen T. Johnson from a location "somewhere in the South Pacific."

In his article, Staff Sergeant Johnson reports that First Lieutenant Carl O. Dunbar's "recent six weeks of aerial combat duty in the South Pacific had few dull moments." Johnson wrote:

As part of a Marine fighter squadron, he accompanied Marine dive bombers while they dropped thousands of pounds of high explosive bombs on strategic Jap-held territory. His squadron played an important role in the softening up process prior to taking Munda Field, a Japanese air base on the northern tip of New Georgia Island in the Solomon group. He was with his squadron when it landed on Munda Field a few weeks after it had fallen into Allied hands. From Munda Field, Dunbar and his fighter squadron formed a fighter cover over American forces landing troops and supplies in a successful offensive against Vella Lavella north of New Georgia Island.[31]

Received September 30, 1943

Sept. 18

Dear Mom and Dad,

The number of letters I haven't written in the past ten days should give you a fairly good idea of how much I am not doing. In the first place, as I wrote you, I stood in need of a rest. And rest is just what I've been getting—volleyball in the morning, followed by a refreshing swim, lunch and siesta. Possibly some more sun later in the afternoon, an errand or a social visit. Finally, the movies after dinner and to bed.

In the second place, there has been cause for much rejoicing as a two-year old triumvirate had its first reunion. I'm speaking, of course, of Jim and Bill and myself. Bill was here (courting the velvet green dove and snatching at blue fish) when we arrived and Jim was not far behind. Aside from the good cheer of the old friendship renewed, there were two bottles of Johnny Walker Black Label which I have been carrying all the way from San Diego. I took them into the front lines with me. At last, they have justified my patience. Bill and Harry and I spent an evening aboard with Jim in positive luxury. Jim and some of his squadron mates then paid us a visit. Rain spattered on the roof the afternoon long, while inside beer spattered on the deck. It stopped raining about four, but unfortunately no one was then ready to be poured into bed. We should have a photo or two forthcoming which I will forward at the earliest development. It seemed scarcely possible when Bill mentioned the fact that, on this day, it was two years ago when we first clasped hands and faced the challenge of Naval Aviation. In his wildest flight of imagination, none of us then expected to meet again in this remote corner of the world. The United States was not even at war then!

In the vein of reunions, I am eagerly awaiting joining hands with Arthur Paton. I may have a chance to see him day after tomorrow.

I think you might enjoy the humorous little book which I just started reading. It's called "Love at First Flight." One of the co-authors is an Eli classmate of mine, Chuck Spalding. He recounts the trials of flight training with keen regard for all the oddities and colorful incidents we all remember well. You will notice the dedication is to Deuce Mead.

Congratulations on the V-garden award! I know now you must have spent an immense amount of time and effort creating the plot. You know it's not impossible, I may get to taste the fruits of your labor if they can last through the winter. Tell me, was the Mayor as entertaining as ever about ensuring his next reelection? I heard him stump at the Hi-S banquet in tones that wreaked of the New Haven Democratic Party—and you know what that means! I am certain that the award was justified in your case, if nowhere else. But when I saw three professors on the list, I began to wonder if the Mayor wasn't up to his familiar tricks.

I hate to be so brief, but I am tired and sleepy and face the prospect of getting up in the middle of the night. So I shall close here. Don't be alarmed if you don't hear from me for a few days. I shall be busy as a beaver. The name Maxwell is not to be trifled with!

My best wishes to you and to Sis.

Love,

Stuff

The letter on September 18 was written at Turtle Bay, and it is the last from the journey that began in December of 1941 at Squantum Naval Air Station. The day after the letter was mailed, the Swashbucklers moved on to Sydney for a week of rest and relaxation. The tension and fatigue of the final weeks in the central islands of the Solomon archipelago are not talked about in the letter, and its content speaks of the opportunity for rest, the mayor's award for the family's victory garden, and Carl's reunion with Bill Stuhlman.

References to Bill appear frequently in Carl's correspondence. The two young airmen had begun the journey together, but their paths parted after the primary flight training at NAS Jacksonville was complete. Stuhlman remained in the Navy when Carl was commissioned with the intertwined globe and anchor of the U.S. Marine Corps. Bill was assigned initially to PBY flying boats when Carl's assignment was to fighters.[32] Later Bill progressed to dive-bombers and finally to torpedo-bombers in the duty assignment that brought him to the South Pacific as part of the Allied offensive.[33]

In Carl's final letter home, he tells of the reunion with Bill Stuhlman on Espiritu Santo more than a year after their separation in Jacksonville. They had reunited briefly in San Diego before their deployment to the Pacific. Espiritu Santo was a second reunion of two friends who had begun their odyssey together in September of 1941 as cadets in the Naval Reserves, reuniting once again far from where it began.

By the time the Swashbucklers of VMF-214 concluded their second trip to Australia, the Allied invasion force on Vella Lavella was driving the last of the enemy troops from the island.[34] On New Georgia, the remaining Japanese resistance had been eliminated, and the Navy Seabees had flattened the surrounding mountainside and expanded the airfield at Munda Point to accommodate B-25 Mitchell bombers.[35] What had been little more than a devastated landscape of mud and filth a month earlier was now a fully operational forward airfield.

With the central islands group in Allied hands, the backbone of the Japanese defensive line had been broken.[36] The enemy airfields and facilities on Bougainville were now within the range of fighter-escorted bombers, and the attention of the bombers began to focus on the well-fortified enemy installations at Kahili on Bougainville.[37]

8

Bougainville and Home

The transports loaded with men and fighting gear moved into positions off-shore, with warships nearby for protection. From our height, they looked like miniatures. I could see boats making their way from ship to shore and back again, leaving a path of white foam behind them. It was a real sight.

Carl O. Dunbar Jr., January 23, 1944

The Swashbuckler pilots were deployed to the South Pacific to serve three combat tours.[1] They had expected to complete their final tour as a unit and return home together.[2] In an unusual administrative move, however, the squadron designation was reassigned to another group of Marine Corps replacement pilots.[3] Shortly after the original pilots arrived on Espiritu Santo for rest and recuperation at the end of their second tour, the Corsairs of VMF-214 were being flown by others.

Under the new squadron commander, Major Gregory "Pappy" Boyington, VMF-214 was renamed the "Black Sheep" squadron.[4] When the Swashbucklers returned from Australia in September of 1943, squadron member Henry Miller recorded in his diary that "the rape of 214 [was] well under way, with our number gone."[5] The returning Swashbucklers were broken up as a unit when they began their third tour, and the individual pilots were reassigned to four different squadrons.[6]

If there were more letters from Carl to his family during his third tour in the Pacific, and presumably there were, the letters did not survive. The logbook continued to record the flight time and the missions of his third tour, however, and copies of the orders that reassigned him to his new combat squadron survived as well.

There are also random accounts from some of his fellow pilots about Carl's activities following the return from Sydney, and there are copies of newspaper articles that relate a few firsthand accounts of the events during his final tour. These are the only documents that remain to describe the conclusion of Carl's journey to war.

* * *

The Swashbucklers of VMF-214 left Sydney on September 21 to begin their return to combat, arriving back on Espiritu Santo at the end of the month. Vince Carpenter, O. K. Williams, Tom Tomlinson, and five other squadron pilots were assigned to VMF-215.[7] Orders that were kept with his letters show that Carl was transferred to VMF-211 when he returned to Turtle Bay, and he was joined by Henry Miller and three other Swashbucklers in the new assignment.

VMF-211 had been a fully operational squadron at the onset of hostilities in the Pacific, and its pilots were stationed at both Ewa Air Station and Wake Island.[8] Within two weeks of the attack on Pearl Harbor, however, the squadron had lost all of its aircraft and many of its pilots to the Japanese military juggernaut.[9] The squadron had been slowly rebuilt at Ewa in the early months of 1942, and in May the rebuilt squadron had deployed in F4F Wildcats to a defensive position on the Palmyra Atoll between Hawaii and American Samoa. In the fall of 1943, after making a transition from Wildcats to Corsairs, VMF-211 was reassigned to Espiritu Santo and began preparations to join the fight as the Allied offensive pushed into the northern Solomon Islands.[10]

Carl and the other Swashbucklers were initially tasked to train VMF-211's new pilots in the characteristics of the Corsair.[11] The orientation on Espiritu Santo continued for the first three weeks of October. While VMF-211 prepared at Turtle Bay, Vella Lavella and its airfield at Barakoma fell to the Allies, and Vella Lavella became the last "stepping-stone" toward Bougainville.[12]

On October 22 Carl's logbook records that he returned to Advance Base Knucklehead on Banika where VMF-211 took up station as part of the planned Allied invasion of Bougainville in an operation code-named "Cherryblossom."[13] On October 25 the first mission of Carl's flight group was to provide fighter escort for a DC-3 military transport ferrying the ground crew for a Marine dive-bomber squadron forward to Segi on the northern coast of New Georgia where they, too, were to join the coordinated Allied effort to neutralize Bougainville.[14]

The island of Bougainville was now all that stood between the Allied forces and the main operational base for the Japanese in the South Pacific theater located on New Britain. It was "the final rung in the strategic ladder up which Admiral Halsey's forces had been climbing to neutralize Rabaul."[15]

Bougainville, the largest and northern-most island in the Solomon archipelago, was protected by thirty-five thousand enemy troops, and it was defended by six airfields—four at Kahili on the southern coast of the island and two more on the northern coast at Buka and Bonis.[16] The inland portions of the island featured dense jungle vegetation and "jungle-clad mountain peaks, two of which were active volcanoes."[17] The coastlines along either side of the fiddle-shaped, 150-mile long island consisted of little more than narrow beaches abutting the dense and uninhabited jungle.[18] To the south and southeast, satellite military facilities on Shortland Island, Choiseul, and the Treasury Islands provided additional defenses to protect the installations on the big island.[19]

As Admiral Halsey's command prepared for the invasion of Bougainville, three diversionary plans were executed on October 27 to preoccupy and confuse the enemy forces about the primary objective of the Allied command. A battalion of the 2nd Marines landed on the northern tip of Choiseul Island southeast of Bougainville for an extended raiding operation before withdrawing, and other American forces made a feint toward Shortland Island off the south coast of Bougainville.[20] The Eighth New Zealand Division landed on the Treasury Islands south of Shortland Island to open an airstrip intended to support the landings planned for November 1.[21]

In his next mission on October 28, Carl moved forward to the airfield at Barakoma on Vella Lavella. From there his fighter group provided air cover for portions of these diversionary operations that preceded the invasion of Bougainville.[22]

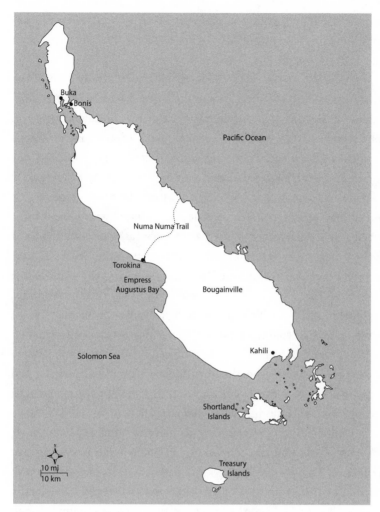

Map 5. Bougainville.

Three days after the diversionary operations were launched, the first wave of the invasion force led by the 3rd Marine Division hit the beaches of Empress Augusta Bay at Cape Torokina on the southwest coast of Bougainville.[23] The Japanese responded to the invasion force with daylight air raids, but their efforts were held at bay by dusk-to-dawn relays of American fighters from airfields in the Central Solomons.[24] The flight sortie for Carl and his squadron on November 1 was to participate as a part of the high-altitude air cover for the Cherryblossom invasion.[25]

Among the others contributing the protective umbrella were the pilots of VMF-215, including Vince Carpenter, O. K. Williams, and Tom Tomlinson.[26]

The combined air cover over Cape Torokina successfully limited the effects of the Japanese air attacks, and the enemy's efforts failed to seriously damage the Allied landing operations.[27] After two days of fighting, the American beachhead at Empress Augusta Bay was secured.[28] Within weeks of the initial invasion, the Seabees had carved three airstrips out of the jungle vegetation to enhance the air defenses for the beachhead.[29]

In addition to being on station over Bougainville on November 1 for the initial landing, Carl and his division were back again a week later as part of the aerial protection over a resupply task force for the invasion.[30] In a newspaper interview after his return to the United States, Carl remembered the scene over Bougainville during these missions, and he described what he had witnessed from twenty thousand feet during Operation Cherryblossom. "It was the most spectacular thing I have ever seen," Carl told the reporter. "The transports loaded with men and fighting gear moved into positions off-shore, with warships nearby for protection. From our height, they looked like miniatures. I could see boats making their way from ship to shore and back again, leaving a path of white foam behind them. It was a real sight."[31]

On November 13, after a refueling stop at the improved complex at Munda Point, Carl was again on station over Bougainville providing task force cover for Navy resupply ships. His logbook entry records the task force escort as the last mission of his third tour, and it is followed by the entry for his return flight to the Russell Islands after a refueling stop in the central islands.[32] When the tour had concluded, twenty-one more hours of flight time had been entered into his logbook during the month of November of 1943.[33]

In all, Lieutenant Carl Dunbar flew eighty-two missions and accumulated 235.3 hours of flight time before his three tours of combat in the Solomon Islands ended. His missions included bomber escorts, dawn patrols, high-altitude missions covering ground forces, Dumbo escorts and searches for missing comrades, scrambles to intercept inbound Japanese bombers and fighters, task force escorts for surface ships moving men and supplies up the Solomon chain, and repeated low-level strafing missions against the enemy[34]—in Carl's words, "the fighter pilot's apple-pie-a-la-mode."[35]

*   *   *

Twenty-seven pilots made up the initial roster of Marine Fighting Squadron VMF-214. They began their individual journeys as ordinary citizens after the bombing of Pearl Harbor, they came together at the Marine Air Station at Ewa from all parts of the country, and together they traveled into the South Pacific to assume their roles in the Battle of the Solomon Islands as a cohesive fighting unit. Of the original group, however, only twenty-one of the pilots made the return trip to the United States, and Carl was one of the fortunate ones.

Bill Steed was lost on the third day of the Squadron's first tour.[36] During the second tour, Bill Pace was the victim of engine failure while trying to return to the airfield on Banika.[37] Bill Blakeslee, flying as a member of Carl's division, was shot down during the photo reconnaissance mission over Shortland Island.[38] And Chuck Lanphier was lost three days before the end of the second tour during a strafing mission against the enemy airfield at Kahili on Bougainville.[39] During the third tour after the Swashbucklers had been broken up as a unit, Jack Petit was lost on a strafing mission against enemy installations on Bougainville.[40] Ledge Hazelwood was lost in a similar attack over the Numa Numa Trail east of Torokina on Bougainville.[41]

"Overlooked by most historians are these gallant, young flyers who fought to preserve the Marine's fragile toehold in the South Pacific during the early months of World War II," wrote David Ekstrand of the Swashbucklers in December of 1989 for the *Marine Corps Gazette*.[42] When they began their training at places like NAS Miami and Corpus Christi, "air combat was still relatively new, much more of an art than a science."[43]

When they came together at Ewa under the command of Major Britt as Marine Fighting Squadron VMF-214, the new pilots were drilled in aerial gunnery and practiced against targets floating on the surface of the ocean.[44] In less than seven months and by the time they had completed their second tour together, the young pilots had become battle-hardened veterans, and they helped to pioneer "important steps . . .

toward a better system of air support. One of the most important, and one for which 214 and other Corsair squadrons could take credit, was proving the effectiveness of the F4U as a gun platform. Its length gave it an extraordinary amount of longitudinal stability, thus enhancing accuracy. It proved its worth in both the air-to-air role and the air-to-ground mode. . . . Finally, Marine fighter pilots played a key role in the all-important battle for air superiority."[45]

*   *   *

On November 24, 1943, ten days after concluding his third tour in combat, Lieutenant Carl Dunbar was transferred from VMF-211 to VMF-123. Four days after his transfer, the members of VMF-123 boarded the troop ship USS *Wharton* and departed the New Hebrides bound for San Francisco; the *Wharton* arrived there on December 17, 1943, without incident. It was two years to the day since Carl had left New Haven to begin his journey to war.

Earlier on the day that the *Wharton* made port in San Francisco, the new Marine Corps pilots of VMF-214 and a squadron of Navy Corsair pilots, the Jolly Rogers of VF-17 commanded by Tom Blackburn, led the first Bougainville-assisted fighter strike against the Japanese fortress at Rabaul in the Bismarck Archipelago.[46] By Christmas of 1943, Bougainville became the final island in the Solomons to be secured under the control of the Allies.[47] The initial sorties from the new airfields at Cape Torokina were followed by a continuous series of fighter-escorted bomber strikes against Rabaul that lasted through the rest of December and on into January of 1944.[48] As the New Year began, Bougainville became the last "hop" in Admiral Halsey's island-hopping campaign to neutralize and isolate the remaining Japanese fortress in the South Pacific.[49]

After spending Christmas and an extended leave at home in New Haven, Carl received his commission as a captain in the U.S. Marine Corps on the last day of January in 1944, a month and a day before his twenty-fourth birthday.[50] Along with fellow Swashbuckler Harry Hollmeyer, orders returned him to the Jacksonville Naval Air Station on the banks of the St. Johns River as a flight instructor for new aviation cadets.[51]

In the South Pacific, Allied bombing raids continued to pound Rabaul into the New Year, and by the middle of February, all active Japanese combat air units had been withdrawn from the island.[52] With the withdrawal of the air units from Rabaul, the influence of the powerful complex of bases that had anchored the military presence of the Japanese Empire in the South Pacific was effectively brought to an end.[53] Within a month of the withdrawal, the eighteen-month campaign for the Solomon Islands, including the neutralization of Rabaul in the Bismarcks, came to an end.[54]

"In retrospect the Japanese air arm suffered the beginning of an irreversible downward spiral in the Solomons," and the Allied successes in the theater broke the back of the enemy's air war offensive capability.[55] The Solomon Islands campaign and fight for Rabaul represented the high-water mark for U.S. Marine Corps aviation during World War II, and the Marine aviators played a central role in the campaign that gained national and worldwide attention.[56] In raw totals, the Japanese lost almost 8,000 combat aircraft in the South Pacific. In contrast, the U.S. Marines lost only 1,673 airmen, most of them in the skies over the Solomon Islands.[57]

As the summer of 1944 approached, the Allied offensive moved north of the equator, and the names of new islands and new island chains came to the forefront of the Nation's consciousness—the Gilberts, the Marshalls, the Marianas, Tarawa, Truk, Eniwetok, Peleliu, Saipan, and, in the fall of 1944, a return to the Philippines.[58]

As 1945 began the Allied offensive continued to press north. In mid-February, the U.S. Marines invaded Iwo Jima midway between the Marianas and Tokyo. After six weeks of bloody fighting, they secured the island during the third week of March.[59] On April 1, American forces launched an invasion of the island of Okinawa, and after a battle that raged into the final week of June, it, too, was wrested from the control of the Japanese.[60]

In June captains Dunbar and Hollmeyer were reassigned from NAS Jacksonville to the Marine Air Infantry School at Cherry Point, North Carolina, to prepare for a return to the Pacific theater of operations, but the orders to return to the Pacific were never issued. The atomic bombs dropped on the Japanese cities of Hiroshima and Nagasaki in August of 1945 effectively ended the conflict in the Pacific, making further troop deployments unnecessary.[61]

In September of 1945 Carl was returned to reserve military status in the Marine Corps, and he entered law school at Yale University.[62] Like millions of others in his generation who made the journey to war, Carl left active military service and returned to civilian life in a mass exodus from uniform that was described by Tom Brokaw in 1998 in his book *The Greatest Generation*.

> When the war ended, more than twelve million men and women put their uniforms aside and returned to civilian life. They went back to work at their old jobs or started small businesses; they became big-city cops and firemen; they finished their degrees or enrolled in college for the first time; they became schoolteachers, insurance salesmen, craftsmen, and local politicians. They weren't widely known outside their families or their communities. For many, the war years were enough adventure to last a lifetime. They were proud of what they accomplished but they rarely discussed their experiences, even with each other. They became once again ordinary people, the kind of men and women who always have been the foundation of the American way of life.[63]

Epilogue

The combat missions of the Swashbucklers of VMF-214 during the Battle for the Solomon Islands that are remembered here did not go unnoticed in the higher echelons of command. The pilots had helped to protect Guadalcanal and contributed to the successes in the central and northern Solomon Islands. In recognition of their contributions, the pilots and their supporting ground crew were awarded the Presidential Unit Citation, and individual pilots of VMF-214 were awarded medals as well, ranging from the Air Medal to the Navy Cross.

The Presidential Unit Citation awarded to the squadron acknowledging their participation in the campaign in the Solomon Islands, the first awarded specifically to a Marine Corps fighter squadron,[1] reads as follows:

> For extraordinary heroism in action against enemy Japanese forces at Guadalcanal, April 7, 1943; Munda, July 17 to August 30, 1943;[2] Northern Solomons, September 16 to October 19, 1943; and Vella Lavella and Torokina, December 17, 1943 to January 6, 1944.[3]
>
> The first squadron to strafe Kahili, the first to operate from Munda while the field was under heavy enemy artillery fire, and the first to lead a fighter sweep on Rabaul, Marine Fighting Squadron TWO HUNDRED FOURTEEN executed bomber escort missions, strafing attacks, search sweeps and patrol missions. Superbly serviced and maintained by its ground crews despite enemy shellfire and nightly bombing attacks, this unit destroyed or damaged 273 Japanese aircraft during these campaigns and, in some

of the most bitterly contested air combats on record, contributed substantially to the establishment of an aerial beachhead over Rabaul and paved the way for Allied bombers to destroy Japanese shipping, supply dumps and shore installations. Frequently outnumbered but never outfought, Marine Fighting Squadron TWO HUNDRED FOURTEEN achieved an outstanding combat record which reflects highest credit upon its skilled pilots, air and ground crews and the United States Naval Service.

For the President, James Forrestal, Secretary of the Navy.

Following the Swashbucklers second tour, Carl was one of the pilots awarded the Air Medal in recognition of his numerous combat missions and the sinking of the Japanese resupply barges in the coastal waters adjacent to Kolombangara. His citation, signed by Admiral William Halsey, reads as follows:

For meritorious achievement while participating in aerial attacks against the enemy as a pilot of a fighter plane attached to a Marine aircraft group operating in the Solomon Islands area during the period from July 22 to September 1, 1943. Lieutenant Dunbar successfully completed numerous flights against the enemy including search, patrol and escort missions often in the face of severe antiaircraft fire and enemy aircraft opposition. On August 29th, he was a member of a strafing mission against enemy fortifications which threatened the positions of our forces. Severe damage was inflicted on enemy ground installations and barge traffic which materially contributed to the security of our advance troops. His courageous conduct and fine airmanship have aided materially in the success of the missions in which his division participated and were in keeping with the highest traditions of the United States Naval Service.[4]

"No pilots," wrote Bruce Gamble in his history of the squadron, "have worn the intertwined globe and anchor of the Marine Corps or flown wearing wings of gold with more valor than the men of Marine Fighting Squadron 214 during World War II."[5]

Carl in Corsair cockpit at Advance Base Knucklehead after the final combat mission of the second tour. (Dunbar family collection.)

In a broader sense, the sentiments expressed by Eric Bergerud in his epic about the Pacific air war mirrored those expressed by Gamble. "Perhaps there is no such thing as a good war," wrote Bergerud. "In rare moments in history there are necessary wars, and the Pacific war was certainly necessary. Allied airmen who fought in the South Pacific, as well as those who supported them, deserve profound recognition from free peoples."[6]

Author's Note

After his return to NAS Jacksonville in 1944, Carl met Ann Peck, a local resident of Ponte Vedra Beach and a recent graduate of the Florida State College for Women. A year later, in May of 1945, Carl and Ann married, and together they returned to New Haven at the conclusion of the war when Carl entered law school.

Carl and Ann's wedding, Jacksonville Beach, May 1945. (Dunbar family collection.)

After law school and a brief period in central Connecticut, the Dunbars returned south to make Florida their permanent home, and together they raised three children. Carl's small-town law practice in Dunedin flourished until his untimely death in 1981. He gave freely of his time to the community; he was an active member of the legal profession; he became a founding member of the Real Property, Probate and Trust Law Section of the Florida Bar; and his time in uniform was left in the past. Although he was issued a commercial pilot's license by the FAA when he retired from the Marine Corps Reserves, Carl did not ever return to the cockpit as a pilot.

Like so many of his generation, Carl rarely talked about the events of war and about his part in those events. During the postwar years, the only acknowledgment of his time in the Pacific was the Swashbucklers squadron patch that he wore on his flight jacket. Neatly mounted in a small, brown wooden frame, it hung on the wall of his law office until his passing.

Now only the logbook and letters survive to tell of his preparations for combat and the details of his time in the Solomon archipelago. During his lifetime, these remained boxed in closets and forgotten, kept first by his mother, Lora, and then by his wife, Ann.

After more than sixty years, the letters and the logbook were given to me, as much as an afterthought as for their content and story, but their words resonated for me. I wanted to know more about my father's journey and more about the story revealed in the letters and logbook.

Their content led me to sources on geography and on the military installations, staging areas, naval ships, aircraft, and battlefields referred to in the documents I had been given. The historical information from my research has been included with these letters to put their narrative into a better context of the times and places of which they speak and to share the story they reveal. It has left me with a profound respect not only for my father but for all the men he fought beside.

Acknowledgments

The search through the historical events found here and the evolution and completion of this project would not have been possible without the time and contributions of others.

Special appreciation is extended to the surviving Swashbucklers who contributed: Vince Carpenter, who shared not only his personal accounts of the difficult times in the Solomon Islands but also the Solomon Island diary of Henry Miller and the transcript of O. K. Williams' oral history of the events, and to Tom Tomlinson for sharing his personal accounts and memories of the time and for his memoir, *The Threadbare Buzzard*. My appreciation goes to Janet Carpenter as well for her kindness and hospitality, and to Larry Carpenter for sharing the passion to know the history of our fathers and for facilitating the rich and productive dialogue with his family.

Lora Johnson and Ann Dunbar witnessed the history found in these pages on the home front, and without their contributions to the events during the time of war, this project would be incomplete.

The narrative that accompanies these letters evolved into its final version with the help of others and the remaining shortcomings are the author's. But the time and critiques of Lieutenant General Robert Milligan (USMC, Ret.), Matt and Susan Dunbar, and R. Z. Safley have helped to bring the manuscript from its rough beginnings to its refined completion.

Finally, the project would not be a reality without the patience, vision, and encouragement of Meredith Babb, and the tenacious attention to detail, quality, and accuracy of the final manuscript by Theresa Zerkle.

I am profoundly grateful to all of those who have contributed to this project.

Notes

Prologue

1. Brokaw, *Greatest Generation*, 3.
2. Burns, *War*.
3. Gamble, *Black Sheep*, 13.

Chapter 1. Squantum Naval Air Station and the U.S. Naval Reserve Aviation Base in Atlanta, December 17, 1941–March 9, 1942

1. Costello, *Pacific War*, 98.
2. Bergerud, *Fire in the Sky*, 36–37.
3. Ambrose, *Eisenhower*, 61; and Bradley, *Flyboys*, 98.
4. Bradley, *Flyboys*, 118.
5. Ambrose, *Eisenhower*, 61.
6. Dorr, *Marine Air*, 7.
7. Lora Johnson letter to Peter Dunbar, February 4, 2010.
8. Gamble, *Black Sheep*, 74.
9. Bishop and McNab, *Campaigns of World War II*, 186.
10. Gannon, *Operation Drumbeat*, 166.
11. Ibid., 74.
12. Ibid., 211–12.
13. Ibid., 166.
14. Bradley, *Flyboys*, 98.
15. Costello, *Pacific War*, 233.
16. Glines, *Doolittle Raid*, 10, 13.
17. Guardia, *American Guerrilla*, 36; and Bishop and McNab, *Campaigns of World War II*, 186.
18. Bradley, *Flyboys*, 124.
19. Bergerud, *Fire in the Sky*, 333–34.
20. Lora Johnson letter to Peter Dunbar, February 27, 2009.
21. Glines, *Doolittle Raid*, 17.
22. Ibid., 19.

23. Lora Johnson letter to Peter Dunbar, February 27, 2009.

24. Hoyt, *Guadalcanal*, 5.

25. Ibid., 16.

26. Ibid., 29, 33.

27. Ibid., 37.

28. Glines, *Doolittle Raid*, 23–25.

29. Ibid., 22.

30. "Naval Air Station Atlanta," GlobalSecurity.org, http://www.globalsecurity.org/military/facility/atlanta.htm.

31. Costello, *Pacific War*, 223.

32. Bergerud, *Fire in the Sky*, 5.

33. Ibid., 6.

34. Prose, "Somewhere . . . in the Pacific," 12.

35. Bergerud, *Fire in the Sky*, 70.

36. Ibid., 25.

37. Hoyt, *Guadalcanal*, 5.

38. Bergerud, *Fire in the Sky*, 73.

39. Ibid., 38.

Chapter 2. U.S. Naval Air Station, Jacksonville, Florida, March 12, 1942–July 12, 1942

1. Blackburn, *Jolly Rogers*, 6.

2. Gannon, *Operation Drumbeat*, 350–51.

3. Dunbar, Flight Logbook, March 18, 1943.

4. Glines, *Doolittle Raid*, 31, 36, 52.

5. Blackburn, *Jolly Rogers*, 6, 7.

6. Matthews, "Esso Bolivar."

7. Gannon, *Operation Drumbeat*, 266.

8. Ibid., 342.

9. Glines, *Doolittle Raid*, 37.

10. Guardia, *American Guerrilla*, 40.

11. Bergerud, *Fire in the Sky*, 72.

12. Ibid., 540.

13. Glines, *Doolittle Raid*, 47, 48.

14. Ibid., 50, 52.

15. Gannon, *Operation Drumbeat*, 347.

16. Ibid., 362, 364.

17. Ibid., 359.

18. Ibid., 364.

19. Ibid., 376–78.

20. Ibid., 366.

21. Ibid.

22. Bishop and McNab, *Campaigns of World War II*, 197.

23. Astor, *Semper Fi in the Sky*, 56.

24. Bergerud, *Fire in the Sky*, 72.

25. Lora Johnson letter to Peter Dunbar, January 2, 2010.

26. Glines, *Doolittle Raid*, 63, 65, 66.

27. Ibid., 67; and Dorr, *Marine Air*, 51.

28. Glines, *Doolittle Raid*, 78.

29. Dunbar, Flight Logbook, April 21, 1942.

30. Ibid., April 30, 1942.

31. Spencer, *Pilots*, xvii, xviii.

32. Glines, *Doolittle Raid*, 147; and Bradley, *Flyboys*, 109–10.

33. Bergerud, *Fire in the Sky*, 40.

34. Costello, *Pacific War*, 236.

35. Glines, *Doolittle Raid*, 218.

36. Astor, *Semper Fi in the Sky*, 56.

37. Bradley, *Flyboys*, 125.

38. Bishop and McNab, *Campaigns of World War II*, 64.

39. Overy, *Air War*, 261.

40. Bergerud, *Fire in the Sky*, 41–42.

41. Hoyt, *Guadalcanal*, 5.

42. Dunbar, Flight Logbook, May 15, 1942.

43. Bradley, *Flags of Our Fathers*, 63.

44. Dunbar, Flight Logbook, May 25, 1942.

45. Bergerud, *Fire in the Sky*, 333–34.

46. Bradley, *Flyboys*, 119.

47. Astor, *Semper Fi in the Sky*, 40.

48. Gannon, *Operation Drumbeat*, 163.

49. Bergerud, *Fire in the Sky*, 89.

50. Dunbar, Flight Logbook, May 31, 1942.

51. Ibid., June 2, 1942.

52. Bishop and McNab, *Campaigns of World War II*, 125.

53. Gannon, *Operation Drumbeat*, 222.

54. Bradley, *Flyboys*, 120.

55. Ibid.

56. Bergerud, *Fire in the Sky*, 41.

57. Ibid., 70.

58. Astor, *Semper Fi in the Sky*, 58; and Bergerud, *Fire in the Sky*, 70.

59. Blackburn, *Jolly Rogers*, 89.

60. Gannon, *Operation Drumbeat*, 379.

61. Ann Peck Dunbar, interview with Peter Dunbar, December 10, 2008, Palm Harbor, Florida.

62. Bergerud, *Fire in the Sky*, 41.

63. Ambrose, *Pacific*, 74.

64. Allison, "Black Sheep Squadron," 78; and Costello, *Pacific War*, 320.

65. Ibid.

66. Bergerud, *Fire in the Sky*, 333–34.

67. Gamble, *Black Sheep*, 7.

68. Dunbar, Flight Logbook, July 7, 1942.

69. Astor, *Semper Fi in the Sky*, 23; and Allison, "Black Sheep Squadron," 64.

70. Gamble, *Black Sheep*, 7.

71. Astor, *Semper Fi in the Sky*, 163; Gamble, *Black Sheep*, 13; and Tomlinson, *Threadbare Buzzard*, 120.

72. Gamble, *Black Sheep*, 14.

73. Bradley, *Flags of Our Fathers*, 62.

74. Ambrose, *Pacific*, 74.

75. Bradley, *Flags of Our Fathers*, 63.

76. Dunbar, Flight Logbook, July 7, 1942.

77. Astor, *Semper Fi in the Sky*, 58.

78. Ambrose, *Pacific*, 94; and Blackburn, *Jolly Rogers*, 89.

79. Allison, "Black Sheep Squadron," 70.

80. Gamble, *Black Sheep*, 14, 16.

81. Astor, *Semper Fi in the Sky*, 161.

82. Blackburn, *Jolly Rogers*, 6, 7.

Chapter 3. U.S. Naval Air Station, Miami, Florida, July 28, 1942– November 11, 1942

1. Blackburn, *Jolly Rogers*, 3.

2. Ibid., 6–7.

3. Dorr, *Marine Air*, 54.

4. Astor, *Semper Fi in the Sky*, 41.

5. Dunbar, Flight Logbook, August 3, 1942.

6. Prose, "Somewhere . . . in the Pacific," 17; Bishop and McNab, *Campaigns of World War II*, 196; and Toland, *Infamy*, 51.

7. Hoyt, *Guadalcanal*, 16.

8. Tregaskis, *Guadalcanal Diary*, 46, 71.

9. Bergerud, *Fire in the Sky*, 95.

10. Tregaskis, *Guadalcanal Diary*, 80.

11. Hoyt, *Guadalcanal*, 59.

12. Ibid., 53.

13. Costello, *Pacific War*, 328.

14. Hoyt, *Guadalcanal*, 60; Bishop and McNab, *Campaigns of World War II*, 196; and Tregaskis, *Guadalcanal Diary*, 126.

15. Hoyt, *Guadalcanal*, 60.

16. Bergerud, *Fire in the Sky*, 41.

17. Costello, *Pacific War*, 328.

18. Bradley, *Flyboys*, 125.

19. Ibid.

20. Bergerud, *Fire in the Sky*, 220.

21. Bradley, *Flyboys*, 125.
22. Bergerud, *Fire in the Sky*, 516.
23. Dunbar, Flight Logbook, February 3, 1943.
24. Bergerud, *Fire in the Sky*, 41.
25. Tregaskis, *Guadalcanal Diary*, 132.
26. Ibid., 147.
27. Gamble, *Black Sheep*, 17, 18.
28. Blackburn, *Jolly Rogers*, 7–8.
29. Ibid., 7, 9.
30. Bergerud, *Fire in the Sky*, 77.
31. Ibid., 17.
32. Hoyt, *Guadalcanal*, 29.
33. Costello, *Pacific War*, 331.
34. Ibid., 343–44.
35. Hoyt, *Guadalcanal*, 101.
36. Tregaskis, *Guadalcanal Diary*, 204–5; and Hoyt, *Guadalcanal*, 101.
37. Ibid., 103–5.
38. Gamble, *Black Sheep*, 17.
39. "Peabody's Man of Four Professions," *New Haven Register*, August 30, 1942.
40. Johnson, "Togo Is Tough," *New Haven Register*, January 1944.
41. Hoyt, *Guadalcanal*, 132.
42. Blackburn, *Jolly Rogers*, 7, 9.
43. Dunbar, Flight Logbook, October 1–26, 1943.
44. Gamble, *Black Sheep*, 8, 9.
45. Hoyt, *Guadalcanal*, 135, 152.
46. Bergerud, *Fire in the Sky*, 83.
47. Hoyt, *Guadalcanal*, 163, 164.
48. Ibid., 270.
49. Dunbar, Flight Logbook, October 26, 1942.
50. Costello, *Pacific War*, 360.
51. Bergerud, *Fire in the Sky*, 423–24.
52. Costello, *Pacific War*, 361; and Bergerud, *Fire in the Sky*, 565.
53. Costello, *Pacific War*, 363.
54. Ibid., 364.
55. Bergerud, *Fire in the Sky*, 424.
56. Ibid., 41.
57. Dunbar, Flight Logbook, November 4, 1942.
58. O. K. Williams, interview with Richard Misenhimer, November 21, 2002.
59. Dunbar, Flight Logbook, November 11, 1942.
60. Hoyt, *Guadalcanal*, 203.
61. Ibid., 205.
62. Bergerud, *Fire in the Sky*, 83, 84.
63. Hoyt, *Guadalcanal*, 209–10.
64. Ibid., 219.

65. Ibid., 222.

66. Ibid., 233.

67. Tregaskis, *Guadalcanal Diary*, 259.

68. Hoyt, *Guadalcanal*, 234.

Chapter 4. San Diego to Espiritu Santo, New Hebrides, December 5, 1942–March 12, 1943

1. Prose, "Somewhere . . . in the Pacific," 12.

2. Williams interview, November 21, 2002; and Gamble, *Black Sheep*, 28.

3. Hoyt, *Guadalcanal*, 238.

4. Dunbar, Flight Logbook, December 12, 1943.

5. Bergerud, *Fire in the Sky*, 667.

6. Bradley, *Flyboys*, 131.

7. Blackburn, *Jolly Rogers*, 38.

8. Dunbar, Flight Logbook, December 26, 1942.

9. Costello, *Pacific War*, 384.

10. Tomlinson, *Threadbare Buzzard*, 54; and Drury McCall, open letter, October 4, 2000, available at http://www.worldwar2pilots.com/USMC-F-McCall.htm.

11. Hoyt, *Guadalcanal*, 252.

12. Ambrose, *Pacific*, image of document in photo signature following page 110.

13. Lora Johnson letter to Peter Dunbar, February 27, 2009.

14. Gamble, *Black Sheep*, 30.

15. Astor, *Semper Fi in the Sky*, 161.

16. Tomlinson, *Threadbare Buzzard*, 55.

17. Hoyt, *Guadalcanal*, 256.

18. Ibid., 270.

19. Williams interview, November 21, 2002; Vince Carpenter interview with Peter Dunbar, August 28, 2010; and Astor, *Semper Fi in the Sky*, 161.

20. Carpenter interview, August 28, 2010; Williams interview, November 21, 2002; and Allison, "Black Sheep Squadron," 72.

21. Gamble, *Black Sheep*, 23.

22. Blackburn, *Jolly Rogers*, 17, 18.

23. Gamble, *Black Sheep*, 25.

24. Blackburn, *Jolly Rogers*, 40.

25. Ibid., 50.

26. Gamble, *Black Sheep*, 33; and Dunbar, Flight Logbook, February 3, 1943.

27. Dunbar, Flight Logbook, February 4, 1943.

28. Ibid., January 31–February 12, 1943.

29. Hoyt, *Guadalcanal*, 269–70.

30. Dunbar, Flight Logbook, February 21, 1943.

31. Gamble, *Black Sheep*, 35.

32. Williams interview, November 21, 2002.

33. Gamble, *Black Sheep*, 35.

34. Ibid., 38.

35. Ibid.

36. Williams interview, November 21, 2002.

37. Gamble, *Black Sheep*, 40.

38. Astor, *Semper Fi in the Sky*, 162.

39. Dunbar, Flight Logbook, March 4, 1943.

Chapter 5. Fighter One Air Base, Guadalcanal, March 13, 1943–May 28, 1943

1. Dorr, *Marine Air*, 44.

2. Bergerud, *Fire in the Sky*, 10.

3. Ibid., 74; and Blackburn, *Jolly Rogers*, 95.

4. Van der Vat, *Pacific Campaign*, 217.

5. Dunbar, Flight Logbook, April 7, 1943.

6. "Lieut. Carl O. Dunbar, Jr., Describes Sky-View of Bougainville Invasion," *Bridgeport Sunday Post*, January 23, 1944.

7. Dunbar, Flight Logbook; Gamble, *Black Sheep*; Carpenter interview, August 27 and 28, 2010; Miller, "Solomon Islands Diary"; Tomlinson, *Threadbare Buzzard*; and Williams interview, November 21, 2002.

8. Ambrose, *Pacific*, 94; and Dunbar, Flight Logbook, March 4–12, 1943.

9. Dunbar, Flight Logbook, March 4–12, 1943.

10. Miller, "Solomon Islands Diary," 9.

11. Dunbar, Flight Logbook, March 13, 1943; and Blackburn, *Jolly Rogers*, 97.

12. Astor, *Semper Fi in the Sky*, 163.

13. Miller, "Solomon Islands Diary," 10.

14. Dunbar, Flight Logbook, March 16, 1943; and Gamble, *Black Sheep*, 67.

15. Miller, "Solomon Islands Diary," 6; and Gamble, *Black Sheep*, 70–71.

16. Blackburn, *Jolly Rogers*, 101.

17. Dunbar, Flight Logbook, March 18, 1943.

18. Gamble, *Black Sheep*, 70–71.

19. Miller, "Solomon Islands Diary," 10; and Dunbar, Flight Logbook, March 18, 1943.

20. Blackburn, *Jolly Rogers*, 18; and Williams interview, November 21, 2002.

21. Tomlinson, *Threadbare Buzzard*, 67–68.

22. Ibid., 63.

23. Quoted in Bergerud, *Fire in the Sky*, 101.

24. Carpenter interview, August 28, 2010.

25. Hammel, *Pacific Warriors*, 93.

26. Tomlinson, *Threadbare Buzzard*, 66.

27. Dunbar, Flight Logbook, March 20 and 21, 1943.

28. Miller, "Solomon Islands Diary," 13.

29. Tomlinson, *Threadbare Buzzard*, 66.

30. Dunbar, Flight Logbook, March 23–29, 1943; and Miller, "Solomon Islands Diary," 14.

31. Astor, *Semper Fi in the Sky*, 165.

32. Dunbar, Flight Logbook, March 20, 1943.

33. Hammel, *Pacific Warriors*, 66; and Bergerud, *Fire in the Sky*, 66.

34. Bergerud, *Fire in the Sky*, 79.

35. Astor, *Semper Fi in the Sky*, 163.

36. Ibid., 83.

37. Overy, *Air War*, 118; and Bergerud, *Fire in the Sky*, 76.

38. Astor, *Semper Fi in the Sky*, 172–73.

39. Williams interview, November 21, 2002; and Carpenter interview, August 27, 2010.

40. Tomlinson, *Threadbare Buzzard*, 71.

41. Miller, "Solomon Islands Diary," 17; and Astor, *Semper Fi in the Sky*, 173.

42. Dunbar, Flight Logbook, April 1, 1943.

43. Ibid., April 2–9, 1943.

44. Ibid., April 7, 1943.

45. Gamble, *Black Sheep*, 96.

46. Carpenter interview, August 28, 2010.

47. Astor, *Semper Fi in the Sky*, 176; and Hammel, *Pacific Warriors*, 96.

48. Gamble, *Black Sheep*, 89.

49. Dunbar, Flight Logbook, April 9, 1943.

50. Carpenter interview, August 27, 2010.

51. Ekstrand, "Swashbucklers," *Marine Gazette*, December 1989; and Williams interview, November 21, 2002.

52. Gamble, *Black Sheep*, 74–75.

53. Miller, "Solomon Islands Diary," 29; and Gamble, *Black Sheep*, 93.

54. Dunbar, Flight Logbook, April 15, 1943.

55. Miller, "Solomon Islands Diary," 31; and Dunbar, Flight Logbook, April 18, 1943.

56. Dunbar, *Flight Logbook*, April 19–22, 1943.

57. Ibid., May 3–13, 1943.

58. Miller, "Solomon Islands Diary," 31; Williams interview, November 21, 2002; Carpenter interview, August 28, 2010; Tomlinson, *Threadbare Buzzard*, 76; and Gamble, *Black Sheep*, 94–96.

59. Astor, *Semper Fi in the Sky*, 180.

60. Ibid., 179.

61. Miller, "Solomon Islands Diary," 31.

62. Carpenter interview, August 28, 2010.

63. Hoyt, *Guadalcanal*, 271–72.

64. Williams interview, November 21, 2002; Carpenter interview, August 28, 2010; and Bergerud, *Fire in the Sky*, 215–16.

65. Bergerud, *Fire in the Sky*, 215.

66. Ibid., 71.

67. Miller, "Solomon Islands Diary," 43.

68. Gamble, *Black Sheep*, 100.

69. Miller, "Solomon Islands Diary," 44.

70. Ibid.

71. Tomlinson, *Threadbare Buzzard*, 81.

72. Prose, "Somewhere . . . in the Pacific," 12.

73. Miller, "Solomon Islands Diary," 45–46.

74. Gamble, *Black Sheep*, 100.

75. Ibid.

76. Ibid.

77. Dunbar, Flight Logbook, March 16–May 13, 1943.

78. Dorr, *Marine Air*, 17.

79. Gamble, *Black Sheep*, 105.

Chapter 6. Advance Base Knucklehead, Banika in the Russell Islands, June 6, 1943–August 14, 1943

1. Astor, *Semper Fi in the Sky*, 193.

2. Hoyt, *Guadalcanal*, 288.

3. Blackburn, *Jolly Rogers*, 88.

4. Hoyt, *Guadalcanal*, 85–86; Bergerud, *Fire in the Sky*, 594.

5. Blackburn, *Jolly Rogers*, 100.

6. Carpenter interview, August 28, 2010; Williams interview, November 21, 2002; and Bergerud, *Fire in the Sky*, 595.

7. Dunbar, Flight Logbook, June 29, 1943.

8. Prose, "Somewhere . . . in the Pacific," 12, 14.

9. Bergerud, *Fire in the Sky*, 69.

10. Miller, "Solomon Islands Diary," 53.

11. "John Lewis & the Flag," *Time*, May 10, 1943.

12. "Until April 1943," *Time*, December 1, 1941.

13. "John Lewis & the Flag," *Time*, December 10, 1943.

14. Miller, "Solomon Islands Diary," 54.

15. Tomlinson, *Threadbare Buzzard*, 83.

16. The "cats-eyes" found while exploring the coastal shallows were brought home and years later made into a bracelet and brooch.

17. Dorr, *Marine Air*, 11.

18. Gamble, *Black Sheep*, 115.

19. Miller, "Solomon Islands Diary," 54–55.

20. Dunbar, Flight Logbook, June 20, 1943.

21. Allison, "Black Sheep Squadron," 87.

22. Tomlinson, *Threadbare Buzzard*, 77.

23. Bradley, *Flyboys*, 128.

24. Miller, "Solomon Islands Diary," 44, 55–56.

25. Gamble, *Black Sheep*, 113, 114.

26. Astor, *Semper Fi in the Sky*, 164.

27. Allison, "Black Sheep Squadron," 93.

28. Quoted in Bergerud, *Fire in the Sky*, 98.

29. Miller, "Solomon Islands Diary," 57.

30. Dunbar, Flight Logbook, June 29 and 30, 1943; and Drury McCall, open letter, October 4, 2000, available at http://www.worldwar2pilots.com/USMC-F-McCall.htm.

31. Dunbar, Flight Logbook, June 29, 1943.

32. Miller, "Solomon Islands Diary," 60–62.

33. Hammel, *Munda Trail*, 48–49; and Blackburn, *Jolly Rogers*, 95.

34. Costello, *Pacific War*, 411.

35. Astor, *Semper Fi in the Sky*, 193, 194.

36. Hammel, *Munda Trail*, 91–100.

37. Bergerud, *Fire in the Sky*, 607–8.

38. Hammel, *Pacific Warriors*, 94.

39. Blackburn, *Jolly Rogers*, 95.

40. Astor, *Semper Fi in the Sky*, 164.

41. Dunbar, Flight Logbook, July 1–16, 1943.

42. Tomlinson, *Threadbare Buzzard*, 89.

43. Bergerud, *Fire in the Sky*, 435.

44. Dunbar, Flight Logbook, June 29–July 16, 1943.

45. Ibid., July 18, 1943; and Astor, *Semper Fi in the Sky*, 203.

46. Gamble, *Black Sheep*, 145–46.

47. Ekstrand, "The Swashbucklers."

48. Ibid.

49. Dunbar, Flight Logbook, July 22–25, 1943; and Gamble, *Black Sheep*, 152.

50. Vince Carpenter letter, August 2, 2010.

51. Allison, "Black Sheep Squadron," 94; and Costello, *Pacific War*, 413.

52. Gamble, *Black Sheep*, 133–38.

53. Ibid., 136–37.

54. Dunbar, Flight Logbook, July 28, 1943.

55. Roosevelt, "On Progress of War."

56. Dunbar, Flight Logbook, July 30, 1943.

57. Ibid., June 30, 1943, and July 31, 1943.

58. Bergerud, *Fire in the Sky*, 607.

59. Hammel, *Munda Trail*, 183–84; and Costello, *Pacific War*, 413.

60. Costello, *Pacific War*, 414.

61. Gamble, *Black Sheep*, 137–38.

62. Dunbar, Flight Logbook, August 1, 1943.

63. Ibid.

64. Burgess, "Dunbar in Air Battles."

65. Dunbar, Flight Logbook, August 2, 1943.

66. Van der Vat, *Pacific Campaign*, 282; "PT-109," Pacific Wrecks, http://www.pacificwrecks.com/ships/ptboat/PT-109.html; and Tomlinson, *Threadbare Buzzard*, 90.

67. "JFK in History: John F. Kennedy and PT-109." John F. Kennedy Presidential Library & Museum online. http://www.jfklibrary.org/Historical+Resources/JFK+in+History/John+F.+Kennedy+and+PT109.htm."

68. Ibid.

69. Lora Johnson letter to Peter Dunbar, February 27, 2009.

70. Dunbar, Flight Logbook, July 18, 1943–August 13, 1943.

71. Blackburn, *Jolly Rogers*, 119.

72. Tomlinson, *Threadbare Buzzard*, 89–90.

73. Allison, "Black Sheep Squadron," 79–80.

74. Gamble, *Black Sheep*, 133.

75. Hammel, *Munda Trail*, 223.

76. Astor, *Semper Fi in the Sky*, 194.

77. Gamble, *Black Sheep*, 141.

78. Bergerud, *Fire in the Sky*, 625; and Blackburn, *Jolly Rogers*, 94.

79. Blackburn, *Jolly Rogers*, 97.

80. Astor, *Semper Fi in the Sky*, 192.

81. O'Hara, "Battle of Vella Lavella," 1; and Blackburn, *Jolly Rogers*, 90.

82. Tomlinson, *Threadbare Buzzard*, 111.

83. Dunbar, Flight Logbook, August 6, 1943.

84. Thomas Tomlinson letter to Peter Dunbar, August 6, 2010.

85. Miller, "Solomon Islands Diary," 72–73; and Gamble, *Black Sheep*, 141–44.

86. Dunbar, Flight Logbook, August 6, 1943.

87. "Lieut. Carl O. Dunbar, Jr., Describes Sky-View of Bougainville Invasion," *Bridgeport Sunday Post*, January 23, 1944.

88. Dunbar, Flight Logbook, August 8, 1943; and Gamble, *Black Sheep*, 166.

89. Dunbar, Flight Logbook, August 13, 1943.

Chapter 7. Airfield at Munda Point, New Georgia Island, August 15, 1943–August 31, 1943

1. Costello, *Pacific War*, 414.

2. Goldstein, "Dolph Camilli."

3. Dunbar, Flight Logbook, August 15–31, 1943; and Drury McCall, open letter, October 4, 2000, available at http://www.worldwar2pilots.com/USMC-F-McCall.htm.

4. Dunbar, Flight Logbook, August 15, 1943; Gamble, *Black Sheep*, 168; and Costello, *Pacific War*, 414, 415.

5. Dunbar, Flight Logbook, August 16, 1943.

6. Lora Johnson letter to Peter Dunbar, March 23, 2009.

7. Laurier, "Black Sheep at Munda."

8. Tomlinson, *Threadbare Buzzard*, 102.

9. Miller, "Solomon Islands Diary," 77.

10. "Jack Petit's Personal Story," http://dfield.home.texas.net/personalstory.html.

11. Gamble, *Black Sheep*, 148.

12. Miller, "Solomon Islands Diary," 77; and Dunbar, Flight Logbook, August 20–31, 1943.

13. Dunbar, Flight Logbook, August 20, 1943.

14. Gamble, *Black Sheep*, 155.

15. Dunbar, Flight Logbook, August 22, 1943.

16. Miller, "Solomon Islands Diary," 79.

17. Dunbar, Flight Logbook, August 25, 1943.

18. Ibid., August 26 and 27, 1943.

19. Allison, "Black Sheep Squadron," 102.

20. Jim Laurier letter to Peter Dunbar, February 10, 2010; Dunbar, Flight Logbook, August 29, 1943; and Gamble, *Black Sheep*, 162.

21. Laurier, *Swashbuckler's Surprise*, 51.

22. Dunbar, Flight Logbook, August 30, 1943; and Astor, *Semper Fi in Sky*, 205.

23. Dunbar, Flight Logbook, August 31, 1943.

24. Miller, "Solomon Islands Diary," 81.

25. Ibid.

26. Gamble, *Black Sheep*, 163–64.

27. Ibid., 161–62.

28. Tomlinson, *Threadbare Buzzard*, 110.

29. Miller, "Solomon Islands Diary," 77, 80.

30. Dunbar, Flight Logbook, August 31, 1943.

31. Johnson, "Dunbar Finds Life of Thrills."

32. Carl O. Dunbar Jr. letter to family, June 9, 1942.

33. Ibid., May 14, 1943.

34. Morison, "Vella Lavella."

35. Bergerud, *Fire in Sky*, 625; and Blackburn, *Jolly Rogers*, 95.

36. Churchill, *Closing Ring*, 558.

37. Allison, "Black Sheep Squadron," 93; Tomlinson, *Threadbare Buzzard*, 91; Astor, *Semper Fi in Sky*, 211; and Bergerud, *Fire in Sky*, 609.

Chapter 8. Bougainville and Home

1. Tomlinson, *Threadbare Buzzard*, 115.

2. Allison, "Black Sheep Squadron," 112.

3. Gamble, *Black Sheep*, 116.

4. Astor, *Semper Fi in the Sky*, 224.

5. Miller, "Solomon Islands Diary," 81, 82.

6. Ibid., 82.

7. Carpenter interview, August 28, 2010; Williams interview, November 21, 2002.

8. Cressman, *Magnificent Fight*, 1.

9. Dorr, *Marine Air*, 4; and Astor, *Semper Fi in the Sky*, 24.

10. "Fighting Squadrons of the USMC in WWII." Acepilots Web site. http://www.acepilots.com/usmc_sqns.html.

11. Miller, "Solomon Islands Diary," 82.

12. Tomlinson, *Threadbare Buzzard*, 111; and Blackburn, *Jolly Rogers*, 112.

13. Blackburn, *Jolly Rogers*, 102.

14. Dunbar, Flight Logbook, October 28, 1943.

15. Costello, *Pacific War*, 422; and Blackburn, *Jolly Rogers*, 115.

16. Astor, *Semper Fi in the Sky*, 211; and Costello, *Pacific War*, 422.

17. Costello, *Pacific War*, 421.

18. Bergerud, *Fire in the Sky*, 635.

19. Gamble, *Black Sheep*, 141–44; and Bergerud, *Fire in the Sky*, 25.

20. Costello, *Pacific War*, 422–23.

21. Blackburn, *Jolly Rogers*, 112.

22. Dunbar, Flight Logbook, October 28, 1943; and Astor, *Semper Fi in the Sky*, 239.

23. Astor, *Semper Fi in the Sky*, 234.

24. Hammel, *Pacific Warriors*, 109.

25. Dunbar, Flight Logbook, November 1, 1943.

26. Carpenter interview, August 28, 2010; and Williams interview, November 21, 2002.

27. Blackburn, *Jolly Rogers*, 112.

28. Bergerud, *Fire in the Sky*, 640.

29. Allison, "Black Sheep Squadron," 128.

30. Dunbar, Flight Logbook, November 1 and 7, 1943.

31. "Lieut. Carl O. Dunbar, Jr., Describes Sky-View of Bougainville Invasion," *Bridgeport Sunday Post*, January 23, 1944.

32. Dunbar, Flight Logbook, November 13, 1943.

33. Ibid., November 25, 1943.

34. Ibid., March 1943–November 1943.

35. Carl O. Dunbar Jr., letter to family, September 7, 1943.

36. Dunbar, Flight Logbook, March 17, 1943.

37. Gamble, *Black Sheep*, 146.

38. Ibid., 143.

39. Miller, "Solomon Islands Diary," 81.

40. "Jack Petit's Personal Story," http://dfield.home.texas.net/personalstory.html.

41. Tomlinson, *Threadbare Buzzard*, 127; and Gamble, *Black Sheep*, 152.

42. Ekstrand, "Swashbucklers," *Marine Corps Gazette*, December 1989.

43. Bradley, *Flyboys*, 125.

44. Williams interview, November 21, 2002.

45. Allison, "Black Sheep Squadron," 102.

46. Blackburn, *Jolly Rogers*, 182; and Gamble, *Black Sheep*, 152.

47. Churchill, *Closing the Ring*, 558.

48. Dorr, *Marine Air*, 37; and Bergerud, *Fire in the Sky*, 648.

49. Bradley, *Flags of Our Fathers*, 82; and Blackburn, *Jolly Rogers*, 180.

50. "Carl Dunbar Visiting after 10 Months in the Pacific," *New Haven Register*, December 12, 1943.

51. Lora Johnson letter to Peter Dunbar, March 23, 2009; and Dunbar interview, November 14, 2008.

52. Bergerud, *Fire in the Sky*, 678.

53. Dorr, *Marine Air*, 44; Bergerud, *Fire in the Sky*, 654–54; and Gamble, *Black Sheep*, 349.

54. Costello, *Pacific War*, 458.

55. Bergerud, *Fire in the Sky*, 676.

56. Allison, "Black Sheep Squadron," 135.

57. Bergerud, *Fire in the Sky*, 668–69.

58. Costello, *Pacific War*, 451.

59. Bishop and McNab, *Campaigns of World War II*, 232–33.

60. Ibid., 242–43.

61. Costello, *Pacific War*, 590, 593; and Dunbar interview, November 14, 2008.

62. Ibid.

63. Brokaw, *Greatest Generation*, 15.

Epilogue

1. Gamble, *Black Sheep,* 152; and Tomlinson, *Threadbare Buzzard*, 421.

2. First two tours by the Swashbucklers.

3. Second two tours by the Black Sheep.

4. Admiral W. A. Halsey, undated letter, 1943.

5. Gamble, *Black Sheep*, 421.

6. Bergerud, *Fire in the Sky*, 676.

Bibliography

Primary Sources

Personal Communications

Carpenter, Larry. Letters to Peter Dunbar, 2010.

Carpenter, Vince. Letters to Peter Dunbar, 2010.

Dunbar, Carl O., Jr. Letters to family, December 19, 1941–September 18, 1943.

Halsey, W. F. Air Medal Citation to Carl O. Dunbar Jr., 1943, South Pacific Force of the United States Pacific Fleet, Headquarters of the Commander.

Johnson, Lora. Letters to Peter Dunbar, 2009–10.

Laurier, Jim. Letters to Peter Dunbar, 2010.

McCall, Drury. Open Letter, October 4, 2000, available at http://www.worldwar2pilots.com/USMC-F-McCall.htm.

Tomlinson, Thomas M. Letters to Peter Dunbar, 2010.

Interviews

Carpenter, Vince. Interviews with Peter Dunbar. August 27 and 28, 2010.

Dunbar, Ann Peck. Interviews with Peter Dunbar. November 14, 2008, and December 10, 2008.

Tomlinson, Thomas M. Interview with Peter Dunbar. August 18, 2010.

William, O. K. Interview with Richard Misenhimer. Center for Pacific War Studies Oral History Program. November 21, 2002.

Documents, Records, and Memoirs

Blackburn, Tom. *The Jolly Rogers: The Story of Tom Blackburn and Navy Fighting Squadron VF-17*. With Eric Hammel. St. Paul, Minn.: Zenith Press, 2006.

Dunbar, Carl O., Jr. Flight Logbook. April 21, 1942–September 17, 1945.

———. MAG Group Transfer Orders, January 1, 1943.

———. Orders to 4th Marine Air Defense Wing, January 29, 1943.

Miller, Captain Henry S., USMC (Ret.). "Solomon Islands Diary: 3 March through November 13, 1943." Self-published, 1988.

Roosevelt, Franklin D. "On Progress of War and Plans for Peace." July 28, 1943. Franklin Delano Roosevelt Presidential Library and Museum, http://docs.fdrlibrary.marist.edu/072843.html.

Tomlinson, Thomas M. *The Threadbare Buzzard*. Minneapolis, Minn.: Zenith Press, 2004.

Tregaskis, Richard. *Guadalcanal Diary*. New York: Random House, 1943.

Secondary Sources

Allison, Fred Harold. "The Black Sheep Squadron: A Case Study in U.S. Marine Corps' Innovations in Close Air Support." PhD diss., Texas Tech University.

Ambrose, Hugh. *The Pacific*. New York: NAL Caliber, 2010.

Ambrose, Stephen E. *Eisenhower: Soldier and President*. New York: Simon & Schuster, 1990.

Astor, Gerald. *Semper Fi in the Sky: The Marine Air Battles of World War II*. New York: Ballantine Books, 2005.

Bergerud, Eric M. *Fire in the Sky: The Air War in the South Pacific*. Boulder, CO: Westview Press, 2000.

Bishop, Chris, and Chris McNab. *Campaigns of World War II Day by Day*. Hauppauge, N.Y.: Barron's Educational Series, 2003.

Bradley, James. *Flags of Our Fathers*. New York: Bantam Books, 2000.

———. *Flyboys: A True Story of Courage*. Boston: Back Bay Books, 2003.

Brokaw, Tom. *The Greatest Generation*. New York: Random House, 1998.

Burgess, Arthur. "Lt. C. O. Dunbar in Air Battles over Solomons," *New Haven Register* (AP). August 15, 1943.

Burns, Ken. *The War*. A Ken Burns film. FUBAR episode. 2007.

Churchill, Winston S. *Closing the Ring*. New York: Houghton Mifflin, 1951.

Costello, John. *The Pacific War 1941–1945*. New York: Atlantic Communications, 1981.

Cressman, Robert J. *A Magnificent Fight: Marines in the Battle for Wake Island*. Commemorative series. Produced by the Marine Corps History and Museums Division. http://www.nps.gov/archive/wapa/indepth/extcontent/usmc/pcn-190-003119-00/sec2.htm.

Dorr, Robert F. *Marine Air: The History of the Flying Leathernecks in Words and Photos*. New York: Berkley Caliber, 2005.

Ekstrand, David J. "The Swashbucklers." *Marine Corps Gazette*. December 1989.

Gamble, Bruce. *The Black Sheep: The Definitive Account of Marine Fighting Squadron 214 in World War II*. New York: Presidio Press, 1998.

Gannon, Michael. *Operation Drumbeat: The Dramatic True Story of Germany's First U-boat Attacks along the American Coast in World War II*. New York: Harper Perennial, 1990.

Glines, Carroll V. *The Doolittle Raid: America's Daring First Strike Against Japan*. Atglen, Pa.: Schiffer Publishing, 1991.

Goldstein, Richard. "Dolph Camilli, Who Led Dodgers to '41 Pennant, Dies at 90." *New York Times*. October 22, 1997.

Guardia, Mike. *American Guerrilla: The Forgotten Heroics of Russell W. Volckmann*. Philadelphia: Casemate Publishers, 2010.

Hammel, Eric. *Munda Trail: The New Georgia Campaign, June–August 1943*. London: Orion Books, 1989.

———. *Pacific Warriors: The U.S. Marines in World War II*. Minneapolis,Minn.: Zenith Press, 2005.

Hoyt, Edwin P. *Guadalcanal*. New York: Stein and Day, 1981.

Johnson, Pen T. "Dunbar Finds Life of Thrills Chasing Zeros." *New Haven Register*. January 1944.

Johnson, Thomas M. "Togo Is Tough—But Not Too Tough!" *New Haven Register*. August 31, 1942.

Laurier, Jim. "Swashbuckler's Surprise." *Foundation* 26, no. 1 (Spring 2005): 50–51.

———. "Black Sheep at Munda." Historical description of painting of same name. Original art by Jim Laurier; online gallery at http://www.jimlaurier.com/details/munda.htm.

Matthews, Ira. "The Esso Bolivar." http://www.40thbombgroup.org/matthews/Ira8.htm, n.d.

Morison, Samuel Eliot. "Vella Lavella: 15 August–7 October 1943." In *Breaking the Bismarcks Barrier*. Vol. 6, *History of United States Naval Operations in World War II*. Boston, Little, Brown, 1950.

O'Hara, Vincent P. "Battle of Vella Lavella, October 6–7, 1943." http://www.microworks.net/pacific/battles/vella_lavella.htm, n.d.

Overy, R. J. *The Air War: 1939–1945*. New York: Stein and Day, 1980.

Prose, Dorothy. "Somewhere . . . in the Pacific: A History of Bauerfield." *Foundation* 29, no. 1 (Spring 2008): 12–19.

Spencer, James. *The Pilots*. New York: G. P. Putnam's Sons, 2003.

Sullivan, Jim. *F4U Corsair*. Squadron/Signal Publications, 1994.

Toland, John. *Infamy: Pearl Harbor and Its Aftermath*. New York: Doubleday, 1982.

Van der Vat, Dan. *Pacific Campaign: The U.S.-Japanese Naval War, 1941–1945*. New York: Simon & Schuster, 1991.

Index

Page numbers in italics refer to illustrations.

Peter M. Dunbar is an attorney and partner with Pennington, Moore, Wilkinson, Bell & Dunbar, and he is a member of the American College of Real Estate Lawyers. He serves as an adjunct professor of law at Florida State University and is the author of five other books, including the very popular *Condominium Concept*, *The Law of Florida Homeowners Associations*, with Charles Dudley, and *The Homeowners Association Manual*, with Marc Dunbar.